Altering Frontiers

Health and Innovation Set

coordinated by
Corinne Grenier

Volume 1

Altering Frontiers

Organizational Innovations in Healthcare

Edited by

Corinne Grenier
Ewan Oiry

iSTE

WILEY

First published 2021 in Great Britain and the United States by ISTE Ltd and John Wiley & Sons, Inc.

ISTE Ltd
27-37 St George's Road
London SW19 4EU
UK

www.iste.co.uk

John Wiley & Sons, Inc.
111 River Street
Hoboken, NJ 07030
USA

www.wiley.com

Library of Congress Control Number: 2021934597

British Library Cataloguing-in-Publication Data
A CIP record for this book is available from the British Library
ISBN 978-1-78630-707-1

MIX
Paper from responsible sources
FSC® C013604

Contents

Foreword by Jean-Louis Denis

Adaptation, Trust and Methodology

The issue of organizational innovation in health is not new, but it is nonetheless topical. All health systems in high-income countries face significant challenges when adapting their health systems to changing demands, knowledge and preferences, economic circumstances or technologies (Denis *et al.* 2018). The current COVID-19 pandemic highlights the need for organizational innovation to better respond to the unexpected and ensure an adequate and accountable response. These organizational innovations are multifaceted and refer to a reconfiguration of the professional, clinical, managerial and civic logics, to name but a few, that structure the functioning of a healthcare system (Thornton & Ocasio 2008). The healthcare system has long been characterized by a significant gap between technical innovation and organizational or institutional innovation. While such a gap is not unique to the healthcare sector, it is surprisingly acute in this sector. Technical innovation in the broadest sense of the term is a powerful driver of change in the healthcare sector. New drugs and diagnostic and therapeutic technologies are penetrating the healthcare system and organizations at a speed that makes them difficult to master. What is looming in terms of cell therapies is described as a tsunami that could sweep away the healthcare system, or at least revive it without being able to escape the difficult question of costs and what should or should not be offered by our social welfare systems. Digital innovation and artificial intelligence will also bring about organizational and institutional transformations (Hinings *et al.* 2018).

Organizational innovation, which can be more broadly described as immaterial innovation, is difficult to bring about, or at least to such a degree that it would allow better control of so-called technical innovations. One need only think of the experience of healthcare systems in the face of the deinstitutionalization of care made possible (in principle) by the arrival of laparoscopic technologies in the 1990s. The development of ambulatory care has been slower than otherwise, and clinical or organizational environments have had difficulty capitalizing on this opportunity.

This is certainly a reflection of reasonable caution, since innovation must make it possible to produce quality care in complete safety. There is also the imprint left by professional, organizational or political rigidities that make this capitalization uncertain or late.

Healthcare is not alone in this fight for innovation. Other sectors of activity, including that of economically oriented companies, have long stressed the difficulty of renewing social relations of production in favor of greater adaptation to a constantly changing environment (Osty *et al.* 2007). In the healthcare sector, organizational innovations, which I would call "basic", are also slow to materialize. Take, for example, the difficulty in linking the designation of responsibility for care, the establishment of incentives to take on this responsibility and the optimization of the use of clinical resources. The interest in France and elsewhere in the implementation of new organizational forms such as Accountable Care Organizations (ACOs) is a major challenge in terms of innovation (Lemaire 2019). More broadly, we could also highlight the difficulty for several healthcare systems to also refocus their mission toward emerging priorities (mental health, frailty, etc.). Obviously, this is not only a question of organizational innovation, but also of innovations in terms of mentalities and social relations between stakeholders. So what does this book offer us? Without claiming to do it justice in a few lines, it serves to better understand the strategies likely to promote and capitalize on organizational innovation. The interest of such a book lies not in its diagnostic scope – the problem is fairly well known – but in the avenues of response it proposes to the tricky issue of the cumbersomeness or inadequacy of organizational innovation in health. I will limit myself to some remarks on the three main theses that make up the three parts of the book. These three themes are partly overlapping and I will come back to them in conclusion.

The first theme of this book, dealt with in Part 1 entitled "Innovations as Seen by Stakeholders", raises the question of the agility of health innovation processes. In this case, innovation means developing a greater scope for the thought and action of stakeholders on the usual channels of power, whether they are professionals or patients. Organizational innovation here involves the ability to generate counter-powers in order to increase the legitimacy of new knowledge, modes of intervention and representations. These counter-powers (Light 2010) are the source of innovation insofar as they are and will be powerful enough to move away from the reproduction of the logics that dictate the current functioning of organizations and the health system. Behind this staging of new stakeholders is a real political project in the sense that organizational innovation consists of fundamentally renewing the social relationships between stakeholders in the healthcare sector (Hallett & Ventresca 2006). Under this topic, a greater or at least more explicit place could be given to stakeholders who live on the limits of the health system but who call for its renewal. I am referring here to people in social situations described as marginal and militant organizations for whom the social and healthcare issues overlap and are confused.

The second topic, dealt with in Part 2 entitled "Innovations on the Collective Side", explores innovation as the product of new agencies. These spaces or collectives of all kinds, communities of practice and innovation laboratories among others, are themselves innovations from the point of view of organizations and the health system. Their establishment questions current practices and expresses a form of productive resistance in organizations and the healthcare system (Courpasson *et al.* 2012). The hypothesis here sees innovation as the product of a protective zone that allows stakeholders to freely engage in exploration and experimentation. The vitality of such spaces depends on the fact that the organization accepts the temporary suspension of environmental discipline to allow innovation to emerge (Zietsma & Lawrence 2010). These spaces testify to the importance of creativity and detachment in rethinking ways of doing things. They also enable the bringing together of stakeholders who usually operate in parallel or separate universes. They will bring innovation insofar as what they produce is taken up and accepted by stakeholders who can influence the decisions made within the organization.

This is the challenge of sustainability and scaling up of healthcare innovations where, too often, successful local experiences fail to be brought to light and institutionalized. Here, the authors do not deal only with innovative spaces but also with innovations in the design of organizations (structuring into clusters, for example) or in public policies (territorialization of policies, for example). It can be hypothesized that innovative design and new spaces of innovation complement each other, perhaps offering the prospect of an institutionalization of innovation. Innovations in organizational design in a sense absorb the logic of the living laboratory by formalizing new frameworks for interaction. They must be accompanied by change and boldness of ideas and mindsets in order for organizational innovations and new practices to emerge. Finally, technologies are called upon to play an increasingly important role in bringing together and creating tension between various stakeholders in search of innovation. Each of the chapters presented in this section could consider the potential of new technologies to create collective spaces that accelerate organizational innovation (Ansell & Gash 2018).

The third topic, dealt with in Part 3 entitled "Reflective Insights on Organizational Innovations in Healthcare", gives way for the systematic analysis of experiences to contemplate change and innovation, whether through research or through evaluation in context. This part highlights, through the various contributions that compose it, the importance of the knowledge-power nexus in understanding and shaping innovations (Ferlie & McGivern 2014). Organizational innovation emerges from a rather deliberate process and does not easily reveal all its subtlety. Systematic processes must be put in place in order to learn from experience and produce knowledge that can accompany and propel innovations. The idea is to produce, by means of a reflexive analysis, knowledge about the conditions for transforming an organization or a health system. The analysis of public healthcare policy offers an opportunity to learn in real time from initiatives aimed at bringing about large-scale transformations and generalizing organizational innovations.

The next challenge is to make this knowledge effective, i.e. to create the conditions for stakeholders to take an interest in it in order to act in favor of innovation. Management tools and policy instruments play a key role here, since they put into circulation representations of activities, behaviors and changes they can induce that were previously less or little known. Ideally, they make it possible to open up new objects to governance, whether it be the state of health of a population, quality of life or healthy living with illness (Jarzabkowski & Kaplan 2015). In all innovation processes, it is important to pay attention to the resource allocation channels that weigh in favor of or against organizational innovation. It is not enough to want to renew primary care or encourage the so-called grassroots innovation; an organization must be able to dedicate the resources that will enable these stakeholders to materialize their projects. These resources are not necessarily new, underlining the importance of being able to reallocate resources to emerging priorities or representations in the healthcare system.

The three parts that structure this book on organizational innovation in healthcare complement one another. Fostering innovation requires stakeholders with the capacity to influence, spaces to create and experiment, and knowledge about processes that can support and accelerate the challenging of the *status quo* and the implementation of new organizational modes or practices. One of the essential conditions for the governance of innovation in healthcare systems is the question of alignment and coherence between public policies and the dynamics and needs found in organizations and clinical settings. This book provides us with the pieces to tackle the puzzle of organizational innovation with seriousness and relevance. It will benefit from being complemented by a reflection on the political and social conditions that enable health systems to adapt better than others to the major contemporary challenges of health and thus to capitalize on innovation on a large scale, whether organizational or not.

Jean-Louis DENIS
CR-CHUM
Université de Montréal
March 2021

References

Ansell, C. and Gash, A. (2018). Collaborative platforms as a governance strategy. *Journal of Public Administration Research and Theory*, 28(1), 16–32.

Courpasson, D., Dany, F., Clegg, S. (2012). Resisters at work: Generating productive resistance in the workplace. *Organization Science*, 23(3), 801–819.

Denis, J.L., Usher, S., Preval, J., Côté-Boileau, É. (2018). Health system reforms in mature welfare states: Tales from the North. *Revista Brasileira em Promoção da Saúde*, 31(4), 1–15.

Ferlie, E. and McGivern, G. (2014). Bringing Anglo-governmentality into public management scholarship: The case of evidence-based medicine in UK health care. *Journal of Public Administration Research and Theory*, 24(1), 59–83.

Hallett, T. and Ventresca, M.J. (2006). Inhabited institutions: Social interactions and organizational forms in Gouldner's Patterns of Industrial Bureaucracy. *Theory and Society*, 35(2), 213–236.

Hinings, B., Gegenhuber, T., Greenwood, R. (2018). Digital innovation and transformation: An institutional perspective. *Information and Organization*, 28(1), 52–61.

Jarzabkowski, P. and Kaplan, S. (2015). Strategy toolsation: An institutional perspective "technologies of rationality" in practice. *Strategic Management Journal*, 36(4), 537–558.

Lemaire, N. (2019). Accountable Care Organizations (ACO) : quelle pertinence pour le système de santé français ? *Les Tribunes de la santé*, 1, 99–107.

Light, D.W. (2010). Health-care professions, markets and countervailing powers. *Handbook of Medical Sociology*, 6, 270–289.

Osty, F., Sainsaulieu, I., Uhalde, M. (2007). *Les mondes sociaux de l'entreprise : penser le développement des organisations.* La Découverte, Paris.

Thornton, P.H. and Ocasio, W. (2008). Institutional logics. In *The SAGE Handbook of Organizational Institutionalism*, Greenwood, R., Oliver, C., Suddaby, R., Sahlin, K. (eds). SAGE Publications, Thousand Oaks.

Zietsma, C. and Lawrence, T.B. (2010). Institutional work in the transformation of an organizational field: The interplay of boundary work and practice work. *Administrative Science Quarterly*, 55(2), 189–221.

Foreword by Norbert Nabet

The Challenges of Altering Frontiers: For Other More Collaborative Approaches

Healthcare systems are complex, the result of historical evolutions that are sometimes contradictory, rich in their diversity but finally well enough organized to resist change, especially institutional change. In France, however, it is the institution that drives change: a hyper-regulated and over-administered system, the fruit of our poorly tamed health history, rich in specificities, achievements and compromises, and therefore of compartments and sectors with their own governance, representations, rates, authorities, hindered or finally protected by their own partitions.

In France, the law and the administration, in the name of quality, safety and equal access to healthcare, use their traditional tools to organize the system, its robustness and universality, as well as its performance and evolution.

On the one hand, spectacular health crises impose strong and visible, and therefore legislative, reactions. Accustomed to dealing with problems at this level of power, governments have become accustomed to the legislative ritual, turning each presidential term into an opportunity to reform, improve and transform the entire healthcare system, which everyone now, certainly for the sake of simplicity, agrees to refer to it as a healthcare "system".

Moreover, since the beginning of the 2000s, two symbolic and operational guardianships have been more or less in competition with each other, each issuing its own rules, recommendations and therefore partitions to redundant central and territorial administrations.

Finally, over the last 10 years or so, as arithmetic control of spending has gone from being an exclusive solution to being a problem, the organization of the system – its governance (ARS[1]), its operation (path) and its evolution (innovation) – has become the embodiment of everyone's attention, hopes and ambitions.

Unfortunately, if the objective changes, the means resist and the law still prescribes these evolutions, which are for many a decompartmentalization. The homeric struggles of lobbies and corporations condemning, most of the time, the mountain to give birth to a mouse. The system devised by the government is thus often cut off from its essence because it was necessary to find a point of balance in the parliamentary debate and negotiations, be they deliberate or political.

The other legislative framework is the annual Social Security Financing Act, which sets the French national health insurance spending target (*objectif national des dépenses d'assurance maladie*, ONDAM[2]). This financial regulation tool has a terrible influence on operational organizations in cities, hospitals and medical-social institutions and services, without any health professional or manager understanding its rationale or the means and methods available to influence it.

With this barely caricatural observation, what can we do? Perhaps, first of all, question our system in order to understand what would make it a readable, controllable and therefore decompartmentalizable organization. Understand in order to act. Choose a reading grid to define a master plan and finally a strategy of actions and innovations that does not erect new partitions and does not increase the cacophony.

Thus, for example, it is not only possible to consider our system, but also our innovation projects, as value propositions addressed to one or more segments of the population or patients, through specific channels and according to specific relationship patterns, relying on resources and activities that mobilize partners. Each of these elements naturally has a cost that must be considered and optimized. It is certainly the methodical, pragmatic and uncompromising analysis of these *processes* or stages that will enable us to understand and build health organizations that are readable, manageable and therefore *decompartmentalizing*.

Then, on this basis, the innovation of practices and organizations is first and foremost conceivable at constant law. It is also necessary to point out the legislator's will to leave a little more room for operators (and not only their representatives) and patients to develop their professional organizations locally and concretely by providing them with contractual and financial tools to help them (art. 51 of the

1 ARS: *Agence Régionale de Santé*; i.e. Regional Healthcare Agency.

2 ONDAM: national health insurance expenditure target.

HPST[3] law on cooperation and the LFSS 2018 on organizational innovations, CPTS, GHT[4], etc.). In all cases, it is necessary to get to know each other, listen to each other, talk to each other, share a common implicit, acquire tools and methods, experiment, observe related experiences and be able to rely, when necessary, on a benevolent and helpful administration.

It is in this context that the innovations reported in this book were conceived. They are most often the work of pioneers whose leadership and charisma have made it possible to create a space of freedom. In this respect, they show us the way and demonstrate the usefulness of decompartmentalization not only in operating theaters, centers or territories, but also in the production of knowledge and professional practices among professionals themselves and with patients.

The question of the transformation of the system rests on our collective capacity to disseminate these innovations: either by rapidly transferring to them the status of common law rules – this is the spirit of article 51 of the LFSS[5] 2018; or by authorizing “at the same time” each person to imagine his or her own organization, according to his or her ecosystem and capacities, and by drawing inspiration from a similar, neighboring achievement and relying on flexible and spontaneously evolving regulations.

In all cases, the methods of benchmarking and exchanging practices are central to the dissemination of innovative practices. Operators are too often totally immersed in their work, looking for solutions that, most of the time, exist just a few kilometers away. Facilitating exchanges, the use of social networks, and the publication and distribution of specialized journals or books – such as the one you are about to read, which demonstrates the will, enthusiasm and competence of all the players in our healthcare system – is undoubtedly the best way to progress.

Norbert NABET
Director
Institutional and partnership relations
NEHS Group
March 2021

3 HPST: *Hôpital, Patient, Santé et Territoire*; Hospital, Patient, Health and Territory.

4 CPTS: *Communauté Professionnelle Territoriale de Santé*; Professional Territorial Community for Health; GHT: *Groupement Hospitalier de Territoire*; Territorial Hospital Grouping.

5 LFSS: *Loi de Financement de la Sécurité Sociale*; Law for the Financing of Social Insurance.

Introduction

The Challenges of "Altering Frontiers": The Multiple Facets of Boundaries to Cross and Articulate

In most developed countries, health systems and organizations at first glance seem a kind of mystery to anyone wishing to understand their mechanisms and dynamics. Their challenges are well known, and meeting them is a challenge (aging population, rise in chronic diseases, technological upheavals made possible by the arrival of Big Data and artificial intelligence, financial equilibrium, increasing inequalities in access to healthcare and healthcare services, the desire for greater patient autonomy and the legitimacy of their voice and experiences, etc.). Conditions are identified as being reinforced by a system that is too procedural, losing its ability to respond in a personalized and individualized manner to the needs of its users and patients. It appears to be "ungovernable" through the usual channels when it comes to dealing with crises with sudden manifestations that are part of a complex network of causes (such as the COVID-19 pandemic or climate change).

Once this diagnosis has been made, the avenues for transformation have also been identified around the central priority of altering frontiers in a system that is too strongly compartmentalized: inventing new forms of governance and cooperation to counter the impossibility of doing things "collectively" in a pluralist system, and giving back room for maneuver and spaces for inventiveness and transformation to local stakeholders in the face of a system that is heavily top-down and has little trust and legitimacy in a number of stakeholders; and yet, health systems remain difficult to transform when there is an extraordinary number of experiments, creative approaches, local dynamics, organizational reorganizations, etc.

Introduction written by Corinne GRENIER and Ewan OIRY.

In order to go beyond this apparent paradox, it is necessary to adopt relevant viewpoints that broaden analytical perspectives that are conducive to transformation.

This is why the angle of this book is that of "altering frontiers", at the micro (stakeholders), meso (various collectives, organized groups) and now macro (organizations) levels. Indeed, the expression "altering frontiers" offers different viewpoints, enabling the researcher and professional and institutional stakeholders to rethink what constitutes a boundary and to act on them in order to organize or coordinate activities differently. This book therefore proposes a new way of analyzing organizational innovations that aim to transform the healthcare system from a vertical and compartmentalized approach to a more horizontal and decompartmentalized one. This approach provides a multifaceted view of the drivers, favorable conditions and methodological principles that can support sustainable transformations in order to "rebuild institutions".

I.1. Altering frontiers: a boundary concept

Thinking of innovation from a perspective of "altering frontiers" invites us, on the contrary, to invest in that which forms a boundary. Indeed, a boundary makes it possible to name, identify, make tangible or visible what is distinctive between what is inside or outside a "space" (Lamont & Molnar 2002). There are thus multiple dimensions (Zietsma & Lawrence 2010; Bucher & Langley 2016): social, relational, cognitive, symbolic, geographical, temporal, material, institutional, etc. (Zietsma & Lawrence 2010; Bucher & Langley 2016). From this perspective, innovation becomes opportune when crossing boundaries, and makes it possible.

Let us consider, for example, the new methods of intervention with the elderly that are currently emerging in France or in other countries and that are described by the still imprecise expression: *EHPAD hors les murs* (EHPAD[1] outside the walls). For such an establishment, it is a question of intervening in the homes of these people by relocating expertise there. The depth of the innovation is measured in terms of the different boundaries crossed: institutional boundaries between the establishment and the home or professional boundaries between the professions of the EHPAD and the home, for example. Some of the contributions in this book shed light on these crossed boundaries that are necessary to support innovation in the field of healthcare: with the emergence of a new "profession", that of advanced practice nurses which, according to Philippe Mossé (Chapter 2), attempts to create a new, autonomous professional space between the nurse and the general practitioner; with entry into the domain of the common stakeholders of care or support, of

1 EHPAD: *Etablissement d'Hébergement pour Personnes Agées Dépendantes*; retirement home.

volunteers who, according to Bertrand Pauget (Chapter 3), seek to make the most of their expertise, which is neither professional nor completely lay.

Another way of rethinking boundaries is to design new spaces conducive to innovation (Grenier & Denis 2017), taking the form of original structural reorganizations, which may be internal and/or external, and bringing together stakeholders from different services or structures. This is the case, for example, of teams reshaping their relationships and knowledge when, according to Delphine Wannenmacher (Chapter 4), they use a new technology (surgical robot) to deliver care differently. In this chapter, the author shows in particular how much, with respect to this robot, visual communication (and associated skills) is reduced and the usual partitions (with regard to time and division of work) are no longer effective. In the same way, the creation of service clusters within hospitals constitutes, for Christelle Havard (Chapter 5), a potential for transformation provided that the stakeholders can carry out cooperative work, at three levels: structural (at the level of the hospital as a whole, to divide and coordinate work), operational (at the level of a department, to organize care tasks around the patient) and trajectorial (around the patient to design and implement a care plan). Finally, we can cite the example of the PTA (*plateforme territoriale d'appui*, territorial support platform), which organizes in an original way the coordination between so-called "front-line" professionals to provide a coordinated response to patients in complex situations. For Matthieu Sibé, Sandrine Cueille and Tamara Roberts (Chapter 7), this organizational innovation will reach its full capacity to provide individualized solutions in the monitoring of trajectories if the stakeholders reinvent their relationships and governance according to the adhocracy model (Mintzberg 1993). This form reflects flexible organizations, combining multidisciplinary and cross-disciplinary skills, capable of adapting to the needs and constraints of the tasks to be accomplished. In this way, another lesson from the various contributions in this book is that the managerial and organizational innovation that accompanies the adoption of new intervention models, new tools or processes only produces its effects if the paradigms relating to modes of governance and decision-making are also transformed (Moore & Hartley 2008).

This calls for a look at a second point to think about innovation, enabled by the boundary concept: creating new networks of knowledge, insights and experience. One way is to introduce new stakeholders who will renew the cognitive reserve of those typically present. With reference to charitable workers working with older people in Sweden, Bertrand Pauget (Chapter 3) examines the interest in encouraging the creation of communities of practice, henceforth called "managed communities" (Bootz 2015), to enable these stakeholders to exchange their experiences in order to improve or even transform them. Focusing on patients, Luigi Flora (Chapter 1) relates the original experience of the "UniverCité" of patients, based in the south of France (Nice). The latter is inspired by similar Quebec models, and brings together health professionals, patients, caregivers, users and civil society to develop experiential knowledge about care, particularly about chronic diseases. It is a double innovation that is thus introduced: the recognition of patients' knowledge and the recognition of experiential knowledge.

Following the example of this type of university, a community of practice forms spaces conducive to building new knowledge, beyond the diversity of stakeholders, and could generate misunderstandings if it is not accompanied in this way. This misunderstanding is of three kinds (Carlile 2004): syntactic, when the misunderstanding concerns words or acronyms; semantic, when it stems from different representations or values; and pragmatic, when it calls into question the re-articulation of interests and areas of power.

These spaces are favorable to the co-construction of knowledge and discursive elements when they have certain characteristics. Thus, Delphine Wannenmacher (Chapter 4) draws our attention to the importance of establishing interactive and reflexive spaces of dialog, in which the stakeholders will define their language and acquire new skills together. Similarly, Boiteau and Baret (2017), studying a working group on new HR practices in a public hospital, show the conditions under which this group was able to support this innovation: by being a "translation center" within which problematization and enlistment made it possible to "tackle subjects considered until then as taboos" by transforming misunderstandings or disinterest around certain questions into controversies that allow stakeholders to express themselves and develop acceptable proposals. It is here that the quality of the controversy enables innovation (Grenier & Denis 2017).

More broadly, we can understand the significance of new stakeholders in the health field, known by the generic term "intermediary organizations", "boundary partners" (Chesbrough & Haas 2016) or "brokers" (Hargadon 1997), whose role (political, cognitive and symbolic) is to bring together professionals who are not accustomed to working together or interacting, in order to build new cognitive and discursive resources together. However, following the example of what is generally observed in third places such as FabLabs, do specific methodological resources (such as those provided by Design Thinking; Grenier *et al.* 2020) still need to be developed to allow stakeholders to cross the boundaries of their institutional embeddedness?

If innovation takes place "at the boundaries", by putting stakeholders in a position to collaborate despite their different cultural or professional spheres, they must also be able to absorb this "novelty" that is made available. Corinne Grenier and

Christine Dutrieux (Chapter 9) question the extent to which organizations can absorb, and thus bring within their boundaries, ideas, models and practices "from elsewhere". Absorptive capacity is understood as a set of organizational routines and processes by which the organization acquires and mobilizes external knowledge to produce dynamic organizational capacity (Todorova & Durisin 2007; Imbert & Chauvet 2012). This capacity is based on four processes (or four stages):

1) acquisition, referring to the organization's ability to recognize, value and acquire external knowledge and ideas;

2) assimilation, referring to the organization's ability to understand, analyze and interpret this knowledge and ideas;

3) transformation, consisting of the organization's ability to develop new routines to facilitate the combination of the old and the new;

4) exploitation, aimed at deploying this renewed stock of knowledge and ideas into new projects, activities and processes.

Entering this process means that some distance is necessary in the exploration of new ideas and knowledge from the acquired stock (to avoid absorbing only those with which individuals and organizations are already familiar). This distance is created *a priori* in the specific places we mentioned above (third places), which host both established operators and start-ups, professionals or entrepreneurs, and very often from various sectors. It is up to Hugo Bertillot (Chapter 10) to offer us an original view on this ability to distance ourselves from habits. He focuses on the comparative management indicators developed since the end of the 2000s, integrated into the certification procedure for public hospitals in France and made public at the national level. They are instruments for regulation, decision support for contractualization and internal drivers for improvement. However, the power of indicators to transform hospitals is far from self-evident. Everything will depend on the ability of the stakeholders to "open the black box" of these indicators, to detect, or even build in, room for maneuver in relation to their habits of doing and thinking.

Finally, this book questions the boundary from a temporal and spatial view by questioning the diffusion of innovation. Many currents are mobilized by the literature investigating the field of health, such as: the adoption of what is new (de Vaujany 2005); a network of stakeholders to advance innovation, by operations of problematization, translation and irreversibility mechanism (Callon 1986), or more recently, by networks of practices (Agterberg *et al.* 2010, 2011) consisting of organizing the circulation of practices and ideas from one place to another. Healthcare innovation has a high degree of contextualization, stemming from in particular the territorialization of the stakeholders' intervention; the question is then approached in terms not of adoption but of adaptation (Sahlin & Wedlin 2008).

This adaptation process requires specific methodologies to capture what has been experimented with in order to disseminate it, and in particular everything that is "invisible", tacit or informal and too often cannot be reduced to "experience capitalization guides". Thus, for Jessica Gheller, Christian Bourret and Gérard Mick (Chapter 8), dissemination appears to be a "journey" reinforced by an exciting, meaningful communication, making it possible to identify the experiences acquired during an expedition, then continuing with the deployment of a living "memory" that will be enriched as innovations are disseminated in other places. This living memory forms a knowledge base that can be subject to questioning and reflexivity for professionals wishing to adopt experiences already developed in other spaces. It promotes learning, an essential element identified by Frédéric Gilbert (Chapter 6) in his study on the dissemination of the family doctor group model in Quebec. In this experience, it is then, *a contrario*, the downside of an evaluative approach that prevents this learning and limits the journey from place to place of this original front-line organizational form.

I.2. Conclusion

The creation of a book is always the fruit of a long process. The present project began in 2019 when, in the vast majority of countries, the transformation of the health system was thought to be a long-term process, with uncertain results, and marked by a fiercely negotiated balance between "high" and "low", between center and periphery, between institutional entrepreneurs and those more inclined to preserve so-called "assets".

However, its manufacture concludes with a context that is completely new for many: the (global) health crisis of COVID-19 and the ways to combat it. Daily reports (TV, newspapers) recount the major difficulties faced by organizations and health professionals in informing, caring for and accompanying patients, users and caregivers: lack of personnel – and those who remain are exhausted – lack of masks and other protection, insufficient intensive care beds, etc. These are all the aspects of the healthcare system that are affected: hospitals, EHPAD, medical and social institutions providing support or accommodation for disabled children and adults, SAAD and SSIAD[2], social services, "front-line" professionals, etc. This crisis will have been a powerful indicator of dysfunctions that have already been in place for a long time.

At the same time, many testimonies have revealed daily the determination of all professionals and other stakeholders (charitable workers and citizens) to continue to

2 SAAD: *service d'aide et d'accompagnement au domicile* (social homecare service); SSIAD: *service de soins infirmiers à domicile* (home nursing service).

practice their "profession for the other". In many countries, everyone seemed to be rallying for the "common good", based on a principle of solidarity in capitalist societies (Tirole 2016). What a lot of tinkering! In the sense that, in a do-it-yourself approach, the stakeholder knows the aims of his or her actions, but at the same time, he or she must identify or locate the resources to achieve them (Levis-Strauss 1962; Garud & Karnoe 2003).

These do-it-yourself projects, as varied as they are ingenious and surprising, are all based on the different facets of action that we have just mentioned, all of which are based on the identification of boundaries and the conditions under which they are crossed. However, they reveal, with renewed acuity, three ingredients for a sustainable transformation of the health system: the autonomy of the stakeholders, enabling them to invent solutions; the benevolence of the supervisory authorities, with a view to mobilize methodological and support resources to assist these professionals and organizations; and the need for a sense of control and evaluation to ensure the sustainability of this inventiveness.

Finally, it emerges from most of the chapters of the book that this crisis is also a call to put an end to a culture of "the fairest". The crisis has revealed what can be called a *slack of solidarity*, when individuals, companies, merchants, etc., spontaneously offer their help and service. The term *slack* refers to the surplus (time, resources) which we do not know *a priori* what it can be used for, except when it has to be used! Schulman (1993) identifies two types of *slack*: that of resources (surplus not strictly engaged in current activities) and that of control relative to the degree of freedom in organizational activities (i.e. a set of actions that are not framed by formal modes of power, and supervision). It is thanks to these that the crisis is overcome as quickly as possible. May this lesson be kept in mind, not only because some people predict the multiplication and complexity of future crises, but more generally because it is an important condition for any innovative organization, when individuals have time, outside of protocolized and routine activities, to imagine how to renew themselves in a different way.

I.3. References

Agterberg, M., Van den Hooff, B., Huysman, M., Soekijad, M. (2010). Keeping the wheels turning: The dynamics of managing networks of practice. *Journal of Management Studies*, 47(1), 85–108.

Agterberg, M., Van den Hooff, B., Huysman, M. (2011). Cracking the core: How core members of electronic networks of practice contribute to organizational learning. *Annual Meeting of the Academy of Management*, San Antonio, Texas, 1–19.

Boiteau, K. and Baret, C. (2017). La conduite du changement en hôpital psychiatrique : le rôle des centres de traduction dans la valorisation des innovations lors d'un projet de promotion du bien-être au travail. *Politiques et management public*, 34(3–4), 231–246.

Boötz, J. (2015). Comment concilier auto-organisation et contrôle au sein des communautés de pratique pilotées ? Une scoping review. *Management international*, 19(3), 15–30.

Callon, M. (1986). Éléments pour une sociologie de la traduction : la domestication des coquilles Saint-Jacques et des marins-pêcheurs dans la baie de Saint-Brieuc. *L'Année sociologique*, 36(3), 169–208.

Carlile, P. (2004). Transferring, translating and transforming: An integrative framework for managing knowledge across boundaries. *Organization Science*, 15(5), 555–568.

Chesbrough, H. and Haas, W.A. (2006). Open innovation: A new paradigm for understanding industrial innovation. In *Open Innovation: Researching a New Paradigm*, Chesbrough, H., Vanhaverbeke, W., West, J. (eds). Oxford University Press, Oxford.

De Vaujany, F.X. (ed.) (2005). *De la conception à l'usage : vers un management de l'appropriation des outils de gestion*. EMS, Caen.

Garud, R. and Karnøe, P. (2003). Bricolage versus breakthrough: Distributed and embedded agency in technology entrepreneurship. *Research Policy*, 32(2), 277–300.

Grenier, C. and Denis, J.L. (2017). S'organiser pour innover : espaces d'innovation et transformation des organisations et du champ de l'intervention publique. *Politiques et management public*, 34(3–4), 191–206.

Grenier, C., Ibrahim, R., Duprat, L. (2020). Comment organiser un tiers-lieu éphémère pour favoriser l'émergence d'innovations institutionnelles ? Le cas d'un pôle d'opérateurs de services à domicile. *Innovations*, 66(1), 89–115.

Hargadon, A. (1997). Technology brokering and innovation in a product development firm. *Administrative Science Quarterly*, 42(4), 716–749.

Imbert, G. and Chauvet, V. (2012). De la capacité d'absorption à la capacité d'insémination. *Revue française de gestion*, 221, 111–127.

Lamont, M. and Molnár, V. (2002). The study of boundaries in the social sciences. *Annual Review of Sociology*, 28(1), 167–195.

Levi-Strauss, C. (1962). *La pensée sauvage*. Plon, Paris.

Mintzberg, H. (1993). *Structure in Fives: Designing Effective Organizations*. Prentice-Hall, Upper Saddle River.

Moore, M. and Hartley, J. (2008). Innovations in governance. *Public Management Review*, 10, 3–20.

Sahlin, K. and Wedlin, L. (2008). Circulating ideas: Imitation, translation and editing. In *The SAGE Handbook of Organizational Institutionalism*, Greenwood, R., Oliver, C., Suddaby, R., Sahlin, K. (eds). SAGE Publications, Thousand Oaks.

Schulman, P.R. (1993). The negotiated order of organizational reliability. *Administration & Society*, 25(3), 353–372.

Tirole, J. (2016). *Économie du bien commun*. PUF, Paris.

Todorova, G. and Durisin, B. (2007). Absorptive capacity: Valuing a reconceptualization. *Academy of Management Review*, 32(3), 774–786.

Wenger, E., McDermott, R., Snyder, W.M. (2002). *Cultivating Communities of Practice*. Harvard Business Publishing, Brighton.

Zietsma, C. and Lawrence, T.B. (2010). Institutional work in the transformation of an organizational field: The interplay of boundary work and practice work. *Administrative Science Quarterly*, 55(2), 189–221.

Part 1

Innovations as Seen by Stakeholders

Introduction to Part 1

Taking up the challenge of "altering frontiers" through organizational innovations raises the double question of the place of different individuals in this profound transformation.

Individuals are first and foremost at the heart of this transformation because they are the driving force behind it. They are singular individuals – the innovators – who develop new interdisciplinary practices, implement decompartmentalization and transform usual routines (Gherardi 2008). They transform their practices by experimenting in "innovative spaces" typically outside the organization, sometimes protected from the rules that usually govern it (Bucher & Langley 2016). They are sometimes tired of the multiple social norms to which they cross in order to innovate (Alter 2011). However, they are clearly, for many, the heart and driving force of the organizational innovation process that enables decompartmentalization.

As for the rest of the professionals, even if they are not exactly innovators, are they not also the target of organizational innovations that aim to decompartmentalize? In this way, they discover and experience on a daily basis the transformations that have been designed for them and that they must appropriate and implement. These innovations transform their ways of working, shake up their skills and sometimes their professional identities (Robelet *et al.* 2005). This can also make them more efficient and even satisfy them by giving more meaning to their work, emphasizing that a decompartmentalized organization ensures better and more effective patient care or support.

"Altering frontiers" through organizational innovations is therefore bringing about interplay of identity dimensions as well as questions of competence or performance.

Finally, we must not lose sight of the fact that compartmentalization cannot be overcome without taking into account the major consequences that this can have. Indeed, in healthcare organizations, compartmentalization is merely a fortuitous and damaging consequence of significant bureaucracy (Weber 2003). Compartmentalization is also that. The sheer amount of bureaucracy means that employees are gradually losing out the overall vision and meaning of the work they do there and reduce their field of intervention to what is their only day-to-day work.

However, silos are also a simple and relatively effective organizational solution for maintaining and deepening employee expertise (Currie *et al.* 2012). In a healthcare activity where expertise is crucial and where its shortcomings can have immediate consequences on the lives of patients, it is understandable that compartmentalization may have appeared to be a satisfactory solution. By asking a radiologist to deal only with x-rays or a surgeon to specialize in the surgery of only one part of the body, a care facility ensures that the expertise will be maximal and that the patient's care will be optimal.

However, it is only recently, with the increasing complexity of care and support (chronic diseases, aging of the population), that the coordination of many stakeholders in a multi-professional approach (different doctors, other health professionals but also patients themselves) has become necessary, revealing even more the restrictive limits of this compartmentalization. Today, when we think about the decompartmentalization of health organizations, it is necessary to also think about organizational devices that will enable the maintenance and the deepening of the expertise of all the professions and expertise (also known as lay) in the field of health and healthcare.

This book, which offers a multidisciplinary and multi-level analysis of current innovations in healthcare systems, had to begin with a reflection on the changing roles and skills of the stakeholders, those who, on a daily basis, act on the healthcare system.

Among these stakeholders, we wanted to analyze first the organizational innovations that are developed around the patients themselves. Although they are the main beneficiaries and stakeholders in the health system, it has long been known that their knowledge and experiences are ultimately difficult to be taken into account by health systems where, often, professional logics dominate.

This section on the players opens with an analysis of the experience of the UniverCité du Soin in Nice by Luigi Flora (Chapter 1). This network makes it possible to work, it seems, on an equal footing – patients, health professionals, caregivers, users and civil society. Its objective is to enable the development of experiential knowledge about care, particularly about chronic diseases. This experiment describes concretely the forms and effects of this "empowerment" of patients, users and civil society.

Chapter 2, proposed by Philippe Mossé, analyzes the new skills that emerge among health professionals as a result of this strengthening of cooperative work (between professionals, with patients and with other users of the healthcare system). The case of advanced practice nurses is a particularly good illustration of the effects of this organizational innovation. In particular, this case highlights the fact that, to be complete, the analysis must go beyond the case of individuals alone to position them within broader frameworks such as those of professional spaces.

Finally, an identical logic is found in the contribution of Bertrand Pauget (Chapter 3) who looks at communities of practice of volunteers in the care of the elderly in the Swedish care system. The analysis clearly shows that the long-term motivation of charitable workers depends on their inclusion in collectives – in this case communities of practice – which enable them to build a sense of purpose for their actions and to disseminate the most effective practices.

References

Alter, N. (2011). Comment les dirigeants des organisations peuvent tuer l'innovation ? *Gestion*, 36(4), 5–10.

Bucher, S. and Langley, A. (2016). The interplay of reflective and experimental spaces in interrupting and reorienting routine dynamics. *Organization Science*, 27(3), 594–613.

Currie, G., Lockett, A., Finn, R., Martin, G., Waring, J. (2012). Institutional work to maintain professional power: Recreating the model of medical professionalism. *Organization Studies*, 33, 937–962.

Gherardi, S. (2008). Aujourd'hui les plaques sont molles ! *Revue d'anthropologie des connaissances*, 2(1), 3–35.

Robelet, M., Serré, M., Bourgueil, Y. (2005). La coordination dans les réseaux de santé : entre logiques gestionnaires et dynamiques professionnelles. *Revue française des affaires sociales*, (1), 231–260.

Weber, M. (2003). *Économie et société*. Pocket, Paris.

1

Recognition of Patients' Experiential Knowledge and Co-production of Care Knowledge with Patients and Citizens in the 21st Century

1.1. Introduction

The expectation of populations to participate in subjects that concern them is a key fact of the 21st century; the health field, a sensitive subject, is only one example. From the emergence in the first part of the 20th century, through the mobilization of citizens and the creation of popular epidemiological approaches (Brown 1987), to participatory research mainly in the environmental field (Houillet 2016), or more specifically in the field of health today, many communities of citizens have initiated practices that call for them to act, actions that have opened the way up to co-construction. It is a continuum organized from initial collaborations through the mobilization of citizens in the face of local intoxication due to industrial pollution, through the reaction of populations affected by the HIV/AIDS pandemic through the development of the Denver[1] Principles, which constitute real collective, individual and interpersonal data.

This movement in favor of patient and user involvement, promoted for example in France by the law of 4 March 2002 on patients' rights and on the quality of the health system, establishing a real framework for health democracy, is part of an international movement with major implications for contemporary health systems,

---

Chapter written by Luigi FLORA.

1 Written by People with Aids (PWA) in 1983, available at: http://lemegalodon.net/a6507-les-principles-de-denver.html.

partly demonstrated scientifically by the increase in the number of articles published over the last 20 years (Boote *et al.* 2002; Crocker *et al.* 2018). A wide variety of co-constructing tendencies have emerged from this change. These trends involve patients, users, citizens and all the stakeholders and institutions that make up health systems, according to different approaches (theoretical, conceptual and methodological).

Since Angela Coulter (2011) identified that 98% of the hours of care given to a person with chronic diabetes is provided by the patient and his or her family, these strategies have been of increasing interest to decision-makers in healthcare systems and their organizations. This English researcher has in fact defined the annual production of care in the context of the chronicization of patients.

Chronically ill people who, depending on their illness(s), spend an average of 5 to 10 hours a year in care with health professionals, while in that time, they and their loved ones spend up to 6,250 hours of care. This knowledge of patients has become a social fact (Durkheim 1988; Flora 2012; Jouet 2014). This chapter therefore deals with what is being organized as a consequence of this ongoing transformation in the organization of our societies as an extension of the changes largely shaped by the rise of science and more particularly of technoscientific approaches in the field of health (Jouet *et al.* 2010).

1.2. From "empowerment" to the "patient revolution", an international trend

With the medical model, which can be described as "organic"[2], imposing itself in the institutionalization of care in Western countries, and relegating the educational dimensions of care to the background, at the end of the 20th century and because of the link between prophylactic policies and the emergence of patient knowledge, it was called into question by the modification of the place of patients' knowledge in the healthcare system. As new figures for patients and citizens who disseminate this knowledge are increasing in the 21st century, it is because of the profitability of their involvement in the management of healthcare systems (Boivin *et al.* 2014). Historically, it was the reaction of patients to the management of AIDS that enabled health democracy to take root and to articulate patient expertise and public health policies. However, the first group of patients mobilizing empowerment processes was initiated in 1934, within the Alcoholics Anonymous movement.

2 From Vesale to the Renaissance, medicine has been defined as being more interested in organs, the fragmentation of the indivisible individual and the aggression of disease, than in the patient (Le Breton 1990).

DEFINITION 1.1. Empowerment. – *The process by which individuals and groups act to gain control over their lives and thus gain greater control over decisions and actions affecting their health in the context of changing social and political environments. Self-esteem is thus strengthened, critical thinking, decision-making and action capacity are promoted. Even people with few abilities or in precarious situations are considered to have strengths and resources. This process cannot be produced, only fostered.*

It was at this very moment that the cornerstones were laid for a new type of exchange based on informal and formal practices between patients. The organizational model that emerged from this was to be extended to other groups, such as drug users in the 1950s and people living with HIV in the 1980s. This phenomenon was then transposed into self-help and self-empowerment movements of user groups in several other addiction pathologies (for example, alcohol in 1935, drugs in 1953, eating disorders or compulsive gambling behavior). This type of interaction, based on mutual aid, information sharing between patients, peer training and developing a global approach to the individual, has gradually challenged and then upset the pyramid of medical knowledge and power alone as a source of healing and disease management. It has also made it possible to meet patients at the very site of their addictions.

The organization of this movement has been formalized according to already operational models, such as those of learned societies or large charitable organizations. This movement thus took this form while, paradoxically, throughout the 20th century, medicine became institutionalized, raising health as a primary value in society in large part thanks to technological discoveries that supported the medical approach, affirming technicality as the spearhead of modern medicine. This institutionalization is accompanied by the displacement of knowledge and care practice from the family sphere to the group and societal spheres, a process which, amplified by societal transformations, sees the development of women's work taking them away from the family sphere. In this redistribution of knowledge, roles and powers, resorting to a "family doctor" and hospital services will become the norm, giving doctors and the medical institution the possibility of seeing themselves higher in the hierarchy because they are able to defy pain and death (Foucault 1963).

In this process at work, the women, ancestral holders of a "care-taking" inherited from one family member to another, used to practice *bona famae* (reputable) remedies, occasionally calling on outside practitioners (binders, healers, etc.) to intervene most often in the final stages of the disease during which the prognosis proved fatal and these forms of knowledge were lost. To conclude on the elements leading to a shift in the distribution of care knowledge, it is necessary to highlight: (1) the death of family members in specialized institutions, first in the hospital where the majority of elderly people died during the 20th century, then to dedicated institutions when signs of old age appeared; (2) the appearance of social protection systems – driven by the economic development of our societies – which, although different from one country to another, provide social added value replacing support cells at the family level.

Economic developments also penetrate the world of healthcare, as the pharmaceutical industry developed and grew throughout the century to become part of the international healthcare system by developing global pharmaceutical trusts whose missions are research and marketing of medicines.

In reaction to this medicine, which is carried and dominated by techniques and technologies, both in the care and in the organization of care, a movement of humanization emerges as a compensation of the dominant medical model with the appearance of listening and accompaniment techniques during the 1970s.

Health professionals are organizing themselves to intervene in this trend, first of all outside the institutional framework that protects these new approaches. Not everything concerning patient information and education has yet been translated into international (WHO 1986) recommendations. At the societal level, new public health policies are needed. The increase in the number of people living with chronic diseases raises the question of the involvement of the patient in the management of his or her treatment. Beneficial effects have been recognized by studies. This involvement improves adherence to treatment in multiple pathologies, and doctors are therefore seeking to develop tools to increase it. This transformation of patient care emphasizes the need not only to inform but also to educate the patient in order to be as close as possible to a so-called "informed consent". This notion of consent initially emerged for research during the Second World War and was the first time that the Nazi regime began experimenting in this field and questioned the behavior of medical doctors who put forward the concept of bioethics. In the course of this process, the patient then began to demand, beyond mere information, a sharing of the decisions that would be taken thanks to free and enlightened information and the right to self-determination.

However, it was during the 1980s that an upheaval was to take place in the attempt to rebalance knowledge and medical power in the context of relationships with patients and populations. It is the result of the emergence of a disease against which, at first, medicine remained powerless: HIV/AIDS. The patient-stakeholder relationship then established itself during the last two decades of the 20th century. This movement added a new element to those previously described and driven by the movement or movements of patients (mutual aid, information and training): the use of an activism that claims to play the role of reformer within a changing society – the information society and then the knowledge society, in the 21st century.

The socialization of action in the field of health then became a fact of society. The approach to health was profoundly modified by the action of these new patients who, as early as 1983, set out new demands through the Denver Principles. They then expressed the need for their participation in everything that concerned them.

At the heart of this change is the desire of patients to become "stakeholders in their own health"; a social reform action explained in 1989 at the World Conference on HIV/AIDS (Canada) by the founding president of the French association AIDES association, Daniel Defert. This period saw the emergence of new types of associations with innovative functions.

These associations were created, from the 1990s on, on inter-associative collectives[3]. These forces and sources of collective knowledge relied on the media to disseminate their message in public opinion and make visible the system's inability to deal with situations. As a result of this shock, patients, through these associations, demanded to participate fully in the organizational processes and in the orientation choices of public health policies. The fact that young people die without the cause being war creates a shock wave among Western populations. Associations are becoming aware of this and are quickly learning to use public opinion to influence political decisions.

The associative movement is then profoundly modified, in its structures and by being partly composed of patients and relatives. The latter act from then on to assert their status as reformers of the health system. They provide a generalized awareness of the fact that the sick individual – as the first person concerned – can become a stakeholder in his or her own health; the idea that one holds knowledge that one can express gradually emerges. This shift questions and upsets the dominance of medical knowledge and powers as the only sources of healing and management of illness. This approach is beginning to appear relevant, even necessary, for the management of chronically ill patients. Indeed, in this field, multiple studies prove the limits of an increasingly technical and efficient medicine in the treatment of the acute phases of diseases and other accidents of life. Thus, the notions of compliance – the ability of the patient to follow medical prescriptions – or more precisely of non-observance are opposed to the solutions, however, which are still largely topical and which propose increasingly specialized medicine, defining the individual according to a mechanistic philosophy. Patients demand that the choices of research, prescription and therapeutic use be explained to them and that their opinions be consulted in the institutional administrative and decision-making bodies. The "AIDS years" and the emergence of this new associative trend are thus modifying the balance of power.

---

3 For example, TRT-5 for "treatment and therapeutic research" and "5" for the 5 associations behind the initiative against HIV/AIDS; then the *Collectif interassociatif sur la santé* (CISS) in France and the European Aids Treatment Group (EATG) in Europe.

Therefore, patients, through associations, demand to participate fully in the organizational processes and in the orientation choices of public health policies, not only for the survival of patients, but also to make proposals in the face of the risk of hecatomb caused by the epidemic. Public policies are gradually changing the place of patient associations in the management of the health system and in the organization of clinical research, at all stages – right up to the marketing of drugs and the care of those affected – thanks to their lobbying actions. To achieve this, the associations have implemented actions and disseminated magazines for people living with HIV. Another situation arising from the shock of the AIDS years, another public health problem that has accentuated the importance of consulting associations of patients and their families: the contaminated blood affair. Although handled differently in the United States and France[4], it had a significant impact on public opinion. This second crisis and all the scandals that have occurred since have been brought up to date with certain regularities (nosocomial infections, asbestos, Creutzfeldt-Jakob disease, drug scandals, etc.) dealt a final blow to the paradigm of management by the monopoly of scholarly knowledge – be it medical, managerial or administrative – as it had been developed until then. Confidence in this paradigm was then undermined; by informing the general public of its problems and thus spreading the mismanagement of public health problems, the media propelled the associations which, supported by public opinion, initiated profound reforms in the management of health systems.

Thus, the emergence of this new associative approach has played on public opinion through the use of communication, with the establishment of large media "Masses" calling for public generosity and the collection of donations – such as the successive Sidaction and Telethon – which have been the impetus to establish new rules. In fact, in parallel with the associations fighting HIV, and while people living with mental disorders within the "Recovery" movement framework are[5] taking up the ideas of the Denver Principles for HIV, the AFM (*Association française contre*

4 While the complaints mainly incriminated the pharmaceutical laboratories in the United States – with foreign plaintiffs to whom the contaminated blood products were exported – in France it was a lawsuit against failing institutions and a questioning of policy that gave rise to the scandal, and in Canada it was the Red Cross and its officials who were quickly targeted by the complaints.

5 Recovery, initially initiated by Alcoholics Anonymous, is based on mutual aid between people living with the same illness, somatic or psychic. Individuals can thus manifest themselves through group dynamics, such as the self-help groups from which they come, or, as is increasingly developing in the 21st century, within a professionalized framework in the dual accompaniment of peers and health and social work professionals whose action is dedicated to their peers. A salutogenesis approach has therefore been developed as an alternative to the historical pathogenesis approach.

les myopathies, French Association against Myopathies) is inventing a model of operation that has been painstakingly acquired and defended with constant vigilance.

This association will clearly intervene without encroaching on the prerogatives of each other and will become as a key player both nationally and internationally. It will be the first association (and the only one to date) to constitute the necessary elements for the production of drugs for orphan diseases that are not of financial interest to the market-driven pharmaceutical industry. In fact, the members of these new associative entities have a better capacity to raise funds and therefore to organize and pilot research tenders.

Through this power, the associations consecrate the place of patients and users in the healthcare system. The HIV-positive movement organized the first general meeting on their problems. These were later followed, in France, by the general assemblies of families and patients living with genetic and orphan diseases (1995) and the *états généraux des personnes touchées par les cancers* (general conditions of people affected by cancer) (1998), leading to the *états généraux de la santé* (general conditions of health national conference (1999), which was the driving force behind institutionalization by legislative means of the possibilities of the 21st century in terms of the potentialities of participation both for *their* health and for health in general. This process culminated in the law of March 9, 2002, relating to the rights of patients and the quality of the health system, which enshrined health democracy in France[6].

In the 1990s, a technological revolution played a parallel role and accompanied this transformation of mentalities, practices and knowledge, both individually and collectively. The advent of the Internet democratized access to medical information, and the media, whether on the Internet or on other types of support, was used to develop the principles of information, training and mutual aid. Associations are rapidly taking over the Internet, as much to raise awareness among the general population (lobbying) as to disseminate to the greatest number of individuals and groups concerned medical information that ranges from popularized information (a term we prefer the expression "democratized information" because it allows everyone to get an idea and participate) to real scientific information delivered as such. The associations subscribe on the Internet to the most renowned scientific journals and learn how to decipher and retranscribe the latest news. They form networks on the Web that are highly reactive. In this way, they have integrated, if not anticipated, the behaviors of the population.

---

6 French health democracy has been initiated in other countries, mainly European, such as Belgium or Germany, without any of them having a framework law of this magnitude.

Indeed, with the arrival of the Internet, new health information and exchange practices emerged. Thus, since the 1980s, citizens and patients developed and implemented framework tools that promoted individual and collective empowerment and had a *de facto* impact on the health system.

1.3. From paternalism to different forms of participation and partnership with patients

Paternalistic approaches to care, which emerged between the 1940s and 1970s from medicine that gradually became all-powerful within health systems structured around acute and highly specialized care offered in health facilities, were gradually combined, or even replaced, to meet the needs of populations.

They are the result of epidemiological mutations, such as the significant increase in the prevalence of chronic diseases and aging populations. They have thus gradually given way, since their timid beginnings in the 1970s, to patient-centered approaches. These take into consideration the particularities, values and experiences of patients.

All over the world, healthcare organizations, institutions and universities have gradually redoubled their efforts to involve patients and make their participation increasingly active, in very different ways and with very different motivations. Recent initiatives, such as shared decision-making, have added to the diversity of approaches in therapeutic patient education (TPE). Then, starting at the University of Montreal at the beginning of the second half of the 20th century, a new approach emerged under the term "partnership approach"; it is a partnership of care with the patient, otherwise known as the "Montreal model" by the Americans since the workshops conducted in 2014 under the aegis of the Macy Foundation.

Thus, there is currently a continuum of models for mobilizing patient and population empowerment (Figure 1.1); it includes access to information for patients and populations, their contribution to all stages and strata of care, their involvement in healthcare organizations through participatory modalities that go as far as co-construction and co-design between patients and healthcare professionals (Pomey *et al.* 2015).

1.4. Innovative practices

As illustrated in Figure 1.1 on the continuum of patient engagement, the care partnership with the patient stemming from the Montreal model can be seen as one of the most innovative practices in collaboration between patients, family members and the public.

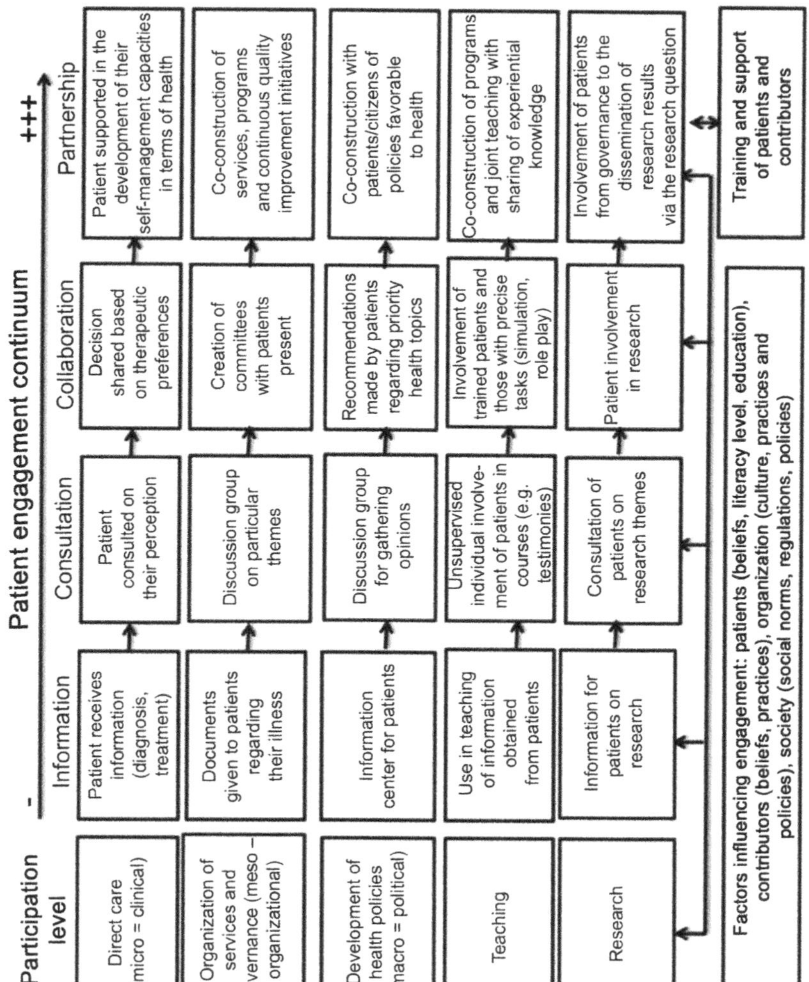

Figure 1.1. *Continuum of patient engagement modalities*

This approach places more emphasis on the sharing of power and responsibility between patients and professionals (from "care for" to "care with") than patient-centered approaches as deployed in care organizations, as presented in section 1.3. This approach proposes that the patient be considered as a caregiver and, consequently, as a full-fledged member of the healthcare team (Karazivan *et al.* 2015). It therefore integrates the capacity of patients and their relatives to produce care (Coulter 2011). Patients are recognized for their experiential knowledge of living with the disease (Jouet *et al.* 2010) and the skills they mobilize (Flora 2012, 2015).

As such, they are considered legitimate persons to make the decisions best suited to their life, in collaboration with health professionals (whom we can no longer call caregivers). The patient is perceived as an individual (indivisible)[7] and is progressively accompanied throughout his or her care journey to make free and informed health choices and take the care decisions that seem best suited to him or her. To do this, his experience of living with the disease and his skills are recognized as contributing to the care that concerns him. Thanks to the skills acquired through therapeutic education and reflexivity based on their own experience (Flora 2012, 2015), patients can strengthen their self-determination and self-management capacities.

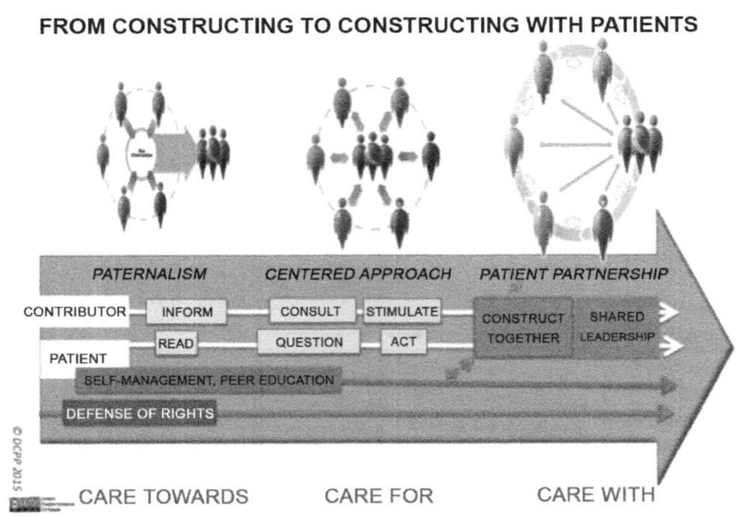

Figure 1.2. *The continuum of care practices. For a color version of this figure, see www.iste.co.uk/grenier/frontiers.zip*

7 The etymology of individual, *individuum* in Latin, calls us precisely to consider the person as indivisible.

This innovative model (Karazivan *et al.* 2015; Pomey *et al.* 2015) is the result of the integration of patients into a Quebec faculty of medicine, thanks to the dean of this faculty, Jean Rouleau, and a patient, Vincent Dumez, who is also a specialist in change management in the faculty of medicine of the University of Montreal (Flora 2012). From this innovative initiative was born a model of co-construction that enabled the emergence of this model launched to enable the medical profession to adapt to the cascading mutations that physicians and healthcare systems have to face (Figure 1.3).

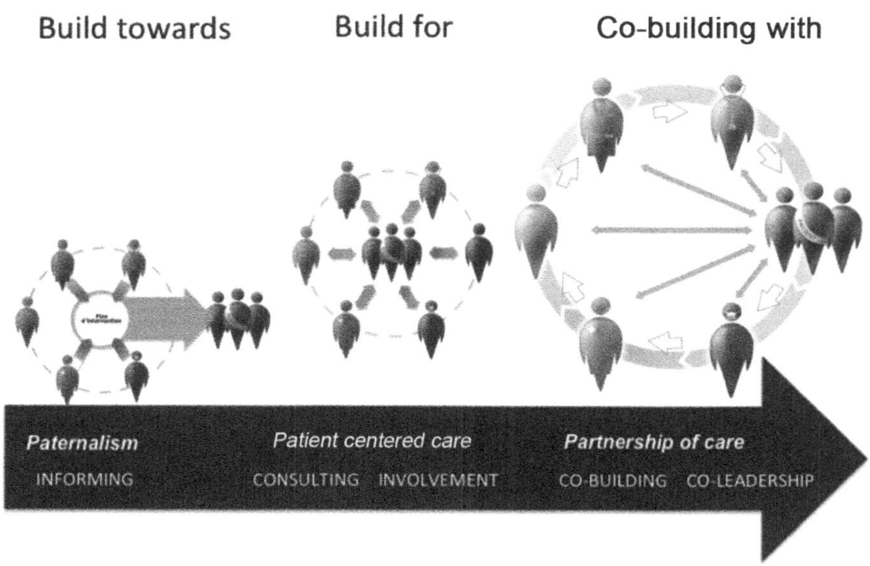

Figure 1.3. *Different approaches to care. For a color version of this figure, see www.iste.co.uk/grenier/frontiers.zip*

On the theoretical and conceptual level of the "Montreal model", the partnership focuses on the recognition of experiential knowledge of patients (Flora 2012; Karazivan *et al.* 2015; Pomey *et al.* 2015), caregivers and citizens. This knowledge, derived from living with the disease, from experience of care and services or from living in the community, is seen as complementary to the knowledge of healthcare professionals (whether clinicians, managers or public decision-makers).

They are anchored in a vision of partnership whose essence is at the level of: (1) the individual care relationship (micro level) (Pomey *et al.* 2015), which is the basis for partnership interventions between patients and healthcare providers (individual and community members, peer associations and health professionals);

(2) healthcare[8], teaching and research organizations (meso level): and (3) government agencies (responsible for developing public policy) (macro level) (Pomey *et al.* 2015).

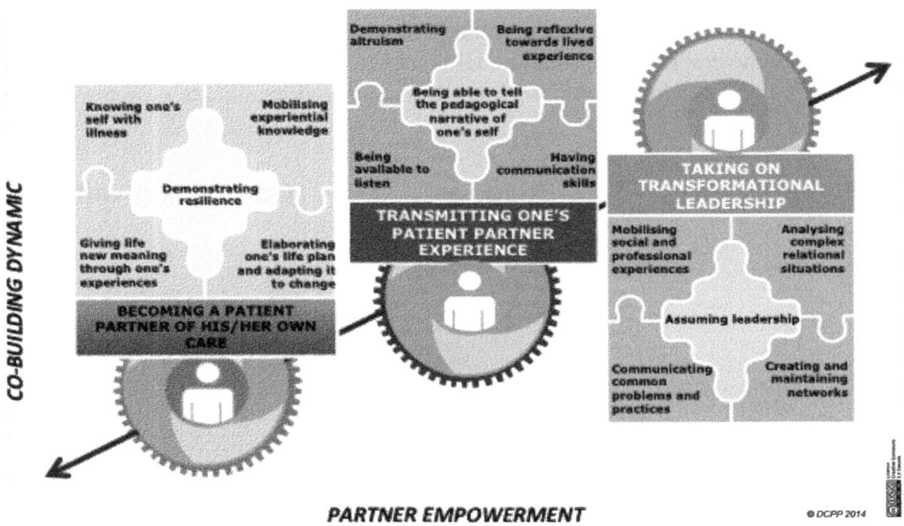

Figure 1.4. *Patients' skills in frame of reference. For a color version of this figure, see www.iste.co.uk/grenier/frontiers.zip*

On the methodological level, the implementation of the partnership at the meso and macro levels, it is through the identification of the experiential knowledge of patients mobilized through skills that the partnerships were organized (Flora 2012).

It is on the basis of a repository of patient partner skills that the means of identifying patients with experiential knowledge to be mobilized according to the situation have been developed (Figure 1.4) (Flora 2015, p. 58).

At the micro level, in order to support a culture of partnership care, courses on interprofessional collaboration in partnership with the patient have been integrated into initial training at the University of Montreal in Quebec (Vanier *et al.* 2014)[9].

8 Organizations ranging from services to regional health agencies (*Agences régionales de santé*, ARS).

9 This has become a recommendation in the United States since the Macy's founding workshop in 2014 and was initiated in 2019 at the Cote d'azur University in France with the Center of Excellence for Patient and Public Partnership (CI3P).

Thus, during the first 3 years of the program, 14 health and psychosocial science professions were taught the five competencies of the reference system that people living with one or more chronic diseases develop. At the same time, the partnership was developed during the course of an interprofessional collaboration competency framework (Figure 1.5) (Raynault 2020).

These cross-references of reference systems integrated during the training of professionals gradually entering the healthcare environment made it possible, with greater frequency, to gradually support patients in making free and informed choices and in assuming them on a daily basis (self-determination), both in the care relationship with the various care providers and in the management of their lives (self-management). To enable the development of this culture of care in partnership with the patient, institutions have been created to support this process.

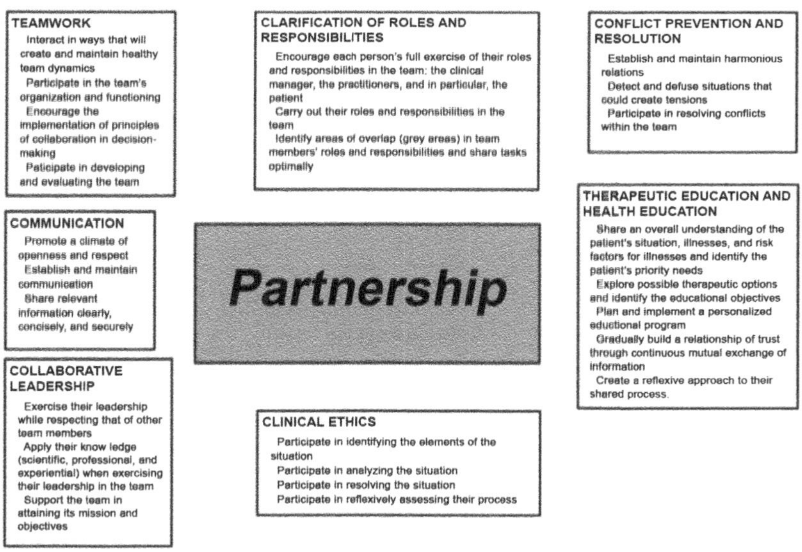

Figure 1.5. *The competence framework for collaborative practice and patient partnership (source: DCPP & CIO-UdeM 2016a, p. 5)*

After the creation of an entity mobilizing patients and their knowledge starting in 2010[10] at the Faculty of Medicine of the University of Montreal, a Canadian Chair

10 *Bureau facultaire de l'expertise patient partenaire* (BFEPP) a Partner Patient Expertise Faculty Office from 2010 to 2013, then *Direction collaboration and partnership patient* (DCPP) from 2013.

on partnership with patients and the public was awarded to Dr. Antoine Boivin. This pan-Canadian initiative has led to the creation of a Center of Excellence for Patient and Public Partnership (*Centre d'excellence du partenariat avec les patients et le public*, CEPPP), combining the research chair and the DCPP.

The CEPPP's intervention model is currently primarily at the meso and macro levels (development of partnership relationships between patients and health professionals at the level of community, teaching, care and research organizations, for example). However, its goal is to foster partnership in individual care relationships at the micro level (e.g. shared decision-making and support for chronic disease self-management between patients and clinicians). To meet this objective, an analysis was carried out to determine the level of engagement between patients and professionals; it shed light on the modalities needed by teams and organizations wishing to move toward an optimal partnership, while taking into account the fact that relationships are dynamic and can change over time (Figure 1.6) (Boivin *et al.* 2017, p. 16).

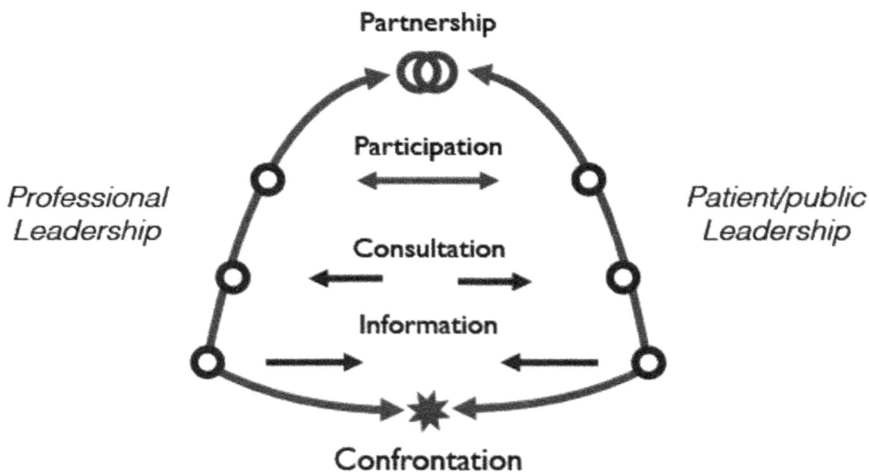

Figure 1.6. *Distinctive record of the nature of patient-professional relationships*

The partnership is a model of *reciprocal* engagement between members of the public (patients, family members and citizens) and health professionals (clinicians, managers, researchers and decision-makers). The partnership is characterized by the *co-leadership* of common actions, *co-construction* (of the understanding of the problem and the solutions) and *co-responsibility* (in relation to the results of the actions carried out jointly).

Partnership differs from models of engagement in which leadership is provided exclusively by professionals: *information to* patients by professionals; *consultation by* survey, interview, focus group or advisory committee; and *ad hoc participation of* patients and members of the public in a working group, citizen panel or deliberative meeting in which leadership is provided by professionals.

The partnership is also distinct from engagement approaches in which the leadership is assumed exclusively by patients taking the initiative to inform or consult with professionals on an *ad hoc* basis. Partnership is built on a relationship of mutual learning and influence within organizations, rather than one in which patients "outside" the healthcare system attempt to influence professionals "inside". The partnership is therefore different from advocacy or activism relationships where patients and professionals confront each other in a dynamic of confrontation (Flora 2012). This model has not only been adopted by the CEPPP and its partnership school in North America[11], but also in several European countries.

Far from being copied, it actually adapts to the context. In France, for example, a grafting of this model in the spirit of Nice gives rise to the emergence of a "UniverCité" of care (Ghadi *et al.* 2019). It is organized around different modalities of action, for example:

– popular and citizen education system;

– action-training seminars for learning and doing together;

– actions carried out by the *Centre d'innovation du partenariat avec les patients et le public* (CI3P). The CI3P brings together patients and their families and integrates them into medical education, healthcare and research environments as part of co-design initiatives, including new technologies.

Citizen education meetings are oriented toward health issues and challenges, through the action of the *Maison de la médecine et de la culture* (MMC). It is a popular university that raises awareness and questions the representations of citizens, whether they are patients, relatives, health science students, practicing professionals, decision-makers or those who have to fulfil several of these roles. Two co-learning modules are associated with this, in which all parties can act, learn to practice and practice together. It is this combination that makes the concept of the "UniverCité" of care relevant and effective. It is therefore from the initiative of a medical school open to citizens that a first step toward the social responsibility of

11 It is one of the proposals of the CEPPP organized around three streams: research, training and animation of communities of practice and therefore networks.

this type of institution is organized. These modules are, on the one hand, an annual international seminar in the field of narrative medicine open to all citizens and, on the other hand, training in the art of care in partnership with the patient, offered both in the initial study courses and in continuing education at the Faculty of Medicine (some seminars, however, are held in various locations in the city). As for CI3P, it is a new entity of the Faculty of Medicine of the University of the Côte d'Azur (Nice) which, as in Montreal, brings together patients, family members and patient-healthcare professional partnership tandems. The members of this center have already co-designed, with patients, tandem teaching for medical students in their initial curriculum at the CHU (Nantes university hospital) and have invested in various physician research groups and interprofessional collaboration (Figure 1.7).

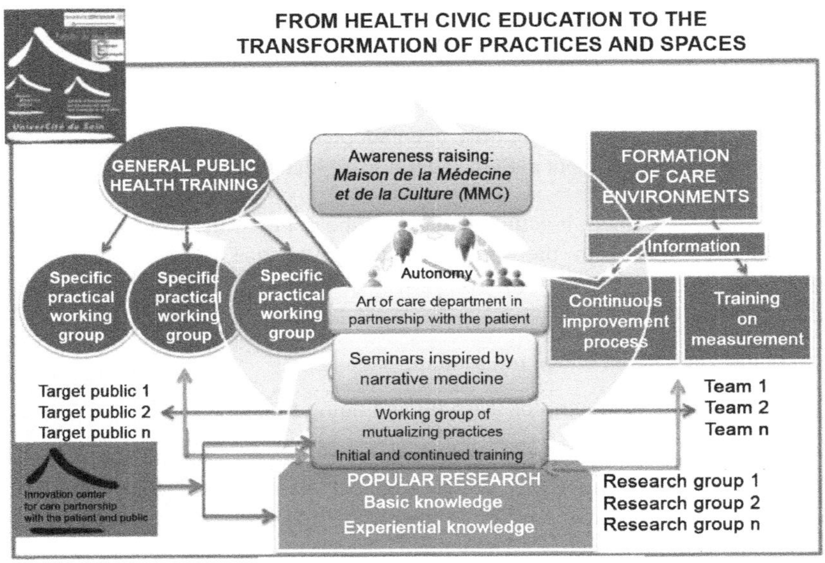

Flora, Banattar 2016 etc inspired by the methodology designed in Quebec
Luigi Flora, Jean-Michel Benattar et al, 8th Health Conference, Marseille, 20 and 21 May 2019

Figure 1.7. *Systemic transformation practice. For a color version of this figure, see www.iste.co.uk/grenier/frontiers.zip*

This moving ensemble, originating from the city, demonstrates the complementarity of knowledge and is oriented in the care(s) according to a paradigm of reciprocity from which contributing research will allow a desired systemic mutation.

However, if this "UniverCité" of care is the first organization in France with this type of partnership, it is not the only one. There is, for example, an initiative in

Rennes, France, coordinated by the public health physician Pascal Jarno, who is responsible for coordinating the improvement of professional health practices in Brittany (CAPPS) in association with a collaborator from the Canadian CEPPP. Other examples include the Savoirs Patients association, mandated by the ARS Occitanie, which has carried out an inventory of co-construction initiatives based on the vision of partnership with patients developed by the Montreal model, or the creation of the *Centre national de ressource et de résilience* (CN2R) in Lille, which opened in 2019, with a partnership unit in its management structure, and which has rapidly created a community of people suffering from psycho-trauma to co-design the implementation of its missions.

However, these companies develop while maintaining their local specificities. For example, we can note the implementation of patient trainers in the teaching of general medicine at the Bobigny Faculty of Medicine in the Paris region; it has chosen to mobilize only patients representing users and has preserved the relational model of the patient-centered approach, unlike the approach implemented in Montreal – although methodologically largely inspired by it. It is this model which, for the time being, is being adopted by the BEPP of the AP-HP, which does not appear to be the choice of Rennes, which is starting from the existing situation to develop it locally. Other attempts to grasp this model are under way in various European countries, such as Italy: since 2013, training in the teaching of family medicine integrates this approach at the Faculty of Medicine and Surgery of Modena. In Belgium, it is at the Free University of Brussels, under the impetus of the Institute of Nursing Sciences and the Department of Public Health, that teaching and research are organized according to the patient partnership. In Liège, a team of researchers, under the impetus of Benoît Petre, is organizing a research partnership between Belgium, Luxembourg and the University of Nancy based on the Montreal model. Switzerland is not to be overlooked with companies initiated by the Geneva (GHUG) and Lausanne (CHUV) hospital centers, through the *Hôpital ami des aînés* (elderly friendly hospital) project, and by the *Réseau santé région Lausanne* (RSRL) through the Anticipated Care Project (*Projet anticipé de soin*, PAS), which aims to accompany patients toward self-determination in the canton of Vaud.

However, if the Montreal model does exist, it is not the result of a rupture but of a new stage (Karazivan *et al.* 2015), as presented in the continuum and implicitly exposed in the introduction in view of the inflation of publications on the different forms of patient mobilization; it is the extension of a current, part of a set of innovations that are part of the duration of representations and practices. The CEPPP has also listed a certain number of resources[12] and other tools for evaluating

12 https://ceppp.ca/fr/ressources/.

collaborative practices, or even partnerships, developed by other currents; it is a real toolbox[13], accessible on the Internet.

If the Montreal model seems to be the most accomplished, it is therefore far from being the only one and it can be considered as a legacy of a fruitful entity. It encompasses the achievements of patient movements invested in the fight against AIDS, and also the socialization of knowledge of people living with mental disorders through the "Recovery" movement. Quebec has largely integrated it into its approach thanks to the *Association québécoise pour la réadaptation psychosociale* (AQRP). Since 2006, the AQRP has been training and accompanying peer helpers integrated into care teams under the leadership of the provincial Ministry of Health, as an extension of a trend born in the United States and much studied in Minnesota. In this state, a program (Minnesota Program 1950) in the field of addictions has already been designed, inspired by the Alcoholics Anonymous model, initiated in 1946 and implemented in the 21st century in some 40 countries, including France, through the APTE center opened in 1994 (Flora 2012, pp. 114–115).

In both cases, the aim is to mobilize peers in multi-professional teams. In the field of addictions, the range of individuals or groups supported by this system has largely developed toward all forms of addiction, with or without products. In the context of people living with mental disorders, various programs exist throughout the world; these are programs that have a strong positive impact on users, as summarized by Patrick Le Cardinal, a psychiatrist who declared himself to be living with mental disorders, in a review of the literature (Le Cardinal *et al.* 2013).

To make the mechanism more explicit, consider the example of the *Housing First* program. Originating in the United States, it is now being rolled out in 14 countries, including France, under the name "Housing First". It is the extension of an experiment initiated in Marseilles through the employment of former homeless people in mobile care teams for street people. After being rolled out in large conurbations, since the end of 2016, this approach has been part of a policy that has been rolled out nationwide and is gradually being extended to medium-sized cities. In practice, this approach is based on the creation of multidisciplinary teams of medico-social professionals associated with one or more peer helpers, known in France as "peer health mediators". It postulates that people, including those who are sustainably homeless, have the skills to access and maintain housing. It proposes direct access to housing as a prerequisite for access to rights, care and social and civic integration. Peer health mediators in France are now trained prior to university through training courses initiated by the WHO Europe Collaborating Center for Mental Health based in Lille and universities (Paris 8, Paris 13, Lille, Marseille) or

13 https://ceppp.ca/fr/nos-projets/boite-a-outils-devaluation/.

by associations to which the regional health agencies (*agencies régionales de santé*, ARS) have delegated this training. Mission – for example, the Federation of Solidarity Actors Burgundy-Franche-Comté for the ARS of this region, which initiated a training program in early 2019. More broadly and beyond the public concerned by these initiatives, some universities in France have been investing in patient training since 2009 with a national law on TPE. A concept of "patient university" initiated in 2006 in Hannover, Germany, and adapted in France with its own specificities. The first patient university was opened in 2009 at the Faculty of Medicine of the Pierre and Marie Curie University. It takes the form of training courses in which all healthcare and medico-social professionals as well as patients are trained in TPE.

This type of university has since multiplied (Paris, Marseille and Grenoble) according to different modalities. They have had the consequence of initially pushing other TPE training courses to integrate patients before opening up to other themes, according to a diverse panel of commitments, some of which train and invite co-construction. Whether or not they are co-designed from the outset in their engineering with patients and health professionals, they generate in healthcare settings as many forms of intervention that can be placed in the categories proposed in Figure 1.1 (Pomey *et al.* 2015). Universities, through medical schools and other paramedical training institutes, are currently working to involve patients. All parties claim the need for this type of approach: the national conference of deans who, in April 2019, commissioned a physician to carry out an inventory of the situation and coordinate action; the National Association of Medical Students of France (*Association nationale des étudiants en médecine de France*, ANEMF), which has issued recommendations on the subject and is campaigning for the introduction of teaching with patients; or a group of healthcare stakeholders and users' and patients' associations who drafted the charter *Associons nos savoirs* (let us combine our knowledge).

1.5. Conclusion

While the experiential knowledge of patients and users has become a social fact, its recognition in France is an ongoing process. In fact, although from the beginning of the 21st century, the voice of users has been put forward at the regulatory level – through a framework law of 2002, followed by contributions to each framework law until a national action law on therapeutic education (TPE) in 2009, experience has only recently begun to be taken into account globally, beyond the epiphenomenon. We have been able to illustrate the process by which various experiences have mobilized various forms of experiential knowledge of users/patients, most often from abroad.

However, the challenge currently lies in the capacity of the health system to allow the widespread use of knowledge for large-scale use, within the framework of a partnership; a widespread use that allows, while respecting invariants that guarantee homogeneity and quality of care, the preservation of a plasticity and flexibility that encourages appropriation and allows for a diversity of local adaptations that preserve the particularity of the environments and populations that reside there. This process, as we have explained, is a major contribution to the re-establishment of the healthcare system, particularly in terms of understanding its complexity. Our societies and healthcare systems are facing several fundamental transformations: epidemiological, with the explosion in the number of patients with chronic generational diseases due to the aging of the population; organizational, with the re-composition of power relationships and the Fourth Industrial Revolution brought about by the advent of digital technology.

The mobilization of patients' experiential knowledge and its translation through knowledge of use in co-construction, collaboration and partnership will contribute to the management of these transformations. All stakeholders in the health system need it.

1.6. References

Boivin, A., Lehoux, P., Lacombe, R., Burgers, J., Grol, R. (2014). Involving patients in setting priorities for healthcare improvement: A cluster randomized trial. *Implementation Sciences*, 9(1), 1–10.

Boivin, A., Flora, L., Dumez, V., L'Espérance, A., Berkesse, A., Gauvin, F.-P. (2017). Transformer la santé en partenariat avec les patients et le public : historique, approche et impacts du "*modèle de Montréal*". In *La participation des patients*, Collection Ethique biomédicale et normes juridiques, Editions Dalloz, Paris.

Boote, J., Telford, R., Cooper, C. (2002). Consumer involvement in health research: A review and research agenda. *Health Policy*, 61(2), 213–236.

Brown, P. (1987). Popular epidemiology: Community response to toxic waste-induced disease in Woburn, Massachusetts and other sites. *Science, Technology and Human Values*, 12(3–4), 76–85.

Coulter, A. (2011). *Engaging Patients in Healthcare*. Oxford University Press, Oxford.

Crocker, J.C., Ricci-Cabello, I., Parker, A., Hirst, J.A., Chant, A., Petit-Zeman, S., Evans, D., Rees, S. (2018). Impact of patient and public involvement on enrolment and retention in clinical trials: Systematic review and meta-analysis. *BMJ*, 363(8178) [Online]. Available at: https://doi.org/10.1136/bmj.k4738 [accessed 1 December 2018].

Durkheim, E. (1988). *Les règles de la méthode sociologique*. Flammarion, Paris.

Flora, L. (2012). Le patient formateur : élaboration théorique et pratique d'un nouveau métier de la santé. PhD Thesis, Université Vincennes Saint-Denis – Paris 8, Paris.

Foucault, M. (1963). *Naissance de la clinique : une archéologie du regard médical.* PUF, Paris.

Ghadi, V., Flora, L., Jarno, P., Lelievre, H. (2019). The engagement conundrum of French users. In *Patient Engagement: How Patient-provider Partnerships Transform Healthcare Organizations*, Pomey, M.-P., Denis, J.-L., Dumez, V. (eds). Springer, New York.

Houillet, F. (ed.) (2016). Les sciences participatives en France : état des lieux et méthodes. Report, Ministères de l'Éducation nationale et de l'Enseignement supérieur et de la recherche, Paris.

Jouet, E. (2014). La reconnaissance des savoirs des malades : de l'émergence au fait social. In *Nouvelles interventions réflexives dans la recherche en santé : du savoir expérientiel des malades aux intervention des professionnels de santé.* Archives contemporaines, Paris.

Jouet, E., Flora, L., Las Vergnas, O. (2010). Construction et reconnaissance des savoirs expérientiels des patients : note de synthèse. *Pratique de formation : analyses*, 58–59, 13–94.

Karazivan, P., Dumez, V., Flora, L., Pomey, M.-P., Del Grande, C., Guadiri, S., Fernandez, N., Jouet, E., Las Vergnas, O., Lebel, P. (2015). The patient as partner in care: Conceptual grounds for a necessary transition. *Academic Medicine*, 90(4), 437–441.

Le Breton, D. (1990). *Anthropologie du corps et modernité.* PUF, Paris.

Le Cardinal, P., Roelandt, J.-L., Rafael, F., Vasseur-Bacle, S., Francois, G., Marsili, M. (2013). Pratiques orientées vers le rétablissement et pair-aidance : historique, études et perspectives. *L'Information psychiatrique*, 89, 365–370.

Pomey, M.-P., Flora, L., Karazivan, P., Dumez, V., Lebel, P., Vanier, M.-C., Débarge, B., Clavel, N., Jouet, E. (2015). Le "Montreal model" : enjeux du partenariat relationnel entre patients et professionnels de santé. *Santé publique*, HS(S1), 41–50.

Raynault, A., Lebel, P., Brault, I., Vanier, M.-C., Flora, L. (2020). How interprofessional teams of students mobilized collaborative practice competencies and the patient partnership approach in a hybrid IPE course. *The Journal of Interprofessional Care* [Online]. Available at: https://doi.org/10.1080/13561820.20.

Vanier, M.C., Dumez, V., Drouin, E., Brault, I., MacDonald, S.A., Boucher, A., Fernandez. N., Levert, M.J. (2014). Partners in interprofessional education: Integrating patients-as-trainers. In *Partnering with Patients, Families, and Communities to Link Interprofessional Practice and Education*, Fulmer, T., Gaines, M. (eds). Josiah Macy Jr. Foundation, New York.

WHO (1986). Ottawa Charter [Online]. Available at: https://www.euro.who.int/__data/assets/pdf_file/0004/129532/Ottawa_Charter.pdf [accessed 8 December 2019].

2

Innovative Organizations and Professional Strategies: The Nursing Professional Space

2.1. Introduction: experimenting experimentation

The main features of the profound changes, which have taken place in the health systems of all developed countries since the early 1980s, have been widely identified. On the one hand, the economic and medico-economic imperatives driven by the search for efficiency have become imperative. On the other hand, the explosion of chronic diseases and multi-morbidities is profoundly changing the demands placed on professionals.

These two phenomena converge to question the industrial approach, which is dominant today. This is based on a health system centered on individualized care and its technical efficiency to the detriment of prevention and the collective or social dimensions of health. Contrary to this approach, current developments are therefore capable of placing public health, which is now neglected, at the top of the list of priorities.

To this end, all stakeholders are now invited to engage in the "experimentation" of new forms of cooperation. It is indeed expected that these experimentations will lead to innovative forms of organization which, in particular, avoid or circumvent the pitfalls of hyper-specialization and hospital centrism. This amounts to erasing the internal and external bounds of the healthcare system by "decompartmentalizing" it, notably through the control of "health pathways".

Chapter written by Philippe MOSSÉ.

Starting from these observations, this chapter is based on the conviction that the quality of the association and the commitment of professionals in this new orientation is the condition for its effectiveness. This is why the division of labor between health professionals and the transformations it is undergoing is a central issue.

Here we find the opposition between innovation and organization; the latter can be an obstacle to the diffusion of the former (Greenhalgh 2004). Alter (1993) referred to it in connection with the "new productive paradigm" when he concluded that there was competition and complementarity between these two legitimacies. However, the literature in health socio-economics shows that, in this sector, this tension is both supported and reinforced by the influence of professional strategies (Robelet *et al.* 2005). These are seen as tending toward the maintenance of identified, if not "closed", "professional markets" that may include competing "segments". Current changes thus take the form of three competing yet complementary dynamics: innovation-experimentation, organization-coordination and profession-corporatism.

Based on the example of the place and role of nurses in these changes, the purpose of this chapter is to highlight this tension and to learn from it about the conditions for efficient organizational innovation.

In a first section intended to frame the problem (section 2.2), we will show how and to what extent, in France, the time for "experimentation" has come. Admittedly, in a national historical context characterized by a centralism perceived as the guarantor of republican equality, the re-emergence of the legitimacy of experimentation may seem surprising. All the more so since the attempt of the 1980s and the city-hospital networks had come to a halt. Today, however, experimentation is seen by the French public authorities as an almost obligatory step before any generalization (section 2.3).

Basing the analysis mainly on official documents and professional literature, two complementary and recent concrete examples will be given of this evolution in the form of collective learning. At the end of this analysis, it will become clear that choosing to "experiment with experimentation" means relying on the capacity of health professionals to redefine locally innovative forms of cooperation and the concrete places where the new skills can be exercised. To conduct this analysis, the notion of "professional space" will be used (Maurice *et al.* 1982).

On the theoretical level, this notion designates the place and the stakeholders of the interaction between the construction of labor supply and demand, which are classically considered to be subject to different logics. Indeed, on the one hand, the supply of labor is constructed through the acquisition of qualifications and skills, in particular through training; on the other hand, the demand for labor is oriented by the modes of organization and the division of labor in firms. The major contribution of the notion of professional space is to put at the center of the analysis the link between these two spheres (supply and demand of labor) that standard economics encourages to consider as independent. Therefore, this chapter pushes forward the idea that mobilizing the notion of professional space enables progress to be made in understanding the changes taking place within and on the periphery of the nursing profession. For this reason, thanks to semi-structured interviews, section 2.4 will be devoted to an analysis of the nursing professional space and its current transformations.

The hypothesis that is favored here is that the principle of the changes underway is the struggle for the consolidation and recognition of new professional practices through the acquisition of new skills. Thus, the creation of *ad hoc* structures and organizations likely to promote them would reinforce professional strategies, and under certain conditions – notably, success – would legitimize them.

2.2. Participatory evidence-based policy: a new conceptual framework?

A priori, in a country with a highly centralized reputation, it is hard to see how experimentation could have its place and, even less so, a place recognized by the State itself. However, in the health sector, this form of commitment by stakeholders who are encouraged by their guardians is not new. However, until recently, it had remained confined and, as it were, tolerated. The fact that, since the beginning of the century, the sequence of experimentation, evaluation and generalization has tended to become a legitimate mode of regulation (i.e. one that is accepted and advocated by the ministry in charge of health and its agencies) is indicative of a shared observation. This can be summed up as follows: after decades of vertical management, the French health system, strictly speaking its organization and financing, must make room for the initiative of those working in the field. However, one condition is set for this new form of regulation: the standard (professional, legal or regulatory) must remain the absolute reference for action and practices. Moreover, the horizon of the experimentation and the sign of its success must be the possibility of generalizing it, i.e., more often than not, its capacity to change the standard. This is why, the first phase of the experimentation is the "waiver". If we consider that experimentation consists of "testing regulations in a defined space and time" (Quet 2005, p. 216), we can see the extent to which it establishes relations between the protagonists of public action that have never been seen before in the French context. Moreover, "experimental laws" have the particularity of being valid only for a given period of time, after which they can be abandoned, extended to the national territory or modified.

Quet (2005) sees in the emergence of social experimentation, and even more so of the “experimental metaphor”, the sign of a renewed relationship between politics and science. Experimentation would be justified by the uncertainty that would preside over all decisions regarding their consequences (especially financial) and which would make it difficult to compare them; even though to compare is necessary for the definition of priorities.

Designed to remove or reduce this uncertainty, the evaluation of practices and its use in decision-making can be considered central. This is why, in the field of health, evaluation methods have converged toward a single technique and criterion in order to be able to compare (*ex ante* or *ex post*) various actions. This is evidenced by the fact that the proliferation that was once the rule (Culyer 1983) was followed in the 1990s by the omnipresence of a criterion for the performance of health actions presented as universal: the quality-adjusted life year[1] (Loomes & McKenzie 1989).

Thus, as in the past in the field of medicine with evidence-based medicine, what is called evidence-based policy has its place in the field of public policy. However, there is a major difference: the effectiveness of social experimentation is deployed over a long period of time and along a complex path (Jullien 2004), whereas in medicine, evaluation is most often based on individualized performance indicators estimated over the short term.

This is why, the search for the most efficient organization in a context of uncertainty, such as that of health, is not the main driving force behind experimental action. The conduct of experiments remains supervised but the initiative most often falls to stakeholders wishing to have their practice recognized and therefore in search of legitimacy and … resources.

From this point of view, it is noteworthy that the first occurrence of the term “experimentation” in the institutional field of health appeared at the crossroads of the political-administrative world and the scientific or academic world. The interministerial mission for research and experimentation (*mission interministérielle Recherche-expérimentation*, MIRE) of the Ministry of Health is in fact “one of the oldest structures aimed at encouraging and supervising local initiatives under the supervision of researchers in charge of their evaluation” (Strobel & Dauphin 1990,

1 Under the acronym QALY, this indicator makes it possible to evaluate the effectiveness of a health program, protocol or action on the basis of the life years they save, weighted by their quality (which is evaluated by the patients themselves on the basis of a questionnaire).

p. 12). In the 1980s, the MIRE was able to benefit from a political context that was favorable both to the development of the human sciences and to the increase in resources allocated to research grants. At the time, this research was already oriented toward the question of professional cooperation and, in particular, health networks. As Bouchayer (2005, p. 242) rightly notes:

> Research on health networks has also illustrated the necessary contextualization of professional dynamics in the health field. In this respect, the successive systems put in place [...] have also served as a real Trojan horse for public authorities to better control professional dynamics that are considered too "corporatist" or disordered.

These dynamics and the political will to control them are part of a fundamental shift. Among others, the research "Hospital, innovations, professions" (Branciard *et al.* 1994) gave an overview of them in the early 1990s. The two examples summarized in the appendix to this chapter (section 2.6) and drawn from this research are representative of this period. In line with Freidson's (1990) reflections on the medical profession, they suggest the hypothesis that, far from a heroic vision of change, the bearers of innovations (technical or organizational) must sooner or later come to terms with the professional projects and hierarchies in place.

During the 2000s, the "Berland experiments" were both the extension and, within certain limits, the consecration of this philosophy. In April 2003, the Ministry of Health entrusted Professor Y. Berland, then dean of the Faculty of Medicine of Marseille, the mission of examining and promoting the cooperation that it would seem possible to develop between the various health professionals. After analysis of the experiments actually carried out (Berland & Bourgueil 2006), the transfer of skills could be extended to other medical and paramedical activities.

In its work to evaluate and monitor these experiments, the French National Authority for Health (*Haute Autorité de santé*, HAS) clearly specified the stakes involved in these new forms of cooperation:

> For physicians, they can help to improve the conditions of practice [...] by enabling them to focus on purely medical activities. For the other health professions, the increase in missions and the recognition of skills development offer career development opportunities other than management positions alone. (HAS 2008, p. 5).

A test of the feasibility of these "new forms of organization" is presented today, in the form of Article 51 of the Social Security Financing Law (*loi de financement de la*

Sécurité sociale, LFSS) for 2018[2]. While it is too early to assess the performance of these experiments, it is already possible and timely to analyze the projects submitted in the framework of this system in terms of their innovative capacity.

2.3. Article 51: a full-scale test

As defined by the Ministry of Health, the purpose of section 51 of the LFSS for 2018 seems broad: it is to allow "experimenting with new health organizations". Yet the purpose is clearly and explicitly more precise. Innovations must first contribute to "decompartmentalizing" a healthcare system that is considered to be composed of elements acting in "silos". The observation is that the lack of coordination between increasingly specialized health actors is becoming an obstacle to improving the efficiency of the system as a whole. This diagnosis, which has been widely shared for a long time, the law of 2018 (as well as, even more strongly, the "Ma santé en 2022" program)[3], makes this its main argument. It intends to fill these gaps by encouraging innovation: "Eligible projects will include experiments relating in particular to the coordination of the healthcare pathway, the relevance and quality of health, social or medico-social care, the structuring of outpatient care and access to care[4]".

2.3.1. *Experimenting for recognition*

The core of the system is that the experimenters will be able to set up financing methods that derogate from the current rules. In fact, the derogatory financing agreement aims to test the feasibility of original modes of remuneration which would free themselves from the fee-for-service payment, which is currently dominant and considered inflationary. It would also organize the sharing of resources between professionals on the basis of a "lump sum" or any other form of resource allocation.

On the incentive side, a decree published in the *Journal officiel* on March 31, 2018 indicates that, under Article 51, 20 million euros per year will be reserved by the French Health Insurance for a "fund for health system innovation". A sum of

2 The Social Security Financing Act, passed by Parliament every year since 1996, authorizes the Social Security budget. Its purpose is to allow elected officials to control a budget that, traditionally, has been beyond their control.

3 In September 2018, under the title "Ma santé en 2022", the French government presented a set of measures aimed at reorganizing the health system. It aims to encourage stakeholders to cooperate more, to organize health pathways and to reduce territorial inequalities.

4 Légifrance, Social Security Code, Article L162-31-1, December 2017.

10 million will be supplemented by funding from the Regional Intervention Fund (*Fonds d'intervention régional*, FIR)[5].

In addition, in order to base the evaluation of experiments and their possible reproducibility on rigorous analysis and advice, a Strategic Council for health innovation (*Conseil stratégique de l'innovation en santé*, CTIS) has been created. It comprises 61 members from the "health ecosystem"; its evaluation reports and opinions are to be forwarded to the government and then to Parliament.

Since its publication, this article has attracted the attention and interest of many stakeholders in the sector. In general, these were professionals who already had a practice of cooperation in an organizational configuration already in place or envisaged and around defined pathologies.

Similarly, the many letters of intent received by the regional health agencies (*agences régionales de santé*, ARSs) since the start of the experiment show that two-thirds of the projects concerned the quality and organization of care activities for specific populations or areas (mental health, obesity, chronic kidney failure, cancer, etc.). The first report to the Strategic Council indicates that of the 250 projects selected by ARSs, only 16% were focused on "coordinating the players". In addition, several ARSs expressed their attention to the coherence between projects and the priorities of their regional health plans, which are often defined in terms of target populations or pathologies.

A reading of the 30 or so projects authorized as of August 28, 2019[6] confirms that their promoters are anxious to find an organizational framework (and, today, a legal one because it is derogatory) for existing or latent practices in order to have them recognized internally and, even more so, by the partners. This is why, most of the experiments in progress follow a classic pattern: identify a particular population; identify the health stakeholders involved in the responsibility of a stage whose fluidity could be improved; and finally, set up a financial incentive along these lines.

Admittedly, at this experimental phase, the project leaders are aware that the "health path" itself is made up of multiple links between various organizations and care structures, that it is made complex by the existence of pluripathologies and that it is part of the long-term course of chronic illnesses. However, the experiments

5 On the basis of projects relayed by the ARSs, the Regional Intervention Fund (*Fonds d'intervention regional*, FIR) supports experiments that should aim to increase the efficiency and coordination of care.

6 Following the favorable opinion of the technical committee, these 30 experiments were the first to be the subject of formal "authorization" in order to be able to derogate from the financing rules.

validated to date have focused on a limited number of actors and participants and, generally, on one point in the process.

This is why, instead of an innovative and unpublished organization, as expected by the legislators, there is a search for a recognition of existing practices and cooperation. *Via* article 51, it is also a question of remunerating them more fairly than the fee-for-service system and the traditional division of labor between doctors and paramedics allow. As a result, the innovative nature of the organization often boils down to the implementation of an original method of financing and remuneration negotiated by the stakeholders.

2.3.2. *An expression of interest*

In the context of this system, an experiment focusing on outpatient care and launched in 2019 in the form of a call for expressions of interest (*appel à manifestation d'intérêt*, AMI) is illustrative of the challenges and limits of the exercise. Under the name of "payment in teams of ambulatory healthcare professionals" (*paiement en équipe de professionnels de santé en ville*, PEPS), this experiment aims to test an original and derogatory method of remuneration. It is presented as both a flat-rate and collective payment for urban health professionals. It will replace fee-for-service payment and the distribution will be left to the protagonists' discretion.

The Ministry of Health (2019) presents this system in terms that are consistent with the incentive logic, and therefore well argued, that it intends to implement:

> Organizational innovation, like technical innovation, is a crucial issue for the future of our health system [...]. For the implementation of these experiments through innovative financing and organization of our health system, most of the tariff rules in cities, hospitals and the medico-social sector can be waived [...] [for example] fee sharing, authorization of health care activities and heavy equipment to groups, waiver of the monopoly of pharmacists [...].

Concretely, health professionals (general practitioners and nurses) working in an already established non-hospital structure (houses or health centers, for example) volunteer to be paid on a lump sum basis. The lump-sum payment can concern either the entire patient, or people older than 65 years of age, or diabetic patients (type 1 or 2). The experiment, which should last 5 years, began in 2019 for 39 pioneering structures. Its evaluation has been entrusted to a team from the *Institut de recherche et documentation en économie de la santé* (Irdes).

In May 2019, the Technical Committee for Health Innovation (*Comité technique de l'innovation en santé*, CTIS) gave a positive opinion on the PEPS project on the grounds that this experiment aims at the emergence of an innovative organization:

> This experiment is admissible in that it aims at the emergence of innovative organizations in the health and medico-social sectors contributing to the improvement of patient care and pathways, the efficiency of the healthcare system and access to care. (CTIS 2018, p. 21)

In order to be candidates for the "second wave" and to begin the experiment in 2020, multi-professional health centers (*maisons de santé pluriprofessionnelles*, MSPs) or health centers will have to include at least three general practitioners and a nurse. In addition, these structures will have to justify at least 250 patients concerned by the package.

One of the *sine qua non* conditions for the acceptance of the project is the existence of a "mature, multidisciplinary and voluntary" MSP-type team. The specifications specify that the "high level of maturity" of the teams is a "key factor in the success of the experiment". The innovative dimension of the PEPS system does not therefore essentially reside in the organization of the work, since this pre-exists to the project and it is not required to modify it. On the other hand, it is centered on the in-professional relations that the lump-sum payment opens up. Thus, organizational innovation, as it is encouraged by various incentive schemes, is immersed in professional issues, essentially linked to the question of access to financial and symbolic resources.

However, the focus on funding (moving from fee-for-service to lump sum) may mark a change in perspective. It consists of desacralizing the traditional doctor-patient relationship, as symbolized by the singular colloquium, and installing it in a collective relationship. This is why, the deployment of these professional logics needs to be examined further, because, more than organizational innovations, they guide the changes underway.

However, it appears that at the center of these issues is the division of labor between doctors and paramedical professionals and, singularly, nurses, because they are the most numerous and, within the care production process, the closest.

This suggests that an analysis of how the nursing profession is constructed and deformed is necessary to illustrate and understand the changes at work in the overall system of care.

2.4. The nursing space: a controlled extension

The notion of professional space is mobilized here to show how, and to what extent, professional logics are at the heart of the creation of innovative organizations. Indeed, the major particularity of this space is to be both moving and heterogeneous.

Thus, at least since the beginning of the 20th century, the nursing profession has been characterized by both the extension and diversification of its space. This double movement has long taken the almost exclusive form of technical specializations. Often sanctioned by diplomas, these specializations authorize the specific functions in settings that are no less so, such as nurse-anesthetists (*infirmières anes-thésistes*, IADE), operating room nurses (*infirmières de bloc opératoire*, IBODE) or pediatric nurses (*infirmières puéricultrices*, IPDE). The whole is underpinned by the principle of the "proper role" and the "decrees of acts" or "competencies" (integrated into the Public Health Code) which delimit the regulatory territory of nursing intervention. However, beyond their specializations, competencies and responsibilities, the nursing professions are characterized by a wide variety of practice modes and locations.

Today, there are more than 680,000 nurses working in a wide variety of positions in an ever-increasing number of different modalities. This diversity of status was confirmed by a questionnaire survey conducted among nurses working in their patients' homes *via* homecare services (*services de soins à domicile*, SSIAD) or home hospitalization services (*hospitalisation à domicile*, HAD):

> Some [...] work in group nursing practices, others in multidisciplinary practices, and still others on their own. Moreover, in one of the SSIADs [...] all were liberal nurses who had individual contracts with the service. In another, there were both salaried and contract nurses. In one of the HAD services, some nurses were salaried but others were liberals under contract. (Mossé *et al.* 2017, p. 54)

This variety would be first due to the polymorphic and changing demand of the patients. It would also be the result of chronic diseases requiring both relational (*care*) and highly technical (*cure*) treatments. However, it also appears that strategies within the profession lead to these configurations. In fact, combined with the desire to distinguish oneself from other professions (particularly doctors and nurses' assistants), these strategies are as many drivers for transforming the professional environment. In the service of these objectives, and as proposed by Albert-Cromarias *et al.* (2018), organizational innovation must follow, as the significant transformations in nursing illustrate the need for innovation in health organizations.

Two recent forms of the extension of the nursing professional space illustrate the challenges, brakes and levers that allow organizational innovation to take (or not) the path of professional innovation.

In this perspective, the experiment *Action de santé libérale en équipe*, known as Asalée, which began in 2004 and which today finds itself, if not failing, at least contested, will be examined (section 2.4.1). Next, the ins and outs of the creation and implementation of a new skill, sanctioned by a diploma at Master 2 level, the "advanced practice nurse" (*infirmière en pratique avancée*, IPA), will be brought to light. On the basis of interviews conducted in June 2019[7] with students from the first graduating class, this analysis will show how this new profession is upsetting the current equilibrium, while remaining in line with the logic, particularly competitive logic, that constitutes the field (section 2.4.2).

2.4.1. *Asalée: a fragile experiment*

Asalée is a collaborative protocol for nurses that gives them the authorization to provide or prescribe certain care, generally reserved for doctors, on a derogatory basis. The Asalée protocol was part of the "Berland experiments" and was authorized under the "Hospital, Patients, Health and Territory" (*Hôpital, patients, santé et territoires*, HPST) law of 2009. In concrete terms, it allows and regulates the delegation of acts from general practitioners to nurses; it essentially concerns screening and follow-up of chronic patients, notably through therapeutic education. Created in 2004, Asalée is first and foremost an association of general practitioners and nurses delegated to public health and trained in this field. For the first few years, nurses were to be salaried employees of Asalée, but at the request of the guardians, independent nurses can now be hired on a part-time basis (generally one day per week); at the end of 2018, they represented about a quarter of the involved staff.

As is usual in *delegation* or task *transfer* experiments, the aim is to "save" medical time. It is from this perspective that the derogatory acts performed by nurses have been validated by the High Authority of Health and are relatively numerous. They concern the prescription and/or performance of certain tests (microalbuminuria, cholesterol measurement, creatinemia, fundus, electrocardiogram, etc.), the prescription of nicotine substitutes, the prescription, performance and interpretation of spirometry, etc.

In addition, the delegation of procedures is governed by four protocols, which are also derogatory, concerning diabetes, cardiovascular risk, obstructive chromogenic bronchopneumopathy (including smoking cessation) and cognitive disorders.

7 These interviews were conducted with Professor Tetsu Harayama (Toyo University, Tokyo) as part of a France-Japan comparative research.

Asalée has signed an agreement with the Ministry of Health and, in this framework, benefits from a budget per nurse paid by the Health Insurance (*Assurance Maladie*); since 2012, it includes a share of remuneration for the doctor.

The system relies exclusively on local cooperation between general practitioners and nurses. The aim is therefore twofold: on the one hand, to develop prevention for patients suffering from chronic diseases, and on the other hand, to relieve the doctor of certain tasks.

However, the *Institut de recherches et de documentation en économie de la santé* (Irdes), which is responsible for evaluating the system in the form of a "quasi-experimental approach", makes a mixed assessment of it. On the one hand, therapeutic patient education is central and, more often than not, effective. But, on the other hand, "statistics show no difference in the number of days worked between GPs who have joined the system and their non-participating counterparts". On the other hand, the GPs' patient load is increased by an average of 7%, although the number of consultations remains unchanged. "Thus, delegating part of the activity of GPs to nurses would seem to free up the medical time that doctors allocate to increasing the size of their patient load" (Loussouan 2019, p. 1).

In an article published in May 2018 under the title "Un flou artistique" (An Artistic Blur), the president of the French National Federation of Nurses (*Fédération nationale des infirmiers*) expressed himself in rough terms. He denounced the "inconsistency of the device" victim of an original sin, since it is a device created on the initiative of doctors. Referring to the Irdes study, the *Fédération nationale des infirmiers* (FNI) insists on the not very innovative aspect of the experiment:

> [...] independent nurses are already doing this: everything is provided for in the nomenclature of nursing acts. We read that the Asalée nurses "[manage] the doctor's patient". However, this is medical secretarial work! [...] Doctors surf on the problems of medical deserts [...] to finally obtain funding for medical assistants from public funds [...]. So, in view of the artistic vagueness revealed by the Irdes, I think that this device is doomed to disappear. (FNI 2018)

This judgment is undoubtedly primarily dictated by professional reflexes, but it shows a significant amount of reluctance and obstacles. It explains that, after 15 years, only 418 nurses and about 1,300 doctors were involved in the experiment.

To a certain extent, the fragility of this experiment illustrates Féroni's (2000, p. 31) judgment about nursing identities:

> By forcing the analysis a little, it is as if the identity issue of nurses was exclusively situated in the interprofessional nurse-physician relationship, their situation as salaried employees of large organizations being obscured or even evacuated. This bias is all the more reinforced because nurses as a profession have developed a coherent discourse on themselves and their activity that is both descriptive and demanding, and which conceals these aspects.

However, in the light of these experiences, it is necessary to qualify this verdict. Indeed, if the "organizational" dimension remains secondary, the question of professional-organizational interactions is now posed in new terms. Advanced practices are a paradigmatic example of this.

2.4.2. *The nurse in advanced practice: spearhead or first in line*

Article 119 of Law 2016-41, known as the "modernization of our health system" law, published in the *Journal officiel* on January 26, 2016, formalizes the notion of "advanced nursing practice". It aims to adapt to the French context a status and role that already exists, and sometimes has existed for a long time, in many countries such as Canada, Japan or the United States (Pulcini 2009). Since then, implementing decrees has been published specifying, in particular, the four specialties sanctioned by a "mention" of a state diploma IPA equivalent to a Master 2 degree and to which IPAs will be able to apply. The state diploma allows the practice of advanced practice nursing in four areas of intervention: stabilized chronic pathologies; prevention and common polypathologies in primary care; oncology and hemato-oncology; chronic kidney disease, dialysis and kidney transplantation. In August 2019, a fifth area, psychiatry and mental health, was added.

In fact, after the two pioneers, Aix-Marseille (in partnership with the École des hautes études en santé publique) and Saint-Quentin en Yvelines, many universities have had their training models accredited. At the start of the 2019 academic year, there was about 10 of them. The government is encouraging this growth, and plans to create 5,000 new IPA positions throughout the country in the short term. We can think that this figure will indeed be reached because expectations are high and the window of opportunity is favorable. Indeed, chronic diseases, doctor shortages and the desire of nurses and doctors to work differently are all signs that the temporal and spatial division of work among health professionals is already changing. In addition, it is likely that, beyond the quantitative aspect (5,000 IPAs would represent less than 1% of the workforce), their location in various sites and settings will have an impact on the way care work is distributed.

The fact that an IPA union was created shortly after the decree was issued is indicative of this awareness. Of course, this creation is probably close to the problems encountered by the institutions in place (associations of nurses, unions, etc.) to fully accept this new practice, the contours of which have yet to be defined. Certainly, the field and experience will tell whether the insertion of these new professionals will be beneficial and efficient.

But already, the commitment of the first promotions heralds profound changes; they first require an awareness of the stakes involved.

2.4.2.1. *Students in training: conscious pioneers*

Today the people enrolled in these training courses know that they are the spearhead of the profession. As the IPAs are justified by the need for a new "intermediate" profession, it is not surprising that it is on this professional register that the students locate both the brakes and the levers for future actions.

Following the example of the nephrology service studied 20 years ago (see section 2.6, Appendix), one of the main obstacles to the integration of IPAs into hospital teams is on the health executive side: "We will not take the place of nurse coordinators or managers .... We have implementation problems with managers" (interview excerpt).

Another student points out the same potential problem with other nurses: "Advanced practice will be an activity with a lot of consultations ... with the possibility of prescribing to our nursing colleagues ... which can complicate representations" (interview excerpt).

For one of the students interviewed, the same stance should be observed with regard to the liberal nurses: "We will not take the place of the independent nurses; we will receive patients in consultation to orient them" (interview excerpt).

This risk is all the greater because this first class of IPAs is made up of nurses with a particularly acute and documented knowledge of the profession.

Many of the students have degrees other than an IDE or have had rich and open career paths and trajectories (living abroad, working in sectors other than health, various forms of mobility, etc.). As a result, in the eyes of this first class, the professional space is not only wide, but it is also possible to move around without major difficulty as long as the desire to progress is present: "Nurses have the choice of where they practice, contracts, etc. I have always chosen, it has always been fluid. I have learned to be autonomous" (interview excerpt).

This is also the reason why future IPAs do not want to compete with established professions or trades, but rather complement them: "There is a place between the nurse and the doctor. We are not capable and we do not want to take the place of doctors" (interview excerpt).

On the whole, the students interviewed put forward two registers of claims: on the one hand, the necessary autonomy vis-à-vis the medical authorities and, on the other hand, the recognition of what is already being done in the secrecy of the services and the cabinets.

In the course of the interviews, it appeared that several of the practices "new" or advocated by the decree are not actually new. Practices (such as the renewal of prescriptions or certain interventions reserved for doctors) were, in reality, already carried out by nurses, always with the agreement of the doctors and often with that of the management: "in private practice, we are taking an increasingly important part … the adaptation of insulin, we inform the doctor *a posteriori*, which is forbidden … and which has been the daily life of the nurses for years"; "in hospital, we sometimes do check-ups... or renew prescriptions... even if we are not allowed" (excerpts from interviews).

These practices are even claimed in the name of acquired skills: "It's not because you're a nurse that you can't auscultate, palpate the abdomen … It's not making a diagnosis, it's objectifying symptoms" (interview excerpt).

IPA training and its recognition are therefore, first of all, part of the process of catching up with the texts' delay in relation to everyday reality.

In this context, the training and diploma in advanced practice will first of all have the effect of regularizing existing more or less illegal situations. But secondly, students are aware that they will open a path: "Our role is to open the doors for the next ones". One of them specifies: "I could be a referent for the trainees in IPA training … play a leadership role with regard to other nurses"; or again: "We will be the first to implement these practices, legitimacy is super important". Even if, of course, "not all nurses can move towards the IPA profile" (excerpts from interviews).

2.4.2.2. *A changing nursing identity*

In spite of this limitation, the nursing identity is qualitatively upset in the sense that, until now, it was limited by a list of roles, specifications or acts recognized on technical bases. With advanced practice, we are moving away from this "Taylorian" logic to inaugurate a logic of "mission". For this student,

> the decree of acts was a big mistake for the profession, compared to the evolution of our missions such as therapeutic education or prevention [...] It would be better to be in missions [...] like midwives.

This is the reason why the reference to medical nosology alone is called into question:

> I find it a pity that the form taken in France is centered on diseases and not on populations or population groups, such as in Canada, for example, it is counter-intuitive for a profession that is meant to be interdisciplinary. (excerpts from interviews)

Yet, unanimously, IPAs do not consider themselves "mini-doctors" nor as "super nurses". They know that competing for the existing professions would make it difficult, if not impossible, for them to be included individually and to be recognized collectively as a "profession in their own right".

From this point of view, the role of hospital internships is important. The quality of the image that the IPAs will give of the relevance of their mission depends on their smooth running. It is during these short periods (about 6 months over 2 years of master's training) that they will get to know each other.

However, for the time being, in the students' discourse, the organizational contexts within which these recognized, snatched or claimed skills are and will be deployed are not spontaneously evoked. Therefore, the question is whether, like the first in line, IPAs will have a training power for the entire profession or, on the contrary, will constitute an autonomous segment.

Aware of this issue, one mental health institution decided to set up a functional unit reserved for the activities of IPAs:

> In order to be able to operate independently from the medical units, the care management and the hospital's decision-making bodies have taken steps to bring the IPAs together under the same functional unit (FU) and in the same geographical location. Indeed, it was important to be able to detach the IPA exercise from the work carried out in the units [...]. They are no longer part of the staff of the units concerned: they do not therefore take the place of other health professionals. (Danan *et al.* 2019, p. 43)

Although the context (medical and legal) is different, the expectations of this organizational innovation are reminiscent of the following evoked in the 1990s for the creation of a department dedicated to hygiene, also with an interdisciplinary vocation (see section 2.6, Appendix).

It is because similar forces are always at work, such as the desire for autonomy vis-à-vis doctors or the will to work on missions and no longer in reference to the straitjacket of the "decree of acts": once defended as a protector, it has become, for many nurses, the symbol of dependence. In this example, we can also add the will to escape the new constraint imposed by the organization.

Thus, advanced practice – the glory of its Quebec model, omnipresent although born and raised in a very different context – is already becoming one of those available solutions in search of a problem.

Attractive, it is not surprising that the "IPA solution" has recently emerged as a relevant solution to the "crisis" of hospital emergencies. This crisis is characterized by a structural overcrowding of emergency departments due to an inexorably increasing number of emergency room admissions. Whether or not they are medically justified, they are often managed in conditions that are not optimal for patients or caregivers. In 2019, this crisis reached a climax in the form of a strike movement that was widely followed throughout France.

A new training program will be created explicitly to help relieve congestion in these services. A real and serious problem, this overcrowding depends less on what happens in the emergency services than on what should happen upstream and downstream (in the hospitals themselves). However, it is not in the name of this argument that the French National Union of Nurse Anesthetists (*Syndicat national des infirmiers-anesthésistes*, SNIA) has opposed this measure since its announcement in early September 2019:

> The SNIA recalls that the emergence of advanced practice was aimed at caring for patients with chronic pathologies. It therefore notes a paradigm shift [...]. The creation of a new "emergency" nursing training in advanced practice leaves a bitter taste in the mouths of those who have entered the IADE profession with the project of practicing in the emergency sector. (SNIA 2019)

Like the FNI's judgment (see section 2.4.1), this judgment is mainly the outcome of a trade union tactic, but it is in line with some of the professional issues raised by IPA students. As we have seen, however, their speeches show that, under certain conditions, the development of this type of inter-medical profession could become legitimate and foster the cooperation that the health system needs.

2.5. Conclusion: new ways of doing things

To a large extent, the various initiatives that are currently being deployed in different derogatory frameworks confirm Grenier's (2006, p. 34) judgment on health networks:

> Few initiatives go beyond the stage of improving interpersonal relations, because this critical phase is never neutral: it leads to a redefinition of professional territories and requires management thinking that health professionals are not accustomed to conducting.

Despite their limitations, the procedural dimension assumed by these initiatives reveals the meaning of the changes underway. The aim is to encourage and support professionals to work together to define, implement and monitor not so much innovative organizations as new ways of doing things. Therefore, one can think that

> the prospect of cooperating around one's own rules (organizational and financial) will improve reciprocal knowledge of the constraints and interests involved. The wager is that this shared knowledge will facilitate the adoption of truly collective practices, i.e. more rational. (Mossé 2018, pp. 131–132).

Neither the fight against the internal and external compartmentalization of the healthcare system, nor the control of their consequences in terms of efficiency and equity cannot be limited to the accumulation of local experiences of cooperation, even successful ones. Whether it is a question of new modes of remuneration, task, function or mission sharing, their acceptance requires more profound changes. These initiatives will, in particular, have to be legitimized by a change in the positions, stances and representations of the health professions vis-à-vis each other. For example, the proposal to reform studies by merging initial training courses into a common core could go in this direction. This type of linkage would help to get to the root of the crucial question of mutual knowledge – a prerequisite for any lasting form of cooperation. Moreover, the conditions seem to be in place today for such a rapprochement. On the one hand, the *universitarization* of nursing and paramedical studies and the opening of long courses up to the doctorate level are now understood and accepted. On the other hand, the forms taken by current experiments and the "advanced" practices to come induce, or demand, cross-learning which, from this point of view, inaugurate a new era.

Thus, slowly but surely, the current discourse of professionals, relayed by the voluntarist policies of the State, is replacing the qualification-recognition diptych, by the tension between competence and trust. In this perspective, in addition to the debates around the polysemy of the terms used and/or the relative nature of what can oppose *competence* and *qualification* (Oiry 2005), it is the very purpose of "innovative experiments" that needs to be re-examined.

To this end, the assessment of these advanced practices should be conducted from a strategic perspective. Indeed, it will first be a matter of demonstrating the radical specificity of the care they allow (management of healthcare pathways, combination of "technical" and "relational" care, etc.). However, at the risk of being excluded from the field of evidence-based medicine, it will also be necessary to play the game of evaluation on the basis of technical and individualized criteria. So far this has not been the case. For example, an analysis based on a corpus of about 50 evaluative studies has shown that advanced nursing practices are efficient (Newhouse *et al.* 2011), but none of these studies used the QALY criterion, which is considered the universal standard. Ultimately, it will probably be necessary to measure the efficiency of advanced practices *via* their relative cost-utility ratios (Kleinpell & Gawlinski 2005; Vanhook 2007).

However, at a time when the nursing professional space is being redefined, the legitimacy of these new practices depends first and foremost on defending and illustrating their capacity to modify the division of labor within the healthcare system. The result is that, contrary to the evaluative logic and the image given by the metaphor of "experimental science", generalization or reproducibility can no longer be the only horizon of experimentation. Indeed, the actors carrying them out are driven by diverse, sometimes contradictory interests, and their success depends on singular conditions, situated, oriented and constructed over a long period of time:

> Obviously, once that has been said, the problem of closure finally becomes a non-problem, to the benefit, perhaps, of stabilization phases, or "rendezvous" that will bring the relevant actors to evaluate and revise the paths explored. But the very idea of a final decision becomes almost a nonsense in this definition of decision. (Callon & Barthe 2005, p. 127).

The generalization in space being made difficult, remains the durability in time. Therefore, beyond the experimental period (generally set at 5 years), it will be a question of guaranteeing continued support for efficient cooperation, while allowing them to continue to innovate. This means that the future is uncertain.

2.6. Appendix: examples of emancipatory innovations in the 1990s

2.6.1. *Nursing specialization versus the place of the manager*

In a nephrology department of a university hospital (CHU), based on the will of a nurse (whose quest for recognition and specialization was relayed by her department head), it was decided to set up a peritoneal dialysis unit. From the outset, this nurse was given responsibility for keeping schedules and monitoring dialysis notebooks, which led to the marginalization of the healthcare setting. In fact, due to a lack of prior reflection on the organization, the unit became autonomous from the rest of the service. It deliberately turned to the outside world and, in particular, to the independent nurses who monitored homecare. However, as the system was being set up, relations became strained. Complementary, respective roles became competitive, particularly with regard to the financing of patient care and education. Together with the presence of a high density of nephrologists on the territory, this configuration explains the low number of patients finally cared for: about a dozen per year at the time of our study.

2.6.2. *Stubborn labor relations*

With the explicit aim of reducing absenteeism of hospital housekeepers (*agents de services hospitaliers*, ASHs) in a large pediatric ward, the management of the establishment decides to create a cross-functional team. Henceforth, ASHs will no longer be attached to a particular unit but, on the contrary, will be able to intervene throughout the whole hospital. ASHs receive specific training and the term “cleaning” is no longer used, but rather “hygiene chain”. This transition from the domestic sphere to the industrial sphere is widely valued by the players concerned, whose absenteeism is rapidly decreasing. However, since ASHs have been removed from the organization chart of care units, other paramedical staff find themselves at the bottom rung of the hierarchy. Moreover, although under the responsibility of a “foreman”, the agents of the new “Hygiene and Cleanliness” department sometimes respond to informal but imperative requests from the heads of the departments to which they were previously attached. Thus, far from rationalizing the division of labor, the change has blurred its boundaries.

2.7. References

Albert-Cromarias, A., Dos Santos, C., Rochette, C. (2018). Innovation organisationnelle à l’hôpital : s’appuyer sur l’évolution des fonctions infirmières. *The Conversation*, 5 November [Online]. Available at: https://theconversation.com/innovation-organisationnelle-a-lhopital-sappuyer-sur-levolution-des-fonctions-infirmieres-105463.

Alter, N. (1993). Innovation et organisation : deux légitimités en concurrence. *Revue française de sociologie*, 34(2), 175–197.

Berland, Y. and Bourgueil, Y. (2006). Cinq expérimentations de coopération et de délégation de tâches entre professions de santé. Report, Observatoire national de démographie médicale, Paris.

Bouchayer, F. (2005). Dynamiques professionnelles dans le champ de la santé. *Retraite et société*, 46(3), 240–244.

Branciard, A. and Mossé, P. (1994). Hôpital, innovations, professions. Paroles II program report, LEST-CNRS, Aix-en-Provence.

Callon, M. and Barthe, Y. (2005). Décider sans trancher : négociations et délibérations à l'heure de la démocratie dialogique. *Négociations*, 4(2), 115–129.

CTIS (2018). Expérimentations innovantes en santé : mise en œuvre du dispositif en 2018. Report, Conseil stratégique. Avis du CTIS, article 51.

Culyer, A.J. (ed.) (1983). *Health Indicators*. Robertson, Oxford.

Danan, J.L., Biglietto, J., Perquier, F., Celer, A.T., Gakou, S., Ostermeyer, M., Giraud-Rochon, F., Chermak, O. (2019). Les infirmiers de pratique avancée français, de la vision à la mise en œuvre au sein d'un établissement de santé mentale. *Revue francophone internationale de recherche infirmière*, 5, 37–47.

Fédération nationale des infirmiers (2018). Asalée : "un flou artistique", estime la FNI. May 3 [Online]. Available at: https://www.espaceinfirmier.fr/actualites/180503-asalee-un-flou-artistique-estime-la-fni.html.

Feroni, I. (2000). L'identité infirmière vue par ses élites : pièges et limites d'une rhétorique professionnelle. In *Professions et institutions de santé face à l'organisation du travail : aspects sociologiques*, Cresson, G. (ed.). Presses de l'EHESP, Rennes.

Freidson, E. (1970). *Profession of Medecine; A Study in the Sociology of Applied Knowledge*. University of Chicago Press, Chicago.

Greenhalgh, T., Robert, G., McFarlane, F., Bate, P., Kyriakidou, O. (2004). Diffusion of innovations in service organizations: Systematic review and recommendations. *Milbank Quaterly*, 82(4), 581–629.

Grenier, C. (2006). Apprentissages de la coordination entre acteurs professionnels. *Gérer et comprendre*, 83(March), 25–35.

Haute autorité de santé (2008). Délégation, transferts, nouveaux métiers... Comment favoriser des formes nouvelles de coopération entre professionnels de santé ? Report, HAS, Paris.

Jullien, F. (2004). *A Treatise on Efficacy*. University of Hawaii Press, Honolulu.

Kleinpell, R. and Gawlinski, A. (2005). Assessing outcomes in advanced practice nursing practice: The use of quality indicators and evidence-based practice. *Clinical Issues: Advanced Practice in Acute and Critical Care*, 16(1), 43–57.

Loomes, G. and McKenzie, L. (1989). The use of QALYs in health care decision making. *Social Science & Medicine*, 28(4), 299–308.

Loussouarn, C., Franc, C., Videau, Y., Mousquès, J. (2019). La coopération avec une infirmière modifie-t-elle l'activité du médecin généraliste ? *Questions d'économie de la santé*, 241.

Maurice, M., Sellier, F., Silvestre, J.J. (1986). *The Social Foundations of Industrial Power: A Comparison of France and Germany*. MIT Press, Cambridge.

Ministère des solidarités et de la santé (2019). Appel à manifestation d'intérêt. Expérimentation nationale d'un paiement forfaitaire en équipe de professionnels de santé. Document, Ministère de la Santé et CNAM, Paris.

Mossé, P. (2018). *Une économie politique de l'hôpital – contre Procuste*. L'Harmattan, Paris.

Mossé, P., Harayama, T., Boulongne-Garcin, M. (2017). Les infirmières travaillant au domicile des patients ; maitriser l'espace et le temps d'un exercice. *Recherche en soins infirmiers*, 4(131), 52–60.

Newhouse, R. (2011). Advanced practice nurse outcomes 1990–2008: A systematic review. *Nursing Economic*, 29(5), 1–21.

Oiry, E. (2005). Qualification et compétence : deux sœurs jumelles ? *Revue française de gestion*, 158, 13–34.

Pulcini, J., Jelic, M., Gul, R., Yuen Loke, A. (2009). An international survey on Advanced Practices Nursing. *Journal of Nursing Scholarship*, 42(1), 31–39.

Quet, M. (2002). La politique, c'est l'expérimentation. *Hermès la revue*, 63(2), 215–220.

Robelet, M., Serré, M., Bourgueil, Y. (2005). La coordination dans les réseaux de santé : entre logiques gestionnaires et dynamiques professionnelles. *Revue française des affaires sociales*, 34(1), 231–260.

SNIA (2019). IPA "urgences" : une annonce "au goût amer" pour les IADE. September 5 [Online]. Available at: https://www.infirmiers.com/votre-carriere/iade/ipa-urgences-annonce-au-gout-amer-pour-iade.html.

Strobel, P. and Dauphin, S. (1990). Présentation de la Mire. GIP Droit et Justice, Paris.

Vanhook, P. (2007). Cost-utility analysis: A method of quantifying the value of registered nurses. *The Online Journal of Issues in Nursing*, 12(3), 5.

3

Managed Communities of Practice in the Gerontology Sector: Case of a CoP of Gerontology Volunteers in Sweden

3.1. Introduction

Sweden ranks among the best nations in the world according to the WHO for its health system. It is second only to the microstates of Iceland and Singapore according to the American Institute for Health Measurement and Evaluation in 2016. This echoes the research of the English institute Legatum which ranked Sweden seventh in the world in 2018. Beyond the difficulties in comparing health systems and the indicators used to measure these rankings, Sweden enjoys a positive aura abroad.

This ranking is clearly out of line with the feelings of the population, for whom the healthcare system has become a priority issue in the face of immigration or global warming. It occupied a large place in the program of candidates for the 2018 general elections.

How can this discrepancy be explained? A person in charge of health and social action in central Sweden explained to us that the health system had been designed to accommodate eight to nine million people. However, due to recent waves of migration and population growth, the threshold of 10 million inhabitants was crossed in 2017. This Scandinavian country is experiencing a system under stress as in other European countries. A total of 90% of the establishments are understaffed according to the Swedish National Institute of Statistics (2019). This is a major challenge as the demand for care increases along with the aging population and the

---

Chapter written by Bertrand PAUGET.

increase in chronic diseases: the proportion of people older than 75 years of age represents 5.2% of the population, an average of one point more than in other countries (OECD 2013).

To meet these challenges, the Scandinavian kingdom has a long tradition of voluntary work which constitutes a more or less institutionalized system. Voluntary work[1] is a particularly common practice in Scandinavian countries. Enriksen *et al.* (2019) noted that volunteering was highest in Europe in Sweden and Norway (except for the Netherlands). They link this high rate to the anthropological structuring of society, which is very horizontal in its relations.

It is this point that will be the subject of this chapter. We will present a case of an emerging community of practice (CoP) in the Swedish gerontological sector.

However, volunteering is not without its challenges. There are currently about 100 volunteers helping the elderly in the studied commune. However, not all of them choose to continue their commitment. This is a problem for several reasons. The first is that the employees of the municipality need to receive new volunteers, to inform them of the practices to follow in terms of volunteering; this is time-consuming. The second, and perhaps the most obvious, is that seniors who ask for help see volunteers leave and have to wait for a new volunteer to arrive. This change can feel disappointing. The reliance on a more managed CoP has therefore emerged in the head of the commune's gerontological service as a way of coping with the increased demand for care.

3.2. Context and questions

Volunteering is worthwhile for several reasons. First, because it is an undervalued point in French-language scientific literature, the subject is little discussed (Saint-Pierre *et al.* 2009). Yet, the integration of volunteers changes interactions in the healthcare system. Volunteers are not subject to the same rules and relational expectations (Rogers *et al.* 2015). Exchanges are not codified in the same way as between a caregiver and a patient. However, these relationships must be framed by an institution (Pauget 2006).

Gerontology is one of the sectors driving the growth in care due to the aging population. Given the growing need for care and the development of homecare, experimental mechanisms have been set up, but few capitalize on these relationships

1 When we talk about volunteering, we are not talking about caregivers, but about people who do volunteer work.

(Pauget & Dammak 2019), experiencing on the contrary multiple relational failures (Grenier & Pauget 2006).

With respect to volunteers, one of the causes is the diversity of those involved and their lack of knowledge of the sector. The relational aspect is a determining factor in understanding how emerging communities can become managed communities and participate in a better functioning health system.

3.3. Conceptual framework

3.3.1. *Volunteering*

Volunteerism benefits from a long tradition of study in English-speaking humanities and social sciences, including management sciences (Henriksen *et al.* 2019). The themes associated with it are varied and include debates on the scope of this research topic (Cellier 1990). The definition adopted is that of Wilson (2000, p. 15), for whom volunteerism can be defined as any form of activity "in which time is given freely for the benefit of a person, a group, or an organization". We postulate that volunteering as an activity involves action and practices.

One of the interesting points raised by Wilson is that the activity can change over time and the status of the volunteer is bound to change. One of the key issues is the role of volunteers in the health system in a system known for its strong organizational and regulatory constraints.

From the manager's point of view, the integration of volunteers can be managed in order to reduce the cognitive distances between the different people involved in projects and provide a coherent framework for volunteer practices. Volunteer practices are potential sources of change, whether at the level of interactions, organization, etc.

In order to understand the relational framework in which volunteering operates in the Swedish gerontological sector, we mobilize the notion of a CoP, particularly a piloted CoP.

3.3.2. *Communities of practice*

The definition of CoPs, after having been debated for its lack of clarity (Abrahamson 1996), is now a source of consensus (Habdad-Rave 2010). This definition contains the main characteristics expected of CoPs. It is the definition of Wenger *et al.* (2002, p. 4) that is the most cited: "A group of people who share a problem or problems, a passion for a subject and who wish to deepen their knowledge and expertise in a sector by interacting". This was to shift CoPs to the field of knowledge management (Amin & Roberts 2007).

Conversely, according to Brown and Duguib (1991) or Lave and Wenger (1991), it is possible to focus on the relational aspect of CoPs. This implies integration into the community, its purpose and sometimes its history (in the broad sense, which includes understanding and sharing contextual values). Did not Lave and Wenger (1991, p. 98) define CoP in their early days as "a system of relationships between people, activities and the world, developing over time, and interrelating with other tangential and overlapping communities of practice"?

This perspective, which developed the relationship as intrinsically linked to the notion of community, has gradually lost importance as if the relational characteristics described by Wenger *et al.* in 2002 constituted *ante-* and *ex-post* relational elements (Murillo 2011).

These changes can be initiated by the stakeholders themselves. Hadley *et al.* (2007), similar to Wenger, highlight the willingness of stakeholders to participate. This should not be limited to a connection because it brings into play an identity process. Thus, when the conditions are not met (for example, in the event of hierarchical failure), stakeholders innovate, transform, etc., through a CoP. This CoP is dependent on already established relational frameworks, often linked to an organization's history, culture, values, etc. (Bootz 2015).

3.3.3. *Managed communities of practice*

The term CoP is now well established within the scientific community. Soenen (2006) pointed out that communities can be a response to organizational prescriptions. If the commitment of members is mainly emphasized in the first writings on CoPs, it is gradually disappearing (Murello 2011). Subsequent studies have focused on the performance of CoPs (Probst & Borzillo 2007) and their management (Bootz 2015).

To date, very few studies have mobilized the notion of CoPs in the health and social field in French-speaking literature. Dameron *et al.* (2007) considered that health networks could be likened to CoPs. These authors put forward the relational perspectives of CoPs. Conversely, English-language literature is much more extensive, emphasizing both the relational character of CoPs (Oborn *et al.* 2010) and their institutionalization. The role of volunteers is comparatively underdeveloped. This is a contribution on the theoretical level.

3.3.4. *The interpretative framework of a piloted community of practice*

The relational perspective of CoPs is present in the health and social system. This is due to the very nature of the field in which relationships are the basis of professions and occupations (Pauget 2006). Stakeholder participation and internal norms mentioned in the literature (Bootz 2015) are also particularly prevalent in the health and social system. These characteristics suggest that the majority of examples in the literature make CoPs spontaneous CoPs.

According to Bouchez (2015), managed CoPs are "a form of polar continuum [...], extending between strong management steering (in the case of certain community-based projects) and quasi-community steering (in the case of communities based on shared affinities)". For Bootz (2015), their institutionalization is based on at least three factors: clearly identified management, a source of knowledge sharing and the selection and dissemination of innovations.

3.4. Illustrations

In this chapter, we want to describe the Swedish context and then that of a medium-sized Swedish town where volunteer work is organized by the municipality to offer shows and create links between people of different ages. This city is located in the center of the Scandinavian kingdom and has a demographic situation similar to the cities to which it can be compared.

3.4.1. *The Swedish context*

A 2009 European Union report on volunteering in Sweden indicated that 48% of people between the ages of 16 and 74 years were involved in volunteering practices, which corresponded to about 3 million people[2] with a total of 400,000 full-time jobs. In comparison, volunteering is around 25% in France[3].

The social sector is the second most popular sector for volunteers (20% of the total). The Swedish statistics Website, the equivalent of INSEE for France, puts forward the figure of 3.7 million volunteers in 2014. Subsequent data from questionable sources suggest that this figure varies little. The economic value

2 The report is available at https://ec.europa.eu/citizenship/pdf/national_report_se_en.pdf [Accessed 12 September 2019].

3 https://ec.europa.eu/citizenship/pdf/volunteering-in-the-eu-final-report.pdf.

created by volunteering is highest in the social sector and amounts to 25 billion crowns per year, or about 2.45 billion euros[4].

3.4.2. *A community of practice piloted in the field of gerontology*

The three crown kingdom has a development comparable to other European countries with 20% of the population older than 65 years old and a greater proportion of older than 75 years old than in the rest of Europe. In order to meet the growing demand for care, the techniques used have been the same, with an increase in prevention among the 60-year-olds, greater use of homecare and, finally, the use of private care alongside public care in retirement homes. Volunteer work is used by the commune both at home and in retirement homes, showing two CoPs that are diversely piloted.

3.4.2.1. *The use of the managed community of practice*

The gerontological and social sector is led in Sweden by the municipalities, which have a much greater weighting, both financially and politically, compared to their French counterparts. The municipalities directly receive about 31% of taxes, which they can vary according to their needs. In practice, however, there is little variation from one commune to another.

The use of volunteers is a culturally accepted fact in all sectors, including gerontology. Their organization has been progressive but is today considered as one of the tools to help in homecare and organization in retirement homes.

Recruitment is primarily done online when volunteers fill out an "Expression of Interest in Volunteer Assignments". The information to be provided is very brief: name, age, email and telephone. The volunteer is then referred to a volunteer coordination unit. In this case, the volunteer has two possibilities: individual accompaniment of an elderly person, most often in isolation, and/or participation in activities during the May-retirement period.

In the central Swedish city we present here, this office is composed of four full-time staff (two coordinators and two administrative assistants), in order to ensure a permanent presence throughout the year.

The integration of the volunteer begins with an information session and the person meets with the coordinator to learn more about his or her motivation(s). The senior coordinator tries to get to know the values, the history and to determine the possible degree of involvement of the volunteer person.

---

4 www.scb.se/hitta-statistik/artiklar/2018/svenskarna-arbetar-ideellt-for-131-miljarder.

This is posted on the Website of the municipality:

> When recruiting volunteers, we try to match wishes and interests so that both parties can exchange satisfactorily. During the first meeting (in our premises), in which we participate, you meet the senior citizen and get to know each other. Then you establish contact with each other. It is important that you have fun together. The most common thing is to meet once a week.

In a few lines, this is very strong if we refer to Scandinavian culture. The first part of the text concerns the reduction of cognitive dissonance in order to allow entry into the CoP. The practice of the meeting between the volunteer and the elderly person is monitored in order to encourage the practice of volunteering. The aim here is to avoid an asymmetrical relationship. If this seems to be characterized by common sense (the volunteer must not be in a position to take advantage of or abuse the elderly person, which would be illegal), it also has a particular connotation in Sweden where society is marked by a strong horizontality of relationships. One of the unofficial rules to be respected is the one that was codified in the 20th century by the writer Aksel Sandemose and for whom no one should be above the others. There must be a relationship of strict equality and there must be no conflict. This is the basis of interaction in Sweden. Thus, the practice enacted here is intended to be a continuation of what the elderly person will have known throughout his or her life. It is a form of de-stigmatization to use Goffman's (1975) expression. The volunteer integrates the isolated person back into society.

Volunteers are often Swedish 60-year-olds who help people of their parents' generation. The coordinator only sees the volunteers about once a year at a party dedicated to them.

Relational patterns at the individual level are crucial for those of the CoP as a whole. Indeed, the CoP framework limits interactions by providing acceptable norms for the relationship between the volunteer and the senior, but steering does not extend beyond that. Keeping volunteers in such a flexible CoP is not a given (Starbird 2011). There is a lack of knowledge sharing, even if only in the form of feedback, or the selection of innovations.

3.4.2.2. *Toward ever more steering of the community of practice*

The second possibility for the volunteer is to participate in the activities of the retirement homes. The place of the volunteers is strictly defined for the participants (elderly person and volunteer). The municipality clearly states that "volunteering is a complement to the help and support provided by the municipality and does not replace the work done by trained and paid staff".

Here, the role of the coordinator is still pivotal in framing practices but there is more scope for creating and innovating practices. Thus, the structuring of the managed CoP is much more complete than in the first case we have described.

There are several types of activities and therefore practices. The first practice is the so-called fika practice. This term, which has no equivalent in English, refers to a ritualized coffee break that is an intense moment of socialization. This is practiced from nursery school onward and continued throughout life. Volunteers serve coffee, clear away cups, dirty cutlery and clean up, leaving staff time to deal with people face-to-face. Here again we are in a practice of de-stigmatization. During these fikas, the coordinator thanks the volunteers with a special emphasis on the most loyal. For example, an 80-year-old person, who has been a volunteer for more than 20 years, was congratulated in front of those present. This kind of mark of individual esteem at public meetings is rare in Sweden.

The second practice shows all the plasticity of the definition of volunteering[5]. For example, music groups playing Swedish standards from the 1950s are invited to perform in retirement homes for a small fee. The musical practice here is a framework in which the different generations mingle, since this kind of concert is open to people outside the retirement homes: the admission fee is in the order of one to two euros, which the residents of the retirement homes also pay.

Or a volunteer of foreign origin has agreed to organize a foreign meal. The idea was validated by the volunteer center and the coordinator and the volunteer bought the ingredients together (selection of innovations). The aim here is to take advantage of the specificities of the volunteers in order to propose and renew interactions between the residents, the volunteers and the volunteer center. Everything is still subject to approval by the supervisory authorities.

We are here in a typical example of a managed CoP with a willingness to control even the purchase of foodstuff. In this case, the innovation appears rather weak but it nevertheless represents a big difference for the stakeholders in place. Indeed, the Swedes are used to very routine activities in their socialization mode. The change induced in the meal is particularly noticeable.

3.5. Conclusion

In the context of the increase in demand for care, the supervisory authorities have been widely solicited and have encouraged health and social organizations to find solutions.

5 There has been much literature on these cases of partially paid volunteering. According to Wilson's definition often used in Sweden (as in the Swedish report on volunteering mentioned above), a low-paid activity is compatible with volunteer status.

One example is the creation of pilot CoPs. Their objective is twofold: to promote the de-stigmatization of old age through social activities and to standardize the practices of volunteers with very different motivations.

It is within this framework that innovations are most perceptible, even if they remain framed and limited. They do not concern care as such, but peripheral activities that are left in other countries to professionals (artists or health professionals).

Faced with the influx of patients, the idea of the pilot CoPs is to allow healthcare professionals to refocus on their primary mission while providing breaks for residents and professionals in the context of globally ritualized activities.

3.6. References

Abrahamson, E. (1996). Management fashion. *Academy of Management Review*, 21(1), 254–285.

Amin, A. and Roberts, J. (2007). Knowing in action: Beyond communities of practice. *Research Policy*, 37, 353–369.

Bootz, J.-P. (2009). Les communautés d'apprentissage : structuration de la littérature, illustrations et perspectives. *Gestion 2000*, July.

Bootz, J.-P. (2015). Comment concilier auto-organisation et contrôle au sein des communautés de pratique pilotées ? Une scoping review. *Management international*, 19(3), 15–30.

Bouchez, J.-P. (2015). Vers l'émergence progressive d'un nouveau cycle managérial hybride ? Le cas des communautés de pratique "pilotées". *Annales des Mines – Gérer et comprendre*, 3(121), 51–60.

Brown, J.S. and Duguid, P. (1991). Organizational learning and communities-of-practice: Toward a unified view of working, learning and innovation. *Organization Science*, 2(1), 40–57.

Cellier, I. (1995). Le bénévolat à travers la littérature : un objet d'étude à redéfinir. *Anthropologies et sociétés*, 19(1–2), 175–190.

Dameron, S. and Josserand, E. (2007). Le développement d'une communauté de pratique : une analyse relationnelle. *Revue française de gestion*, 174(4), 131–148.

Goffman, E. (1975). *Stigmates : les usages sociaux des handicaps*. Les Éditions de Minuit, Paris.

Grenier, C. and Pauget, B. (2006). Les défaillances et les recompositions professionnelles et relationnelles induites par la création de réseaux de santé. *Sociologie et santé*, 26.

Habdad-Rave, S. (2010). Le rôle des communautés de pratique dans le processus de gestion des connaissances dans les entreprises innovantes : une étude de cas par comparaison intersites. *La revue des sciences de gestion, direction et gestion*, 241, 43–56.

Hadley, K., Sturdy, A., Finchman, R., Clarck, T. (2007). Within and beyond communities of practice: Making sense of learning through participation, identity and practice. *Journal of Management Studies*, 43(3), 641–653.

Henriksen, L.S., Strømsnes, K., Svedberg, L. (2019). *Civic Engagement in Scandinavia: Volunteering, Informal Help and Giving in Denmark, Norway and Sweden*. Springer, Cham.

Lave, J. and Wenger, E. (1991). *Situated Learning: Legitimate Peripheral Participation*. Cambridge University Press, Cambridge.

Murillo, E. (2011). Communities of practice in the business and organization studies literature. *Information Research*, 16(1), 1–18.

Oborn, E. and Dawson, S. (2010). Learning across communities of practice: An examination of multidisciplinary work. *British Journal of Management*, 21, 843–858.

OECD (2013). Panorama de la santé : les indicateurs de l'OCDE [Online]. Available at: https://www.oecd.org/fr/els/systemes-sante/Panorama-de-la-sante-2013.pdf [accessed 21 February 2021].

Pauget, B. (2006). La connaissance relationnelle comme aide à la compréhension de la structuration d'une organisation. PhD Thesis, Université de technologie de Troyes, Troyes.

Pauget, B. and Dammak, A. (2018). Towards a relational innovation. *Society and Business Review*, 13(1), 5–14.

Probst, G. and Borzillo, B. (2007). Piloter les communautés de pratique avec succès. *Revue française de gestion*, 1(170), 135–153.

Rogers, S.E., Rogers, C.M., Boyd, K.D. (2015). Strategic human resource management of volunteers and the link to hospital patient satisfaction. *Nonprofit and Voluntary Sector Quarterly* [Online]. Available at: https://scholarship.sha.cornell.edu/articles/810/ [accessed 9 December 2019].

Soenen, G. (2006). Les déterminants du fonctionnement communautaire. Une étude comparative. *Revue française de gestion*, 4(163), 139–153.

St-Pierre, M., Sévigny, A., Gauthier, J., Tourigny, A., Dallaire, C. (2009). Une nouvelle approche pour la gestion de l'intégration dans le système de santé : le cas des bénévoles et des professionnels. *Management & Avenir*, 26(6), 177–189.

Starbird, K. and Palen, L. (2011). Voluntweeters: Self-organizing by digital volunteers in times of crisis. *Proceedings of the SIGCHI Conference on Human Factors in Computing System, CHI 2011*, Vancouver, Canada, 7–12 May.

Wenger, E., McDermott, R., Snyder, W.M. (2002). *Cultivating Communities of Practice*. Harvard Business Publishing, Brighton.

Wilson, J. (2000). Volunteering. *Annual Review of Sociology*, 26(1), 215–240.

PART 2

Innovations on the Collective Side

Introduction to Part 2

The analysis of innovations has often valued innovators in academic and professional literature. It is often individuals who are put in the foreground, considering that they have played a crucial role in the transformations studied.

However, in order to consider the alteration of frontiers produced in healthcare institutions by organizational innovations, it is essential to broaden this individualistic perspective and to consider the collective and organizational forms on which these innovators rely to produce these innovations (Boiteau & Baret 2017).

Current changes in health demands (pandemics, aging population, chronic diseases, patient autonomy and the legitimacy of their voice and experiences) explain why healthcare professionals are increasingly intervening simultaneously, ideally in a coordinated and concerted manner, with patients (and their caregivers). The sequential dynamic of care is less and less possible and the practices delivered at each stage have profound consequences on the following stages. Operating practices depend, for example, more and more often on what may (or may not) have been done in the preoperative phase, and all these practices have a direct impact on the postoperative phases and the well-being of patients at the end of treatment (Myriokefalitaki *et al.* 2016).

Thinking about altering frontiers of healthcare organizations means thinking very broadly about the organization and intervention of interprofessional teams with patients.

These new dynamics of care also require us to think about the governance of care. Indeed, these flexible collective dynamics, adapted to the specificities of the needs of patients, can no longer be administered "from the top" as it was often the case in healthcare institutions. Frameworks and general principles can be defined by the hierarchy, but it is becoming essential to develop governance that leaves more room for local adaptations to diverse and changing realities. This more decentralized governance of interprofessional activities is a major challenge for all health systems and organizations.

This renewed focus on groups and organizations that enable organizational innovations to lead to alter frontiers also makes it possible to focus on a factor that is often forgotten: technology. Indeed, the analysis of these groups requires us to consider humans as well as "non-humans" (Akrich *et al.* 2002a, 2002b). Humans are the driving force behind innovation, but they rely on tools, machines, management indicators and documents for these organizational innovations to transform care practices. The analysis of the alteration of frontiers of healthcare organizations therefore involves studying the groups of stakeholders and the technologies they use in their interprofessional practices.

Finally, the analysis of organizational innovations that enable altering frontiers also involves thinking beyond the boundaries of healthcare institutions and considering care at the territorial level. It is easy to see here the major challenge posed by altering frontiers brought about by profound changes in the demand for care. Thinking in terms of altering frontiers means conceptualizing and promoting the practices and governance of teams that are highly interprofessional, using multiple and sometimes complex technologies spread over an often large territory.

This section analyzes how organizational innovations are transforming work teams, groups and, more broadly, territorialized care networks.

Chapter 4, proposed by Delphine Wannenmacher, focuses on surgical robots that are implanted in some operating rooms. This technical innovation allows efficiency and surgical procedures that were impossible before. However, it reduces visual communication (the surgeon is forced to have his eyes glued to the screen – and only him) and renders obsolete the divisions of labor that visual communication (e.g. with the doctor in charge of anesthesia) previously allowed. This technical innovation leads to the development of new collective technical skills, but above all non-technical collective skills, such as situational awareness and new forms of decision-making, teamwork and leadership. This technical innovation even leads to the development of forms of communication aimed at conveying emotions. This chapter concludes by emphasizing that the structuring of interprofessional discussion spaces would be very useful to enable and strengthen the development of these new collective skills.

Christelle Havard, in Chapter 5, analyzes several cases of organizational innovation that are clinical poles. The analysis in several French hospitals shows that this organizational innovation leads stakeholders to build new forms of interprofessional and interorganizational cooperation. By analyzing the tools for steering, exchange and decision-making, the contribution shows three forms of articulation that are developing: a structuring articulation (at the level of the hospital as a whole, to divide work and coordinate it), an operational articulation (at the level of a department, to organize care tasks around the patient's trajectory) and a trajectory articulation (around the patient to design and implement a care trajectory). Three tools are used by the clinical pole head, the deputy director, the senior health executive and the management assistant to build this cooperation: the clinical pole project, the pole contract and the medico-economic indicators. This analysis finally identifies the factors that enable this cooperation to be developed.

In Chapter 6, Frédéric Gilbert uses the example of family doctor groups, which, in Quebec, are an organizational innovation designed to meet the major challenges of primary care (emergency room overcrowding, aging population, chronic diseases, etc.). The author notes, however, that despite overall agreement on the relevance of this organizational innovation, it is struggling to spread and that its effects are often limited. He explains these difficulties by the fact that there has been little feedback and little circulation of knowledge about these organizational innovations. To remedy this situation, he proposes a meta-evaluation of organizational innovations in healthcare systems. This new form of evaluation would make it possible to value the results of these innovations and thus contribute to their dissemination.

Finally, Chapter 7, proposed by Matthieu Sibé, Sandrine Cueille and Tamara Roberts, focuses on territorial support platforms, which aim to organize cooperation between the various professionals involved in caring for people in complex situations in a given territory. The cases analyzed show that adhocracy is the organizational structure that allows the best performance of these organizations. The analysis also makes it possible to identify the internal and external contingency factors for these organizations.

References

Akrich, M., Callon, M., Latour, B., Monaghan, A. (2002a). The key to success in innovation part I: The art of interessement. *International Journal of Innovation Management*, 6(02), 187–206.

Akrich, M., Callon, M., Latour, B., Monaghan, A. (2002b). The key to success in innovation part II: The art of choosing good spokespersons. *International Journal of Innovation Management*, 6(02), 207–225.

Boiteau, K. and Baret, C. (2017). La conduite du changement en hôpital psychiatrique : le rôle des centres de traduction dans la valorisation des innovations lors d'un projet de promotion du bien-être au travail. *Revue politiques et management public*, 34(3–4), 215–230.

Myriokefalitaki, E., Smith, M., Ahmed, A.S. (2016). Implementation of enhanced recovery after surgery (ERAS) in gynaecological oncology. *Arch. Gynecol. Obstet.*, 294(1), 137–143.

4

Moving from Partitioning to Transversality in Operating Rooms using Robot-assisted Surgery

4.1. Introduction

In this chapter, we are interested in the effects of the introduction of technology such as the surgical robot on the activity that takes place in an operating room located within a regional university hospital center in the Grand Est region of France, and more particularly on the individual and collective skills of the work team.

In a pragmatic perspective aiming at sensemaking with stakeholders in the field, we have analyzed documents on the subject, observations within the operating room, a video recording and photographs of a surgical intervention in urology, self-confrontation interviews with the members of the team who participated in the filmed intervention, as well as an interprofessional and interdisciplinary workshop on the surgical robot.

After having exposed the context of operating rooms using the surgical robot and the questions it raises in terms of skills, we will specify our theoretical grounding, then illustrate the effects of the surgical robot on individual and collective skills that are deployed in an operating room specialized in urology, before ending with a discussion on the perspective of interactive and reflexive discussion spaces supported by mediating artifacts.

Chapter written by Delphine WANNENMACHER.

4.2. The context of operating rooms mobilizing the surgical robot

Originally, surgery was performed through an open incision, which consists of making a large incision in the patient until the organ or tissue involved in the procedure is exposed. While open surgery has advantages in terms of patient set-up and procedure time and does not require very large investments, it requires more recovery time and hospitalization, and creates more risks for patients in terms of infection and complications.

Laparoscopy, which has been developing since the end of the 1980s, consists of performing a "mini-invasive" surgical operation. It is different from open surgery since it is performed through incisions just large enough to accommodate the "trocars", which are a kind of transparent tube through which the surgical instruments pass, as well as the endoscope that will capture the internal image of the part of the patient's body involved in the operation, and display it on a screen. Compared to open surgery, laparoscopy offers benefits in terms of a reduced hospital stay, a lower rate of parietal complications and postoperative pain, improved cosmetic results and a faster return to normal activity (Pugin *et al.* 2011). However, certain areas, such as the abdomen and shoulders in particular, may remain sensitive for a few days after the operation due to the carbon dioxide injected into the body to expose the areas to be visualized and operated on.

However, laparoscopy has intrinsic limitations and requires a long and difficult learning curve for the surgeon because it imposes non-physiological gestures, constrained by two-dimensional (2D) vision, a gap between the anatomical target and the control screen, reduced hand movements, inversion of gestures (to move forceps to the right, the hand holding the forceps must go to the left), and difficult ergonomic postures for the operator (Pugin *et al.* 2011; Valverde *et al.* 2014).

In comparison, the surgical robot that entered operating rooms in the early 2000s provides a more intuitive surgical act and brings solutions to the intrinsic limits of laparoscopy. The instruments are remotely controlled via a video console that offers a 3D vision and includes an information system that improves the transition between the different control modes (Pugin *et al.* 2011).

While the direct cost of the robot is very high compared to simple laparoscopy and open surgery, studies show its advantages in terms of lower hospital costs, including less postoperative pain for the donor, with a decrease in the use of morphinans and an earlier stopping of their prescription, lower overall consumption of analgesics, a shorter hospital stay and an earlier return to work, improved cosmetic results, fewer postoperative complications and a lower morbidity rate, particularly for obese patients and/or patients on anticoagulants (Pugin *et al.* 2011; Defortescu & Tillou 2016).

Robot-assisted surgery is not yet used in all operating rooms and can never be completely generalized as it does not apply to all specialties and all patients. It is destined to coexist with other techniques such as open surgery or laparoscopy. The majority of hospitals today have a surgical robot, even if it is sometimes relegated to a corner to collect dust, due to a lack of trained personnel to use it. Indeed, the use and installation of the surgical robot requires the development of specific skills.

4.3. The issue of technical and non-technical skills in the context of robotic surgery

With the development of robotic surgery, the mastery of technical skills is necessary. These refer to psychomotor action and mental skills acquired through practice and learning, manual dexterity and good hand-eye coordination (Agha *et al.* 2015).

While technical skills are necessary, they are not sufficient to maintain high levels of performance (Yule & Paterson-Brown 2012). Non-technical skills are equally, if not more, important to achieve an optimum outcome for the patient undergoing surgery. Hull *et al.* (2012) have shown the beneficial impact on technical performance of feedback and management of stressful events in the operating room, and the existence of a link between high levels of fatigue and teamwork failure, and technical errors in the operating room. Non-technical skills include situational awareness, decision-making, communication, teamwork and leadership (Agha *et al.* 2015).

Yule and Paterson-Brown (2012) identify two categories of barriers to communication: "internal" barriers, which refer to differences in language, culture, motivation, expectations, past experience, status, emotions or mood; and "external" barriers, which refer to noise, voice range and level of deafness, electrical interference, spatiotemporal separation and lack of visual cues (body language, eye contact, gestures and facial expressions).

Based on a categorization of the main types of communication that take place during surgery (Table 4.1), Nyssen and Blavier (2009) found that, compared to laparoscopy, robotic surgery results in a greater overall number of communication acts and a higher use of orientation, manipulation, order and confirmation type communications. The authors also showed that the number of communication acts decreases globally with the level of experience and that the communications related to orientation, manipulation and strategies decrease strongly when the pair is composed of experts. On the other hand, communication acts such as orders and confirmations are more important in the presence of an expert-novice pair.

Type of communication	Content
Perception-based communications and orientation	Communications on the perceptual processing of related visual information such as the perception of distances and depth, spatial orientation or organ recognition.
Manipulation-oriented communications	Communications on gestures and manipulations of instruments and organs.
Communications related to operational strategies	Communications related to operating strategies, procedure choices and procedure planning.
Order-related communications	Communications related to orders given to a team member, often corresponding to requests from the department.
Confirmations	Verbalizations attesting to the good reception of certain messages.
Release communications	Communications involving humor and relaxation.

Table 4.1. *Categorization of main types of communication (Blavier & Nyssen 2010)*

If the question of competence is already addressed in the literature on robotic chiropractic surgery, it mainly concerns the technical and non-technical performance of the surgeon or of the surgeon-assistant pair, often with a normative and evaluative aim. We propose to conduct a more detailed analysis of the effects of the introduction of the surgical robot on the activity of an operating room, starting from a theoretical framework around the effects of new technologies in terms of individual and collective skills.

4.4. The effects of new technologies in terms of individual and collective skills

Without yielding to the temptation of technological determinism, it is clear that the introduction of new technologies is not without consequences for the organization. Technology incorporates the technical and social vision of its designers, and is accompanied by a certain type of organizational design and a certain structuring logic, even if this logic is not fixed and can evolve. Technology also has "specific effects" on the organization, linked to the organizational constraints and opportunities of technology, which are however "modulated" by the way in which technological change is managed (Alsène 1990).

We will focus here on the specific effects of technology on the individual and collective skills that are deployed in a collective activity situation. An activity can be considered collective when the execution of a task involves the coordinated intervention of several operators (Leplat 1993), each with their own functions and skills. Multiple definitions coexist of the notion of individual competence as well as collective competence. There is, however, a relative consensus on the definitions and characteristics to which we shall refer here.

The notion of competence refers to the knowledge and know-how, typical behaviors, standard procedures and types of reasoning that can be implemented without new learning and that allow the anticipation of phenomena (Montmollin 1997). Individual skills are dependent on work situations and are distributed among operators who interact within the framework of a collective activity (Largier *et al.* 2008). During a collective activity, cooperation leads operators to articulate their individual skills, giving rise to collective skills that are new and different from the initial, group-specific, shared skills (Leplat 2000).

This notion of collective competence refers to common operational knowledge and referents and to cognitive representations shared by the members of a team (Largier *et al.* 2008) that enable them to work together and cooperate to achieve a common goal or solve problems collectively (Wittorski 1994; Amherdt *et al.* 2000), whether in a routine situation or in the case of difficult or unusual situations (Dubois & Retour 1999; Michaux 2005). Thus, we can speak of collective skills "when, within a team, information is exchanged, representations are standardized, know-how is articulated, reasoning and strategies are elaborated in common" (Montmollin 1997, p. 99).

The quality of the exchanges and the accuracy of the co-constructed representations in inter-action depend in part on the collective skills that develop in the shared practices and times of a collective (Largier *et al.* 2008). And these collective skills are the knowledge and know-how of a collective to coordinate professional worlds related to different professions, people, resources and actions to carry out a collective task such as caring for a patient (Grosjean & Lacoste 1999).

Collective and individual skills are co-determined (Leplat 2000) insofar as the areas of overlap of individual skills in a work team are decisive for the construction of collective skills and the latter enrich individual skills (Largier *et al.* 2008).

4.5. Viewing at the heart of robot-assisted surgery in urology

4.5.1. *A pragmatic approach to analyzing the activity of an operating theater*

In order to understand our problematics, we adopted a pragmatist approach (Lorino 2016) in which thought and action participated in the continuous process of construction of meaning and transformation of the world, and human experience being an ever-renewed quest for meaning, anchored in the pursuit of practical ends. More precisely, we studied the case of an operating room using robotic surgery based on several methodological tools (Yin 2008).

We filmed and analyzed a three-hour surgical procedure. To complete the observations and video recording, self-confrontation interviews with each member of the surgical team were conducted. Finally, a debriefing was carried out, followed by a discussion of the results with some of the stakeholders involved.

The analyzed activity took place in an operating room composed of a highly experienced urology surgeon, a young resident who assisted the surgeon during the operation, a state-qualified operating room scrub nurse who supplied the instruments to the resident or to the surgeon, a circulating operating room nurse who operated certain machines and left the operating room to look for instruments when needed, an anesthesiologist who is in charge of several operating rooms at the same time and a state-registered nurse anesthetist who assisted or took over from the anesthesiologist when he or she was in another room (Figure 4.1).

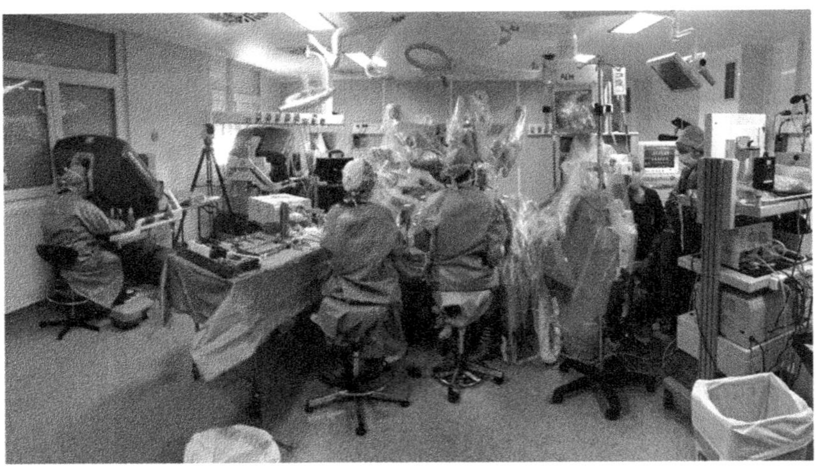

Figure 4.1. *Configuration of the team and operating room during the filmed procedure. For a color version of this figure, see www.iste.co.uk/grenier/frontiers.zip*

4.5.2. *A configuration of the operating room and an installation of the patient constrained by the surgical robot*

The robotic device was originally designed to be able to operate remotely from a console at a given location, as a patient could be hundreds or thousands of miles away, on a battlefield, for example. For this reason, robotic surgery devices have integrated a computer control system into the surgical console to improve the transition between the different control modes and to allow the digitization of the surgical gesture and image through an electromechanical and computer interface (Pugin *et al.* 2011).

However, due to transmission technical problems during several tests of remote deployment of the robotic device, it was finally confined to a single operating room and consists of three elements that are connected to each other by electrical cables: the patient cart, the video column (light source, camera and insufflator) and the console (Valverde *et al.* 2014).

The logic behind robotic technology in surgery has resulted in separation and relative distance of the surgeon from the patient and the rest of the team, which affect the configuration of the operating room, and communication and teamwork (Table 4.2).

The robotic system consists of a console, a patient cart and the robot's arms. Depending on the location of the entrance door, the size of the operating room, the cables and the monitors provided for anesthesia, there are not multiple possibilities to position the console and the robot arms in the space. In any case, the robot arms will be installed on one side of the patient, while on the other side will be the resident and the scrub nurse. The console will be positioned back from the patient and the rest of the team, forcing the surgeon to operate away from the rest of the team. Compared to laparoscopy and even more so to open surgery, the relationship of the surgeon to the patient changes. At the beginning of the operation, the patient's installation is longer because the position must be adapted to the robot, which also takes time to set up, and the support points must be well studied since the operation will be relatively long. Thus, the surgeon will initially be preoccupied by the patient's installation. However, during the intervention, the surgeon will operate from his or her console, which is installed behind the patient and the rest of the team.

<table>
<tr><td>Console 2
(rarely used)</td><td>Robot arms</td><td>2D screen</td><td rowspan="2">Shield</td><td>Monitoring towers
and wiring</td></tr>
<tr><td>Console 1
Surgeon</td><td colspan="2">Patient</td><td>Anesthesiologist
and nurse</td></tr>
<tr><td>Circulating nurse</td><td>Scrub nurse</td><td>Resident</td><td></td><td>Monitoring towers
and wiring</td></tr>
</table>

Table 4.2. *Typical configuration of the operating room using the surgical robot*

4.5.3. *A spatiotemporal separation and limited communication between team members*

In an open channel or conventional laparoscopic procedure, the surgeon and his or her assistant are face-to-face and share the same image, either directly or on the screen. In robot-assisted surgery, on the other hand, the surgeon sits facing the console and manipulates joystick-like controllers using 3D vision. The manipulations of the joysticks are transmitted to the computer which delivers an impulse which, transmitted remotely by a long cable, activates the articulated arms of the slave part of the robot, which reproduces in real time the movements of the surgeon sitting at the console. The assistant is located at the slave part and has the task of changing the instruments of the trocars attached to the robot's arms, exposing the organs and cleaning the operating area (regular aspiration of fluids and irrigation of the site). Thanks to this proximity to the patient and these accesses, the surgeon-assistant keeps a return of force that the surgeon at the console has completely lost. On the other hand, he or she only sees in 2D and practices fairly simple and limited technical gestures, in response to the surgeon's strong instructions.

With the robotic device, the surgeon does not see objects that pass out of his or her visual field, such as a needle or a compress, nor does he or she see what the scrub nurse and the resident are doing, so verbal communication becomes essential to ensure the health and safety of patients, for example by preventing objects from remaining in the patient's body. Although team members are aware of safe communication, it is important to verbalize that the message has been heard – often by repeating it aloud – and the actions taken so that the person who cannot see what is happening in the room – in this case the surgeon here – knows what is happening. The scrub nurse and the resident regularly fail to verbalize what they do following a surgeon's instruction, which can create impatience for the surgeon and irritation for the scrub nurse who has taken the instruction into account but has not verbalized it.

In general, there is less tension at the beginning of the procedure when the surgeon is setting up the patient and the robot, surrounded by his or her team. Communication then seems more "natural" and relaxed, as verbal interactions are accompanied by gestures and looks. On the other hand, interactions are tenser during the procedure, when the surgeon is facing the console and is away from the rest of the team.

Although noise pollution in the operating room is not only related to the robotic device, but it also amplifies the communication problems related to the distance between the surgeon and the rest of the team. In addition to these "useful" noises related to the technical environment of the procedure, there are also avoidable noises, such as the scrub nurse's stool that creaks with every rotational movement.

Given the spatial configuration, all this surrounding noise and a voice that does not carry very far from being directed to the console and not to the team, the scrub nurse and the resident admit that they do not always hear the surgeon's instructions, which is problematic given the stakes. The robotic device included a headset and microphone to facilitate communication between the surgeon and the assistant, but this was not activated because the microphone was crackling. The latest versions of the robot have improved the technique, but it is only available on the newer devices. It would therefore be necessary to acquire a new robot whose cost is very high.

In addition, the field shield separates the anesthesia cluster from the rest of the team and creates an impression of confinement, especially since the anesthesiologist and the nurse anesthetist are surrounded by monitoring towers and cables. Here again, the presence of a field shield is not specific to the robotic device but reinforces the effect of confinement and distance given the distance of the surgeon and the imposing place taken by the robot's arms. This impression of compartmentalization is amplified by the failure of the second 2D screen (repeater) which normally allows the anesthesiologists to follow the operation and to know the status of the operating protocol.

Finally, because of the robotic device and the distance between them, the surgeon's communication acts toward the resident are very directive and leave little opportunity for learning or companionship, which are more developed in other types of surgery.

4.5.4. *The impoverishment and disarticulation of individual and collective skills in the operating room, mobilizing the surgical robot*

As we have seen, the development and articulation of individual and collective skills are based above all on work situations in which information and knowledge are easily shared; people exchange and coordinate to carry out a task or solve a problem collectively, and have shared time for this. The conditions in the operating room studied do not seem to offer a favorable breeding ground and seem to lead more to an impoverishment and disarticulation of individual and collective skills.

Indeed, as we have seen, the surgeon exchanges during the operation almost exclusively with the people nearby, in particular the scrub nurse and the resident, and has, apart from the beginning and the very end of the operation, no direct interaction with the anesthesiologist team. And if they have a privileged relationship, it is important to note that the surgeon's communication with the resident is very directive and leaves little opportunity for learning.

Partitioning	Space	Temporal
In the block	– Modification of the spatial configuration of the block and the patient. The surgeon operates from his or her console and is away from the other team members, who are tightly packed around the patient. – All this creates more verbal exchanges but poorer (strong instructions, reduced responses) and less non-verbal exchanges. – The many objects in the block (console, robot, monitoring towers, cables) create boundaries, including those that are supposed to make the link (visualization screens). – Interaction is cut off between certain members (in particular, between the anesthesia and surgery divisions). – The breakdown of the second 2D screen (repeater), which normally allows the anesthetists to follow the operation and to know the status of the operating protocol, amplifies the phenomenon of compartmentalization. – The mediation between the anesthesia unit and the surgery unit is broken.	– At the time of the checklist (beginning of the procedure), the anesthesiologist is in another room and cannot answer questions about antibiotics. – Lack of exchanges and collegial decision-making at a time that seems crucial. – When the surgeon makes a request (need for a compress, change of instrument, etc.), the absence of visual communication generates impatience. – Exchanges sometimes take place under tension. – Anesthesiologists and surgeons are not concerned in the same way by the different stages of the protocol. This leads to differences in interest and attention.
Out of the block	– The medical team (which includes the surgeon and the resident) meets for briefings while the rest of the operating room team (anesthesiologist, scrub nurse, anesthetist nurse) is seeing the patient or is already in the operating room. – Team members do not share much with each other and therefore do not have the same level of information. – The break areas are different for scrub nurse, anesthetist nurse, anesthesiologist, surgeon and resident. – There is little interaction between team members and few opportunities for interaction outside the operating room.	– Team members have different work rhythms and hierarchical relationships. Thus, the nursing staff can be less abstracted from planning constraints to participate in possible moments of exchange. – This strongly limits exchanges between members outside the block and the possibility of organizing common discussion spaces.

Table 4.3. *Spatial and temporal partitioning within and outside the operating room*

In addition, the surgical robot, which is added to the already extensive equipment (monitoring towers, cables, field shields, etc.), further separates the anesthesia unit from the rest of the team and creates an impression of confinement. The stakeholders speak of a “border” or even a “bubble”. These feelings of confinement and isolation do not only concern the anesthesia team. Indeed, the surgeon who operates in front of his or her console sometimes asks questions or expresses feelings that remain unanswered. Finally, the circulating nurse is also distant from the rest of the team and can sometimes stay for more than an hour without any interaction with the other members.

Beyond the sources of compartmentalization within the operating room, interviews with team members reveal other sources of compartmentalization that are not specific to robotics but rather to the organizational context of the hospital (Table 4.3). For example, the medical team (which includes the surgeon and the intern) meets for briefings while the rest of the operating room team (anesthesiologist, scrub nurse and anesthetist nurse) is already in the operating room or with the patient. The strong constraints of both teams (different work rhythms, operating in several rooms at the same time, etc.) make it difficult to schedule collective briefings or debriefings. Exchanges between members outside the operating room are also severely limited.

In the end, technology has an effect on the configuration of the operating room and the activity that takes place there, which in turn affects individual and collective skills, which are impoverished and less articulated with each other.

4.6. Discussion

As we have seen, the introduction of robotics in the operating room creates a specific configuration of the operating room that amplifies the feeling of confinement and isolation of the team members, particularly due to the distance between the surgeon and the rest of the team and the imposing presence of the robot arms, and modifies the interactions during the operation.

Some of these effects seem irredeemable, at least as long as the technology does not evolve. However, a number of pitfalls could be avoided if all the features of the technology were used. The use of microphones could undoubtedly improve communication and patient safety. The repair of the second screen could reduce the feeling of confinement of the anesthesia center. We also saw that the surgeon was very directive with the intern assisting him or her, leaving little room for learning. However, since 2009, the robotic device offers the possibility of coupling a second console to that of the surgeon. This innovation allows a novice surgeon to be accompanied by a mentor during an operation, increasing safety during the learning curve. The studied block is equipped with a second robotic console that could be used for internal learning.

The partitioning that exists outside the operating room does not help. Meetings never bring together all the members of the operating room: briefings are held in the presence of the surgeon and the resident while the anesthesiologist, the anesthetist nurse and the scrub nurse see the patient and/or prepare the operating room. The work rhythms and break areas are different between team members. The strong constraints of each team member, such as different working hours or the fact of sharing between several rooms at the same time, make it difficult to plan collective briefings and debriefings and limit exchanges between members inside and outside the operating room.

From the above analysis, we conclude that technology can generate a more or less significant conflict between the members of a work team that is detrimental to the development and articulation of skills, and also that its effects are amplified when the organization itself creates compartmentalization. Thus, the situation could be less problematic if the organizational context were more favorable to interprofessional spaces and exchanges (Wannenmacher 2018).

In collective discussions (Detchessahar *et al.* 2015), the learning process is contextualized and centered on work and action, and produces results directly applicable to real situations, thanks in particular to reflexivity which allows a return on oneself and on events and a projection of the professionals in the universe of possibilities (Seppänen *et al.* 2017). By mobilizing different hierarchical levels and different professions around a common activity and a collective experience, these discussion spaces make it possible to develop and articulate skills, and even to innovate (Rocha 2016). Indeed, the space would allow innovation to emerge, be applied and disseminate, which can be seen as a progressive elaboration of problems and solutions through the networking of stakeholders and as a path through trial and error and adaptation until dissemination by different means (Grenier & Denis 2017).

Of course, several conditions are necessary to be able to talk about spaces and innovation in these spaces, including discussion engineering and recognition of the space for action (Rocha 2016; Grenier & Denis 2017).

In short, the discussion spaces developed from a pragmatic perspective and based on artifacts are a very exciting avenue, as they allow us to share and articulate the knowledge and skills of each person in order to build together innovative solutions that take into account both the specific context and the more global environment of the management situation experienced. We believe that researchers can play the role of translating the different points of view and mediating within these spaces, by facilitating discussion and exchanges between stakeholders through reflexive and constructive processes based on artifacts made during the work activity, such as a video capture for example. These spaces can be a source of transformation of practices, provided that they bring together all the stakeholders involved in the work activity, and that they are recognized and supported at the institutional level.

4.7. References

Agha, R.A., Fowler, A.J., Sevdalis, N. (2015). The role of non-technical skills in surgery. *Annals of Medicine and Surgery*, 4, 422–427.

Alsène, E. (1990). Les impacts de la technologie sur l'organisation. *Sociologie du travail*, 32(3), 321–337.

Amherdt, C.H., Dupuich-Rabasse, F., Emery, Y., Giauque, D. (2000). *Compétences collectives dans les organisations : émergence, gestion et développement*. Les Presses de l'Université Laval, Quebec.

Blavier, A. and Nyssen, A.-S. (2010). Étude de l'impact des nouvelles technologies sur les modes de coopération des chirurgiens par l'analyse des communications sur le terrain. *Le travail humain*, 2(73), 123–140.

Defortescu, G. and Tillou, X. (2016). La chirurgie robot-assistée en transplantation rénale. *Progrès en urologie – FMC*, 26(4), F67–F72.

Detchessahar, M., Gentil, S., Grevin, A., Stimec, A. (2015). Quels modes d'intervention pour soutenir la discussion sur le travail dans les organisations ? Réflexions méthodologiques à partir de l'intervention dans une clinique. *@GRH*, 3(16), 63–89.

Dubois, M. and Retour, D. (1999). La compétence collective : validation empirique fondée sur les représentations opératoires de travail partagées. *Psychologie du travail et des organisations*, 5(1–2), 225–243.

Grenier, C. and Denis, J.L. (2018). S'organiser pour innover : espaces d'innovation et transformation des organisations et du champ de l'intervention publique. *Revue politiques et management public*, 34(3–4), 191–206.

Grosjean, M. and Lacoste, M. (1999). *Communication et intelligence collective : le travail à l'hôpital*. PUF, Paris.

Hull, L., Arora, S., Aggarwal, R., Darzi, A., Vincent, C., Sevdalis, N. (2012). The impact of nontechnical skills on technical performance in surgery: A systematic review. *J. Am. Coll. Surg.*, 214, 214–230.

Largier, A., Delgoulet, C., De la Garza, C. (2008). Quelle prise en compte des compétences collectives et distribuées dans la gestion des compétences professionnelles ? *Perspectives interdisciplinaires sur le travail et la santé*, 10(1) [Online]. Available at: https://journals.openedition.org/pistes/2167.

Leplat, J. (1993). Ergonomie et activités collectives. In *Les aspects collectifs du travail*, Six, F., Vaxevanoglou, X. (eds). Octarès, Toulouse.

Leplat, J. (2000). Compétences individuelles, compétences collectives. *Psychologie du travail et des organisations*, 6, 47–73.

Lorino, P. (2016). L'apport de la pensée pragmatiste à l'approche processuelle. In *Théories des organisations. Nouveaux tournants*, de Vaujany, F.X., Hussenot, A., Chanlat, J.F. (eds). Economica, Paris.

Michaux, V. (2005). Performance collective et compétences individuelle, collective et organisationnelle : construction d'une grille d'analyse unifiée. In *16ème Conférence de l'AGRH-Paris Dauphine*. Paris, 15–16 September.

Montmollin, M. (ed.) (1997). *Sur le travail. Choix de textes (1967–1997)*. Octarès, Toulouse.

Nyssen, A.-S. and Blavier, A. (2009). Verbal Communication as a sign of adaptation in socio-technical systems: The case of robotic surgery. In *9th Bi-annual International Conference on Naturalistic Decision Making*, Wong, B.L.W., Stanton, N.A. (eds). London, June.

Pugin, F., Bucher, P., Morel, P. (2011). Histoire de la chirurgie robotique : d'AESOP à Da Vinci® en passant par Zeus®. *Journal de chirurgie viscérale*, 148S, S3–S8.

Rocha, R. (2016). Du silence organisationnel au débat structuré sur le travail. *Revue cadres*, 468.

Seppänen, L., Kloetzer, L., Riikonen, J. (2017). Encourager la réflexion en chirurgie robotique : l'autoconfrontation croisée comme instrument de développement du travail interprétatif dans un environnement technologique complexe. *Psychologie du travail et des organisations*, 23(2), 117–136.

Valverde, A., Goasguen, N., Oberlin, O. (2014). Chirurgie robotique ou cœlioscopie assistée par télémanipulation : généralités. *Journal de chirurgie viscérale*, 151, 215–225.

Wannenmacher, D. (2018). Les défis socio-économiques liés à la chirurgie robot-assistée dans les blocs opératoires : espaces d'échanges et artefacts médiateurs. *Management & Avenir*, 100, 209–223.

Wittorski, R. (1994). Analyse du travail et production de compétences collectives dans le contexte de changement organisationnel. PhD Thesis, Conservatoire national des arts et métiers et Université de Sherbrooke, Paris and Sherbrooke.

Yin, R.K. (2008). *Case Study Research. Design and Methods*, 4th edition. SAGE Publications, Thousand Oaks.

Yule, S. and Paterson-Brown, S. (2012). Surgeons' non-technical skills. *Surg. Clin. N. Am.*, 92, 37–50.

5

Clinical Poles of Activity, an Opportunity for New Cooperation Between the Actors? The Case of a Hospital

The implementation of a "clinical pole" structure is one of the notable changes in the evolution of French hospitals over the last 15 years (Nobre & Lambert 2012). This change, governed by the Order of May 2, 2005 and the "Hospital, Patients, Health and Territories" (*Hôpital, Patients, Santé et Territoires*, HPST) Act of 2009, has been gradually implemented in hospitals through the creation of clinical, medical-technical or administrative clinical poles bringing together different departments and representing an intermediate level of management between management and departments. The creation of these clinical poles has led to the appointment of new actors (clinical pole head, clinical pole manager and clinical pole assistant), the establishment of institutional governance bodies to ensure coordination between hospital management and the clinical poles, and the creation of management tools enabling the implementation of a certain degree of management delegation (clinical pole projects, clinical pole contracts and monitoring indicators) (Nobre & Lambert 2012).

The deployment of these clinical poles therefore represents a real organizational innovation for the hospitals that have adopted them. One of the stakes in the creation of the clinical poles is to establish new ways of cooperating within hospitals and to allow a certain altering of frontiers between the different professional components of the hospital (medical, nursing and administrative) (Domy 2012).

The objective of this chapter is to analyze the way in which clinical pole actors can create new forms of cooperation within the clinical poles but also with other

---

Chapter written by Christelle HAVARD.

hospital authorities or actors outside the clinical poles, thus helping to alter frontiers and reduce certain boundaries within hospitals. The new decision-making and collaboration bodies and management tools can indeed be important supports for internal and external cooperation within the clinical poles.

This analysis is based on a longitudinal case study conducted in a University hospital between 2009 and 2012. The study involved 41 interviews and the analysis of numerous hospital documents. Three areas of activity were studied in particular. The results of this study shed light on the role of the different actors in the clinical poles, their interactions and the way in which management tools are mobilized to work differently within the clinical poles and with other hospital actors.

5.1. Key elements and objectives of polar reform

The outlines of the implementation of clinical poles in hospitals have been defined by various regulatory texts during the 2000s. The ordinances of May 2, 2005, the HPST law of 2009 and the application decrees of June 11, 2010 and March 11, 2016 specified the objectives of the establishment of the clinical poles and the procedures for their operation.

According to article L6146-1 of the Public Health Code, public health establishments must structure their organization around clinical, medico-technical or administrative clinical poles of activity. Each clinical pole is made up of a set of internal structures (or services). A clinical pole manager is appointed at the head of each clinical pole to organize its functioning and the allocation of human resources with the clinical pole's medical, nursing, administrative and supervisory teams. Depending on the wishes of the hospital director, the clinical pole manager may be granted a certain management delegation within the framework of an internal clinical pole contract and a clinical pole project (Lachenaye-Llanas 2012). The clinical pole contract signed between the hospital director and the clinical pole manager determines the objectives and resources granted to the clinical pole and sets the indicators for evaluating the achievement of the objectives. The clinical pole project sets out the missions and responsibilities entrusted to the clinical pole's internal units and the structure to achieve the objectives assigned to the clinical pole. To support the clinical pole's decisions, institutions can create "clinical pole councils" that can contribute to the development of the clinical pole project and the internal clinical pole contract as well as the clinical pole activity report, and promote the expression of the clinical pole's personnel within the clinical pole itself.

The clinical polar reform objectives were numerous and ambitious. The clinical polar structuring of the activities is not only aimed at grouping the different medical specialties within the same unit in order to guarantee better coordination in the management of care and quality of service (DHOS 2008; Domy 2012), but also making certain human and financial resources shared and facilitating collaboration between the different professions (medical, nursing and administrative) (Vallet 2012) within the same collective unit (Domy 2012). The appointment of a clinical pole head aimed at facilitating collaboration between doctors and management by involving the medical profession in decisions and facilitating decision-making at the most relevant level, that of the clinical pole (Fourcade 2011). The clinical pole council, a collective consultation entity composed of a clinical pole head physician, an administrative manager and a care manager, was to allow the clinical pole staff to express their views and facilitate the circulation of information within the clinical pole. The mission of the clinical pole councils was to draw up the clinical pole project and the clinical pole contract. The aim of the clinical pole project was to facilitate consultation and collaboration between medical and non-medical professionals at the clinical pole level and the accountability for a common project (application decree of June 11, 2010). Finally, the clinical pole contract aimed at giving responsibility to the different actors of the clinical poles, particularly the doctors (Dechamp & Romeyer 2006), around objectives validated by the management of the institution and making sense for the members of the clinical pole.

The polar reform thus changed the way in which these activities were divided and coordinated. One of the major challenges of this reform was therefore clearly to improve the conditions for cooperation within hospitals between several actors and several levels, within the clinical poles and between the clinical poles and hospital management (Domy 2012).

5.2. Improving cooperation and better articulating the logics present in the hospital: challenges and theoretical identification

Various reports produced on the clinical pole organization or the hospital in the early 2010s (Zeggar *et al.* 2010; Acker *et al.* 2012) revisit the challenges of better cooperation between hospital actors and take stock of the improvements brought about by the polar reform. According to Zeggar *et al.* (2010), clinical pole structuring has broken down certain barriers between medical and management teams. At the level of the polar teams, it has fostered regular exchanges of information and better "collaboration between often opposing worlds" (Domy 2012, p. 29). Between the clinical poles, it has led to a certain pooling of resources and a "horizontalization" of hospital organization (Acker *et al.* 2012). However, these reports do not show how cooperation between actors has improved with the implementation of the polar reform.

In order to analyze how the cooperation between actors with different logics can take place within the framework of polar structuring, we mobilize different theoretical works. The first works show that hospital organizations are described as "problematically compartmentalized organizations" (Krief 2012, p. 45) or "balkanized" (Gheorghui & Moatty 2013). These compartmentalized organizations are linked to the presence of established professional categories (Zardet *et al.* 2011) that develop their own professional logic (Sainsaulieu 2006) based partly on the training received, and also on the differentiated hierarchical position (Strauss *et al.* 1985; Strauss 1992) and on the exercise of a professional identity constructed in daily action and reinforced by career management systems.

Several studies (Glouberman & Mintzberg 2001) show that cooperation between the different hospital actors (doctors, nurses, administrative and technical staff, and management) is difficult. In particular, Zardet *et al.* (2011) highlight three dysfunctions in interprofessional cooperation linked to work organization, communication-coordination-concertation and the lack of use of steering tools. These authors therefore mention the interest of mobilizing management tools such as projects or contracts to facilitate exchanges and consultations between actors in different professions. Glouberman and Mintzberg (2001) suggest setting up working groups involving several actors, or even pooling decision-making between managers and physicians (Mintzberg 2012). Then it is necessary to consider how the actors can find new ways of cooperating and acting together through the introduction of steering tools and exchange and decision-making mechanisms.

The Strauss's notion of "articulation" offer an interesting framework for analysis of the modalities of cooperation between different actors with different professional logics through (Strauss *et al.* 1985; Strauss 1992). Strauss shows that "articulation work" (Corbin & Strauss 1993) takes place between several hospital professionals at several levels (tasks, units and professions). This articulation work is carried out by "articulation agents", such as doctors or health managers, and may involve discussion, negotiation, persuasion or sanction (Strauss *et al.* 1985; Strauss 1992; Corbin & Strauss 1993). Following on from the Strauss interactionist work, Grojean and Lacoste (1999) point out that articulation work, consisting of establishing coherent links and introducing interdisciplinarity, can be carried out at three levels referring to three types of articulation:

– at the level of the hospital institution, the "structuring articulation" aims to set up standardized processes for the division and coordination of work;

– at the level of a department, the "operational articulation" consists of organizing the care tasks around the patient's journey;

– as close as possible to patients, the "articulation of trajectories" aims to define and identify the pathology in order to design and define the care trajectory.

Articulation work involves operations of "mediation, translation and problematization, anticipation and organization, coherence and decision, control and evaluation" (Grosjean & Lacoste 1999, p. 191). It requires the mobilization of skills of several kinds (technical and communicational, in particular) and presupposes the legitimacy of the actor who assumes this work (a technical legitimacy, and also a statutory legitimacy); it can therefore be provided by several people.

Other work has clarified the conditions for carrying out this articulation. The interdependent links planned by the hospital institution around a "multi-professional collective" can facilitate articulation and acting together (Dehame-Leleyter *et al.* 2008). And the stability of a group of actors makes it possible to develop the "habits" of meeting formally or informally, exchanging ideas, working together (Dehame-Leleyter *et al.* 2008), *or* even developing reciprocal knowledge (Schmidt 1994), which will also allow articulation.

From the same interactionist perspective, Gheorghiu and Moatty (2013) analyzed the modalities of cooperation in operating theaters, an emergency department and a psychiatric establishment. They highlight the forms of "institutional cooperation" taking place in the activities of meetings, training and partnerships, forms of "horizontal cooperation" (such as mutual aid) and stress the need for long-term cooperative relationships.

This interactionist research thus makes it possible to specify this articulation work and to define its modalities within hospital organizations, and it also makes it possible to make it visible, or even to institutionalize it. Indeed, according to Bouret (2008), this articulation work is often invisible for most professional categories, or even little valued by healthcare managers. However, it is necessary to make it visible (Grosjean & Lacoste 1999) as hospital establishments have undergone major changes leading to greater diversification of their missions, the development of medical specialties and demands for economic profitability.

While articulation work has been analyzed at the level of care trajectories or certain hospital services, it has not been analyzed at the level of clinical poles, which were created after the research work mentioned above. We therefore wish to highlight, through a case study, the articulation work that can be carried out at clinical pole level. The following questions will guide our analysis: Which actors carry out this articulation work at the clinical pole level? What management tools are mobilized by the actors? In what spaces of exchange and decision-making does the articulation work take place? How is this work valued or made visible?

5.3. Context and methodology of the study

The case study[1] was carried out between 2009 and 2012 in a university hospital that in 2011 had nearly 1,800 beds and employed more than 7,000 people. The choice of this establishment was guided by the fact that the institution had been engaged in a polar approach since the early 2000s before the 2005 ordinance was promulgated. The articulation work had therefore begun several years ago and could be more easily identified and analyzed. The data analysis was based on documentary data collected within the establishment (the 2007–2012 medical project, organization charts for the clinical poles and the establishment, a clinical pole guide, clinical pole contracts, function sheets, etc.). 41 individual interviews were conducted with the general management and functional departments (Care, CME, HR, Medical Affairs, Management Control and Financial Affairs) and three clinical poles (Neurosciences, Emergency and Imaging). In each of the divisions, we met with the head of the division and his or her deputy, the deputy director, the senior health executive and the division management assistant. Three observations were made within the Neurosciences clinical pole and one observation of a board meeting bringing together representatives of the general management and representatives of the clinical poles.

5.4. Modalities of cooperation permitted by the establishment of the clinical poles

The articulation work not only took place within the clinical poles but also between the clinical poles and the general management of the establishment. It was based on individual actors, management tools, and exchange and decision-making bodies. Certain organizational conditions shaped this articulation work.

5.4.1. *The articulation actors*

In the three clinical poles studied, the actors facilitating the linking of activities and professional logics were the clinical poles head, the senior health executive, the deputy director and the clinical pole management assistant. The nature of the linkage work was, however, slightly different for each of them.

The *clinical pole manager* was responsible for most of the coordination of the clinical pole's activities: "a clinical pole manager's job is first and foremost to

1 This case study is part of a research program funded by the Institute of Public Health Research coordinated by Annick Valette. Data collection was conducted in collaboration with Marie-Thérèse Rapiau.

ensure coordination within all the departments" (clinical pole manager). He or she organized the circulation of information and spaces for exchange and discussion within the clinical pole; made decisions to ensure consistency between the different units of the clinical pole and with the clinical pole medical project; made trade-offs in complex situations (for example, between financial constraints and medical and healthcare operational constraints), or even negotiations with the clinical pole's doctors. He or she also acted as an interface between the clinical pole's departments and the institution's management, both bottom-up (when a department manager expresses a need) and top-down (when senior management or functional departments need to communicate or discuss issues relating to delegated management). The coordination work thus took different forms: communication, decision-making, consistency, translation, intermediation and negotiation. As the holder of the clinical pole's authority, this articulation work was strongly marked by decisions and arbitrations.

The *senior health executive* implemented care projects at the clinical pole level in collaboration with the care management and the clinical pole's care and medical teams. He or she monitored the clinical pole project and institutional projects within the clinical pole. "We support the projects, it's not us who lead them directly but we support them. We make the links, give advice, etc." (senior health executive). He or she coordinated paramedical activities and managed healthcare resources in a forward-looking and operational perspective (organization of substitution). This led him or her to carry out a work of intermediation, discussion, negotiation and persuasion in an attempt to reconcile budgetary constraints and quality of care and to deal with contingencies. By ensuring the implementation of institutional projects within the clinical pole, the senior health executive contributed to the articulation between the clinical pole and the institutional level. "The clinical pole manager, [...] must always work to ensure that everyone can work together. And this is not always easy" (senior health executive). Without having any hierarchical power over the clinical pole's actors, the senior health executive played an important role in the clinical pole's coordination work and could form a real partnership with the clinical pole leader: "If it doesn't work, senior executive/clinical pole leader, the clinical pole doesn't work" (management).

The *deputy director* was a functional director assigned to one or two clinical poles. His or her work was essentially carried out between the clinical pole and the functional and general management through communication, translation and persuasion in two ways. In a top-down manner, he or she guaranteed the representation of the interests of the hospital institution at the level of the clinical pole. In a bottom-up manner, the delegated director could inform or assert the interests of the clinical pole at the level of the general management.

> It is true that there are many boards where one is led to play this role of explanation, argumentation, and sometimes to be an advocate for the institution's management. [...] We play a bit of a regulatory role because they come out with a bit more information and so do we. (Deputy director)

This articulation work between the clinical pole and the general management complemented, and sometimes competed with, that of the division head, with the deputy director being more or less involved in the management of the division.

Finally, the *clinical pole management assistant* was under the responsibility of the clinical pole manager and played a fairly important role in the concretization of the medico-economic logic within the clinical pole, thus articulating the medico-healthcare and management logics. He provided budgetary information to the head of the unit and the senior health executive so that they could interpret management indicators and make medico-economic decisions. He could thus translate economic language for the head of the center and the senior health executive.

> In my opinion, we have a very important role as an interface between the administrative community for questions of financing and budgeting [...] and the members of the clinical pole, i.e. both the decision-making body, which is made up of the clinical pole office and also the departments, department heads, health executives and sometimes even staff more generally. (Clinical pole management assistant)

This role of "disseminating" the managerial logic was more or less assumed by the management assistants depending on the relationships they had established with the clinical pole members (in particular with senior healthcare managers) and on the legitimacy accorded to them by the clinical pole's staff.

The articulation work in this establishment was therefore "distributed" among the members of the polar team and takes different forms. It also relies on certain tools.

5.4.2. *Tools supporting articulation work*

The articulation work within the clinical poles and between the clinical poles and management was based on three types of management tools: the clinical pole project, the clinical pole contract and medico-economic indicators.

As described in the polar guide, the *clinical pole project* was a tool resulting from a confrontation and negotiation of medical, care and administrative logics, as it needed to be developed on the basis of an "internal consultation process involving all categories of personnel". The interviews showed a diversity of situations: while two clinical poles (Neurosciences and Emergencies) had involved the members of the clinical pole in the development of their project, the third (Imaging) had mainly involved the medical and nursing professions.

> On the medical project, which was new, the clinical pole head invited the senior health executive, the management assistant and the clinical polesecretary, they blocked a half-morning, and they asked each department head to come and present their medical project. And he made a polar medical project. (Senior health executive Neurosciences)

Once developed and validated, the clinical pole project could be support exchanges between the actors of the clinical pole.

The *clinical pole contract* was a tool expressing the articulation work mainly between the clinical pole and the general management, and also to a certain extent within the clinical pole. This contractual document (the structure of which was defined by management after a period of experimentation) contained, for a defined period, the objectives, the lines of work, the resources made available to the clinical pole, the areas of management delegation and the clinical pole's medico-economic indicators. The development of the clinical pole contract had been the subject of a real articulation work between the medical and economic logics since the clinical poles had to arbitrate between various objectives and projects within a framed budget envelope and define medico-economic indicators to ensure the monitoring of projects and operations. This work of negotiation, argumentation and arbitration (more or less difficult depending on the clinical pole) was initially carried out within the clinical pole between the medical actors (clinical pole head and clinical pole doctors), healthcare professionals (senior health executive and healthcare managers) and administrative staff (clinical pole delegate and management assistant). However, the clinical pole's representatives were then coordinated with the general management team, which met each clinical poles during the contract construction phase on the occasion of strategic committees; the clinical pole contract was then validated by both the clinical pole manager and the general management team.

Once drawn up and validated, the clinical pole contract was monitored both by the clinical pole's actors (most often the management assistant and the senior healthcare executive) and by the management control department, who needed to collaborate. It regulated relations between general management and the clinical pole by recalling, if necessary, the commitments made by both sides and by making the clinical pole's actors aware of their responsibilities.

> The contract that the clinical pole head signed with management, in which there may be objectives for the activities, was somewhere a

> commitment by the clinical pole head and his entire clinical pole, i.e. all his colleagues. So a small means of pressure, which was worth what it was worth, was to say to his colleague: "the clinical pole has contractualized on this objective, if we don't reach it, work with me to respect this commitment". So the contract is still a tool for the clinical pole and the clinical pole leader. (General management)

The clinical pole contract had also gradually made it possible to facilitate certain trade-offs within the clinical pole by orienting the clinical pole's actions according to the defined objectives.

The *management indicators* operationalized the clinical pole contracts and concretized the articulation of the economic and medical care logics. The main dimensions of the medico-economic indicators were defined by the management control department and these indicators were common to the divisions, which could adapt them according to the areas chosen in the division contract. These indicators enabled clinical pole heads and senior healthcare executives to gradually integrate economic logic into their reasoning and to promote it to the clinical pole's actors (doctors and healthcare professionals), particularly during clinical pole meetings. "With a lot of indicators, we manage to be credible, so we are credible with the administration, because we come to them and say 'I did this, I know, there are our weaknesses, there are our strengths'. With respect to the doctors, tell them 'Stop condemning the administration, the administration has its strengths and weaknesses, but you have your strengths and weaknesses' (clinical pole leader)". Clinical pole management assistants were responsible for monitoring these management indicators, but some division heads also monitored them closely.

5.4.3. *The instances of exchange and articulation*

The articulation work between the different actors took place during informal contacts between the actors and also through several formal bodies of exchange and decision: the clinical pole office and the clinical pole council at the clinical pole level, the board of directors and the operational committee of the clinical poles.

The *clinical pole office* was made up of the clinical pole manager, the deputy clinical pole manager, the senior health executive, the deputy director, the clinical pole management assistant and the clinical pole secretary. According to the clinical pole guide, its purpose was to assist the clinical pole manager in the elaboration and implementation of the clinical pole project and the clinical pole contract, in the coherence of the distribution of means, in the evaluation of the clinical pole's activity and in the animation of the clinical pole's life. In a formal and prescribed manner, the clinical pole office could therefore be a body that could articulate the medical, care and management logics. However, the reality of clinical pole offices varied from one clinical pole to another, with some clinical pole offices operating in a restricted manner around the head of the clinical pole, his or her assistant and the senior health executive (Emergency and Imaging), while others followed prescribed procedures (Neurosciences). The observation of a clinical pole office revealed that the clinical pole office could be a place for discussion on operational issues of clinical pole and institutional projects. "I have a clinical pole meeting with two senior managers, with a deputy director, with a management assistant, and then a deputy clinical pole leader, and the five or six of us solve all the day-to-day problems" (clinical pole leader). It could be a place for comparing the points of view of different professionals, a space for negotiation and collective decision-making, or even a space for the collective construction of an argument to be defended to general management by the division manager. "The clinical pole office is a lot of what you can ask of management, how you can position yourself, what you can bring up" (deputy director).

The *clinical pole council* brought together the members of the clinical pole office and the heads of department, full practitioners and health managers. As a consultative body, it participated in the development of the clinical pole project and the clinical pole contract and expressed its views on the strategic orientations of the clinical pole (organization of the activity, management of paramedical jobs and investments). It mainly ensured the transmission of information in a top-down manner on issues relating to the operation of the clinical pole and the institution. The observation of a clinical pole council showed that the clinical pole council could be a forum for discussions between participants, allowing them to work on persuasion. The clinical pole council could also be a forum for arbitration during the development and validation of the clinical pole project. In the clinical pole council,

> there is a great deal of information on the situation of the University Hospital […]. They receive […] all the measures taken at the level of the establishment. And then they receive the decisions taken in the clinical pole office. […] Next time, I'm going to present to them the medical project for our clinical pole's establishment: we give them, and then we have the decisions validated. (Clinical pole head).

There was also articulation between the divisions and management through the *Board of Directors* and the *divisional operating committee*. Just before the 2005 law creating the executive board, the establishment set up a "strategic council" made up of equal numbers of members representing management and the medical profession, and on which three clinical pole heads were present. The strategic committee was then extended to include all the clinical pole heads and deputy heads and the main functional departments (care, finance, management control, human resources and information systems). This strategic council was designed as a forum for discussion and strategic orientation, with the mission of preparing certain strategic decisions and following up on questions relating to the polar operation (which is notably the case for the negotiation and monitoring of clinical pole contracts). It was also a forum for argumentation and decision-making, allowing the clinical poles to formulate and validate certain proposals, and to "take the heat off each of the clinical poles before making a decision" (deputy clinical pole leader). This body could also be a forum for consultation, sometimes a confrontation of opinions, as we observed during a strategic advisory session on the scope of the clinical poles. In this respect, the strategic council could be considered as a place where the administrative and medical logics were articulated (the strategic council "is made so that doctors and directors can talk about things" – president of the medical commission establishment – *Commission médicale d'établissement*, CME), often setting aside the care logic according to the people we met, as Gheorghiu and Moatty (2013) point out.

In order to overcome certain limitations in the functioning of the strategic advisory board (linked in particular to the use of the body as an instrument and an over-abundance of operational questions from the divisions concerned) and to comply with the HPST law, in 2010 the strategic advisory board became the "Executive Board", which not all division heads could attend. The Executive Board remained a discussion and decision-making body, but was more selective. The establishment then created a "clinical pole operational committee" (*comité opérationnel des pôles*, COP) in which all clinical pole heads and their deputies participated, as well as the president of the CME, the Care Commission and some functional departments (DCG, DRH, DAF, etc.). According to management, the COP was intended to be "a real steering, consultation and debate body, and not simply a top-down information body". It was also seen as a space for exchanging practices between clinical pole heads, which could contribute to a certain degree of coordination between clinical pole heads.

5.5. Conditions for the use of articulations

The different articulations highlighted in the establishment studied were therefore supported by several actors and media. They were based on certain conditions which, if they were not met, could weaken cooperation and interdisciplinarity.

The articulation work within the clinical pole or between the clinical pole and management relied on a knowledge of working together that was built over time and therefore required a certain stability of the actors. The clinical poles that managed to cooperate were therefore those that had been formed around members who had developed certain work habits ("the clinical pole is the translation of teamwork" – Healthcare Directorate), particularly between the clinical pole head and the senior healthcare executive and also gradually with the management assistant. This was also the case for cooperation between management and the clinical pole heads. The habit of working together made it possible to better understand the professional logics of the other actors and to identify possible complementarities (Detchessahar 2001; Dehame-Leleyter *et al.* 2008).

> It is through complementarity that we will make progress, no one can solve a problem alone, at least not in hospital, it is impossible. But it is also true that it is not easy to ask people whose training or primary function is not theirs to slip into a logic that is not initially theirs. Nor is it easy for people who are initially there to manage, to slip into logics that are not necessarily theirs either. But I believe that we will not get out of it otherwise than by mixing these skills. (Managing director)

Articulation work requires certain skills. Managerial and relational skills are crucial, depending on the person you are dealing with (especially the heads of health centers and senior health managers): the ability to listen and diplomatic or pedagogical skills are essential to be able to argue, convince and negotiate.

> It is necessary to have pedagogical skills because it is absolutely necessary to be able to convince people, to lead, to animate. On a daily basis, when you are face-to-face with authorities or teams or even managers, sometimes you have to accept decisions that have been made higher up, with which you do not agree. (Senior health executive)

While these skills were targeted in the professional training of healthcare managers, this was not the case for the clinical pole heads, who had to develop them through professional experience. Articulation work also made it possible to develop certain skills, particularly in medico-economic management. This skill had developed to a greater or lesser extent among clinical pole heads and senior healthcare managers in contact in particular with clinical pole management assistants, and also thanks to training followed by senior healthcare managers and by certain clinical pole heads (which we were able to observe during the last interviews conducted). These skills gave legitimacy to the clinical pole actors facilitating the articulation work, in particular for the clinical pole heads, who had to have both medical legitimacy (allowing them to argue with doctors, to be persuasive and to legitimize medical decisions) and managerial legitimacy in the eyes of the establishment's management (who appoints them to their position). This legitimacy was all the more critical in a context of budgetary restrictions.

Finally, articulation work needed to be made visible and recognized so that it could be sustained over time. This visibility was achieved through the Polar Guide, which institutionalized the various mechanisms of polar structuring (polar authorities, clinical pole actors, the project and the clinical pole contract, and delegated management). However, this organizational artifact only reflects part of the reality of the articulation work. Thus, at the time of the survey, although the articulation activities of the clinical pole managers and senior health managers were explicitly included in the sheets for these two functions and, to a lesser extent, in the sheet for the delegated director, the function of linking and raising awareness among the management assistants was not included in their description.

The articulation work could also be made visible through the means put at the disposal of the actors to carry out the arbitrations and to weigh in the negotiation. However, the clinical pole head only had functional authority over the clinical pole members, with the exception of the clinical pole management assistant. His or her authority over physicians therefore depended mainly on his or her medical legitimacy and power in the allocation of resources between the clinical pole's internal services. Moreover, the workload of the articulation work carried out by the clinical pole managers was not evaluated at the time of the survey; this articulation work was sometimes added to other functions occupied by the head of the clinical pole without the latter easily giving up other prerogatives. For their part, senior health executives may have done much of the articulation work at the clinical pole level, but their status did not give them the same power or institutional recognition as the clinical pole head. Within the clinical poles, doctor-healthcare and care-giver-administrative cooperation was crucial. But it did not seem to be as easy within governance bodies such as the board of directors or the operational committee of clinical poles in which the healthcare community was poorly represented and which seemed to rely mainly on a combination of general management and medical staff (represented by the president of the CME and the clinical pole heads). Finally, coordinating the work of the management assistants was recognized by the members of the clinical pole office, particularly through their requests and the presence of management assistants in the office. However, it was not necessarily recognized by some functional directors who saw this function as a certain decentralization of managerial competence. They were not recognized as managers at the time of the survey. "I'm lucky to have my clinical pole managers and the clinical poles office recognizing my work" (clinical pole management assistant). Status issues here raised the problem of supporting the articulation work with HR recognition processes (Gheorghiu & Moatty 2013), while hospital HR management remained compartmentalized, with doctors being managed differently from administrative and nursing staff.

5.6. Cooperation in a polar structure, some research avenues

The analysis of the different forms of articulation work associated with polar structuring is limited here to a single institution, so the results mentioned cannot be generalized. However, they reveal certain key elements of the development of cooperation and interdisciplinarity permitted by the polar structure. First of all, cooperation took place at several levels through polar structuring within the clinical poles and between the clinical poles and management. It was made possible through articulation work carried out by several actors within the clinical pole, in particular by the clinical pole leaders, senior health executives and management assistants. These actors mobilized several organizational mechanisms to work on the articulation of logic: the clinical pole project, the clinical pole contract, medico-economic indicators, the clinical pole consultation and decision-making bodies and certain hospital governance bodies (such as the board of directors or the clinical pole operational committee specific to the studied establishment). These "structuring articulations" (or "constrained cooperations") (Gheorghiu & Moatty 2013, p. 41) were supplemented by habits of interpersonal cooperation that increased their effectiveness and relied on individual skills carried by clinical pole heads and senior healthcare managers. They could be reinforced if they were made visible and recognized.

These results may open the door to further research that would show how these practices of cooperation between actors and interdisciplinarity of logic at the clinical pole level have evolved since the end of 2010. Several avenues of research could be explored.

1) First of all, to complement the work of Grosjean and Lacoste (1999), a more detailed analysis of the skills required for articulation could be carried out, highlighting the nature of the individual and also collective skills for cooperation within the clinical poles and between the clinical poles and the members of the hospital management. The conditions for the training of these skills and their recognition (notably through HR processes) (Dumas & Ruiller 2013) should also be studied, taking into account the evolution of new professions and functions that have emerged – clinical pole head (Valette & Burelier 2014) and management assistant (Gavault *et al.* 2014).

2) A second avenue for future research would consist of further investigating the "spaces for discussion" (Detchessahar 2003) created by the clinical pole reform (i.e. decision-making and consultation bodies at the level of the clinical poles and governance) and to see how they have evolved over the last 10 years to create a cross-cutting approach between medical, care and management logics. These spaces can be places where collective medico-economic skills can be built.

3) Several works have been carried out on the management tools associated with polar structuring, notably clinical pole contracts and delegated management (Zardet *et al.* 2011; Martineau 2014; Flachère 2015; Vallejo *et al.* 2015; Vallejo *et al.* 2018), but it would be interesting to examine how the processes for developing and monitoring clinical pole projects, clinical pole contracts and management indicators

facilitate learning about the interdisciplinarity of logics and the constitution of articulation skills, thus creating "technical solidarity" around cooperation (Gheorghiu & Moatty 2013, p. 235).

4) Finally, the analysis of this articulation work carried out at the level of the clinical poles leads us to question the "shifting of boundaries" within the hospital institution (Gheorghiu & Moatty 2013, p. 101). At the same time, as it has sought to alter frontiers and instigate interdisciplinarity between medical, care and administrative logics, polar structuring has been able to create new boundaries between the clinical poles. To what extent will the institution's management and its governing bodies avoid competition between the clinical poles in a context of scarce (human and financial) resources and will they maintain institutional coherence?

5.7. References

Acker, D., Bensadon, A.-C., Legrand, P., Mounier, C. (2012). Management et efficience hospitalière : une évaluation des déterminants. Public Report, Inspection générale des affaires sociales, April.

Bouret, P. (2008). Encadrer dans la Fonction Publique hospitalière : un travail de lien invisible. *Revue française d'administration publique*, 128, 729–740.

Corbin, J.M. and Strauss, A.L. (1993). The articulation of work through interaction. *The Sociological Quarterly*, 34(1), 71–83.

Dechamp, G. and Romeyer, C. (2006). Trajectoires d'appropriation des principes de nouvelle gouvernance hospitalière par les médecins. In *XVème Conférence internationale de management stratégique*. Annecy/Geneva, 13–16 June.

Dehame-Leleyter, M., Lancry, A., Valléry, G. (2008). Travail d'articulation et organisation du travail : étude dans un collectif de l'enseignement public. *Psychologie du travail et des organisations*, 14(4), 345–368.

Detchessahar, M. (2001). Quand discuter c'est produire. Pour une théorie de l'espace de discussion. *Revue française de gestion*, 132, 32–43.

Detchessahar, M. (2003). L'avènement de l'entreprise communicationnelle. *Revue française de gestion*, 142, 65–84.

DHOS (2008). Résultats de l'enquête nationale de la nouvelle gouvernance. Report, Ministère de la Santé, de la Jeunesse et des Sports, Paris.

Domy, P. (2012). L'impact de l'organisation polaire sur le pilotage des établissements. In *Le management de pôles à l'hôpital : regards croisés, enjeux et défis*, Nobre, T., Lambert, P. (eds). Dunod, Paris.

Flachère, I. (2015). Comment les instruments de gestion interviennent-ils dans la constitution de rôles organisationnels ? Le cas des contrats de pôle et instruments de suivi financiers dans un hôpital public français. PhD Thesis, Université Paris 1 Panthéon-Sorbonne, Paris.

Fourcade, J.-P. (2011). Rapport au Parlement du Comité d'évaluation de la réforme de la gouvernance des établissements publics de santé, institué par l'article 35 de la loi du 2 juillet 2009 portant réforme de l'hôpital et relative aux patients, à la santé et aux territoires. Report, Ministère du Travail, de l'Emploi et de la Santé, Paris.

Gavault, S., Laude, L., Baret, C. (2014). L'institutionnalisation des pôles d'activité médicale : entre agir stratégique et agir projectif. *Journal de gestion et d'économie médicales*, 32(7), 463–480.

Gheorghui, M.D. and Moatty, F. (2013). *L'hôpital en mouvement : changements organisationnels et conditions de travail*. Liaisons, Paris.

Glouberman, S. and Mintzberg, H. (2001). *Managing the Care of Health and the Cure of Disease – Part I & Part II*. Aspen Publishers, Inc., New York.

Grosjean, M. and Lacoste, M. (1999). *Communication et intelligence collective – le travail à l'hôpital*. PUF, Paris.

Krief, N. (2012). Les préoccupations des acteurs hospitaliers en question : analyse croisée et dynamique de construction collective. *@GRH*, 3, 43–67.

Lachenaye-Llanas, C. (2012). Délégation de gestion et cohérence institutionnelle – une impérative obligation mais une construction pas à pas. In *Le management de pôles à l'hôpital : regards croisés, enjeux et défis*, Nobre, T., Lambert, P. (eds). Dunod, Paris.

Martineau, R. (2014). Proposition d'une grille d'analyse de l'usage des outils de gestion : application à un outil de reporting hospitalier. *Gestion et management public*, 2(4), 21–43.

Mintzberg, H. (2012). Managing the myths of health care. *World Hospitals and Health Services*, 48(3), 4–7.

Nobre, T. and Lambert, P. (eds) (2012). *Le management de pôles à l'hôpital : regards croisés, enjeux et défis*. Dunod, Paris.

Sainsaulieu, I. (2006). Les appartenances collectives à l'hôpital. *Sociologie du travail*, 48, 72–87.

Schmidt, K. (1994). Cooperative work and its articulation: Requirements for computer support. *Travail humain*, 57(4), 345–366.

Strauss, A.L. (1992). *La trame de la négociation : sociologie qualitative et interactionnisme*. L'Harmattan, Paris.

Strauss, A.L., Fagerhaugh, S., Suczek, B., Wiener, C. (1985). *The Social Organization of Medical Work*. University of Chicago Press, Chicago.

Valette, A. and Burelier, F. (2014). Quand l'habit fait le moine les chefs des pôles hospitaliers : devenir des hydrides "malgré tout" ? *Gérer et comprendre*, 116, 4–13.

Vallejo, J., Sampieri-Teissier, N., Baret, C. (2015). Comprendre les difficultés de la mise en œuvre de la délégation de gestion à l'hôpital. Une lecture par le concept d'anarchie organisée. In *3ème Congrès ARAMOS 2015*, November, Marseille.

Vallejo, J., Sampieri-Teissier, N., Baret, C. (2018). La mise en place des pôles d'activité médicale à l'hôpital public : quel est l'impact d'un changement de structure organisationnelle sur le processus de décision ? In *6ème Congrès ARAMOS*, May 25, Paris.

Vallet, G. (2012). Préface. In *Le management de pôles à l'hôpital : regards croisés, enjeux et défis*, Nobre, T., Lambert, P. (eds). Dunod, Paris.

Zardet, V., Fier, D., Savall, H., Petit, R. (2011). Gestion de la coopération interprofessionnelle à l'hôpital. *Journal de gestion et d'économie médicales*, 29, 277–293.

Zeggar, H., Vallet, G., Tercerie, O. (2010). Bilan de l'organisation en pôles d'activité et des délégations de gestion mises en place dans les établissements de santé. Report, IGAS, Paris.

6

Learning from Reforms Aiming to Disseminate Innovative Organizational Models: The Case of Family Medicine Groups in Quebec

6.1. Introduction

Improving primary healthcare is seen as a pillar for improving the performance of health systems (Starfield 2012). Several reforms are being implemented to replicate organizational models considered innovative. Developed locally, they are generally characterized by the grouping of physicians joined by other professionals to offer a registered clientele care that is accessible, comprehensive and integrated with the other components of health systems. In Quebec, such a transformation began in 2003 with the establishment of family medicine groups (*groupes de médecine de famille*, FMGs). Patient-Centered Medical Units in the United States and health centers or multi-professional health centers in France pursue similar objectives. Despite the consensus on the attributes of these models, there are obstacles to their widespread dissemination and their effects are often limited. Some conclude that, overall, such reforms have improved patient and professional satisfaction, but their impact on access is less clear (Lévesque *et al.* 2012). Access to primary healthcare remains problematic for certain clienteles in several countries (OECD 2019). Tensions between the medical and social spheres, the presence of private organizations, and the variety of contexts targeted by transformations are among the challenges complicating the dissemination and effects of innovative organizational models.

Chapter written by Frédéric GILBERT.

The capacity to generate and mobilize knowledge would be central to support such large-scale projects (Wu *et al.* 2015). In addition to identifying promising models and attributes, learning can shed light on why and how these transformations are being implemented and how they are producing effects (OMS 2018). Learning capacities aim to update beliefs about an object and mobilize this increased understanding to support action (Radaelli 2009). Despite their potential, the capacity of governments and health systems to learn and to benefit from these learnings remains limited (Judge & Bauld 2006; Howlett 2009; Denis *et al.* 2015; Turner *et al.* 2016).

In this chapter, we look precisely at this limitation. Our goal is to provide a framework for analysis to better understand the extent to which the evaluation of reforms to primary care organizations contributes to learning. This objective can be associated with meta-evaluation, since it involves assessing certain dimensions of evaluations (Cooksy & Caracelli 2009; Scriven 2012; Baslé 2013).

The chapter is structured into two main sections. First, we draw on the fields of evaluation and public policy learning to support the proposed analytical framework. This framework is then illustrated by an analysis of the main evaluations of the reform aimed at disseminating FMGs in Quebec.

6.2. Conceptual framework

The learning capacities of health systems are related to two main dimensions: (1) the level of precision and understanding of the causal relationships involved in the dissemination of the innovations sought; and (2) the evaluations carried out (Turner *et al.* 2016).

6.2.1. *The impact of intervention precision on the ability to learn*

Learning ability is often hampered by the limited precision of intervention theory (Michie *et al.* 2009 in Moore *et al.* 2015); Turner *et al.* 2016). Intervention theory provides an understanding of the causal relationships that explain how desired effects are produced (Coryn *et al.* 2011; Turner *et al.* 2016) as well as the components of the intervention to be implemented to produce this change (Moore *et al.* 2015). The level of precision of the intervention theory is a determining factor in the learning that can result from its evaluation. Without an intervention theory that describes these mechanisms, evaluation risks limiting itself to analyzing the presence or absence of changes and associated effects, thus removing from the evaluation all the mechanisms involved in the change process being evaluated (Howarth *et al.* 2016).

Ideally, the intervention theory would be explicit and complete at the time of design. However, the complexity of interventions, the multiplicity of implantation contexts, the dynamic nature of the environment and the latitude of stakeholders are among the factors explaining why, in practice, intervention theory is not very detailed (Turner *et al.* 2016; Dunlop & Radaelli 2018).

6.2.2. *The impact of evaluations on learning capacities*

Transformation assessments can be initiated for a number of reasons, such as accountability (Sanderson 2002), political (e.g. to influence or convince) or tactical considerations (e.g. to delay a decision) (Vedung 2006; Denis *et al.* 2015), or to support learning and improvement (Radaelli 2009). Reflexive processes contribute to service improvement when they enable learning and when learning is mobilized to improve services (Dunlop & Radaelli 2018). In this analysis, the focus is on the learnings from the evaluations, not on their use or other impacts (Dunlop & Radaelli 2018). Learnings from the evaluations depend as much on the methods used, the unanswered questions and the objectives pursued.

The methods used can be evaluated using traditional criteria of scientificity and others specific to the field of evaluation (Scriven 2012). Their explanation, however, goes beyond the purpose of this chapter (see, for example, Patton 2008; Posavac 2015).

With regard to the questions addressed by the evaluation, different aspects can affect learning capacity. First, the nature and scope of the evaluation questions may vary. The nature of the evaluation questions can be distinguished by the dimension of the targeted intervention: its relevance, intervention theory, implementation, process, resources mobilized or results achieved (Brouselle *et al.* 2009).

Strategic evaluation is designed to assess the relevance of addressing a particular problem in light of other issues that could have been addressed by an intervention (Brouselle *et al.* 2009). Intervention theory evaluation investigates the relevance of the causal relationships between the different components of the intervention and their potential to achieve the desired policy objectives (Coryn *et al.* 2011). These evaluations can be conducted prior to implementation to verify the potential of an intervention or policy.

Evaluations of implementation seek to know the impact of implementation conditions on its implementation (Perret 2008). They make it possible to assess compliance with the plan, the nature of the adjustments made and the impact of these changes on the effects of the intervention. These evaluations can contribute to a better understanding of the role of contexts in implementation (Durlak & DuPre

2008). Whether they are considered as local variations that improve the intervention for its context or as unwanted diversions, it is useful to identify these variations, to better understand why they are present and the resulting impacts (Moore *et al.* 2015). The evaluation of the implementation thus makes it possible to shed light not only on the implementation issues but also on the mechanisms involved in the production of effects.

The evaluation of effects concerns the assessment of the results obtained, from the most proximal (e.g. the evaluation of services offered) to the most distal (e.g. the evaluation of health impacts). A distinction can also be made between the evaluation of intended, secondary, perverse, unintended and null outcomes (Vedung 2006). In health, the evaluation of results most often focuses on the main dimensions of services: accessibility, continuity, coordination, relevance, technical quality, etc. (Kringos *et al.* 2010; Lévesque *et al.* 2013). Finally, economic evaluations aim to better understand the link between the effects obtained and the resources deployed to produce them.

The scope of the questions concerns the dimensions of an intervention assessed in an evaluation. Evaluation questions are often combined, for example when one wishes to assess the effectiveness of an intervention (e.g. by evaluating its capacity to produce the expected effects) and to better understand how the observed effects were produced (e.g. by evaluating the implementation process) (Perret 2008).

The objectives pursued by the evaluation may vary regardless of the questions investigated. Indeed, the same evaluation question may reflect distinct objectives and interests. For example, the evaluation of the implementation of one intervention may aim to support its implementation, without questioning its relevance, while another may seek to transform the theory of change (Heikkila & Gerlak 2013). Similarly, an outcome evaluation might seek to verify the presence of an expected result, while another might focus on unexpected or undesirable effects. Finally, an analysis of the mechanisms by which effects are produced may aim to incrementally improve the intervention or question its foundations (Patton 2016).

The relevance of the questions and objectives pursued by the evaluation varies according to the knowledge available. If the mechanisms linking a change to its effects have already been demonstrated, process evaluation may offer limited additional learning potential. Conversely, if these mechanisms are poorly understood, an evaluation that excludes process evaluation may lead to invalid conclusions by assuming that the observed effects are the result of the intervention. As we have seen, the often partial mastery of causal relationships involved in large-scale interventions in complex systems can be compensated for by deploying evaluations aimed specifically at clarifying mechanisms that are poorly mastered.

In summary, the learning capacities of systems derive both from the level of precision of the transformation being pursued and from the nature of the evaluations in terms of method, questions and objectives.

6.3. Illustration of the analytical framework: the reflexive processes related to the implantation of family medicine groups in Quebec

The illustration presented here is a summary analysis of learning capacities of the two evaluation projects initiated by the Quebec Ministry of Health and Social Services (*ministère de la Santé et des Services sociaux du Québec*, MSSS) to investigate the deployment and effects of primary care reform through the creation of FMGs.

6.3.1. *Method and context of the study*

The analysis was carried out in three stages. A literature review (evaluation reports, government documentation describing the policy, etc.) allowed us to present the intervention theory disseminated during the adoption of the public policy and in the report of the two evaluation projects evaluated. Next, we assessed the different dimensions integrated into our analytical framework and, finally, we were able to identify the strengths and limitations of the evaluations with respect to intervention theory and the evaluation projects.

The creation of family medicine groups was intended to disseminate a model of primary care organization that was considered innovative. This model, developed locally by a group of professionals, had been identified through a task force established in the early 2000s. FMGs are intended to improve primary care considered too inaccessible and poorly integrated with other components of the healthcare system (Haggerty *et al.* 2004). At the time of its adoption, the MSSS (2002) described the policy's objectives as follows:

> (1) Give all Quebecers access to a family physician; (2) ensure greater accessibility of services and overall management (continuity of services) and follow-up of patients who register with a family physician who is a member of a FMG; (3) improve the delivery and quality of medical care and the organization of front-line services offered to the population; (4) develop greater complementarity of services with local community service centers; (5) recognize and enhance the role of the family physician.

FMGs are not new organizations. They correspond to accreditation in the form of a contract involving a group of 6–12 physicians working in one or more existing organizations (public or private). This contract provides the group of physicians with additional resources (computer systems, two nurses, administrative and clerical support, and various increases in physician remuneration) in exchange for the establishment of and compliance with organizational attributes. Among other things, the physicians commit to collaborate to improve continuity of care and to respect a minimum service offer to a registered clientele. The minimum service offer refers to specific opening hours with and without appointments and the implementation of an on-call system for more vulnerable patients. Nurses integrated into the FMG must assume expanded responsibilities.

Following the launch of the FMG policy, two evaluations were set up by the MSSS to assess the first years of implementation. One evaluation (project A) was carried out by the evaluation department of the MSSS (MSSS 2008). Another (project B) was piloted by a team of university researchers following a call for proposals initiated by the MSSS (Beaulieu *et al.* 2006). The author of this chapter was involved as a member of the reading committee (project A) and as a researcher (project B).

6.3.2. *Results of the analysis*

As we have seen, evaluation-related learning capacities depend on the level of detail in the policy and the evaluation questions, objectives and methods chosen.

Concerning the level of precision of the intervention theory, the analysis reveals that the theory provided limited details. The policy essentially presents a series of objectives followed by a list of attributes to be put in place to achieve them. The mechanics of impact or the theory of change are not presented explicitly. No distinction is made between intermediate targets (e.g. individual or organizational capacity, stakeholder motivation or environmental support) to produce the desired changes and impact mechanisms that explain how the policy attributes should achieve the targets (Michie *et al.* 2011). The theory of policy intervention presented by the MSSS can be illustrated in Figure 6.1.

The questions and objectives pursued by the FMG evaluations were primarily focused on implementation and effects. The mandate given by the MSSS (2008, author's translation) to its evaluation team stipulated that the evaluation was intended to:

> describe the pace and methods of implementing the FMG model, specify the factors, stakeholders, and circumstances that facilitate or

hinder the implementation of this model, and establish the effects of FMGs on the accessibility, continuity, and use of health services, as well as on the organization of medical practice and professional satisfaction.

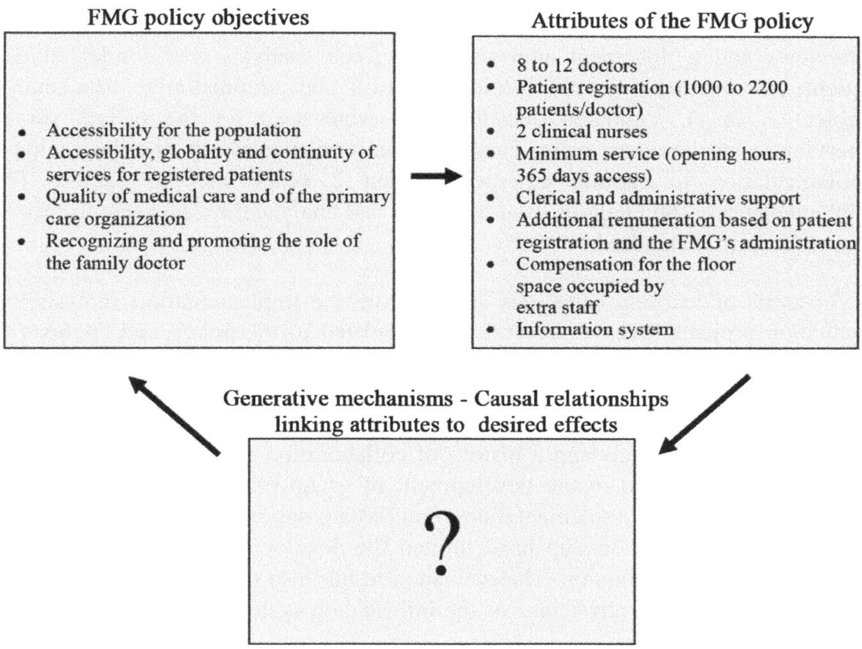

Figure 6.1. *Illustration of the theory of intervention described in the MSSS policy and the reports of the two evaluation projects. For a color version of this figure, see www.iste.co.uk/grenier/frontiers.zip*

The evaluation of the academic team (Beaulieu *et al.* 2006):

> it examined how operating in FMG mode could redefine group practice and collaboration between professionals (between physicians and between physicians and nurses); it also examined the outcomes of this redefinition for registered clients. The influence and the effect of structural and organizational factors in the internal and external environments were also taken into account, as well as ethical issues related to this redefinition of collaboration between professionals.

Neither of the two evaluation projects addressed resource assessment (e.g. cost-effectiveness analysis). The evaluations did not question the relevance of the FMG

Policy in light of its objectives. While the questions and objectives help to assess part of the potential of the evaluations, the analysis of their methods used allows us to assess the resulting learning capacities more precisely.

In terms of the methods used, the two evaluation projects adopted a multiple case study design (24 FMGs in total). The implementation analysis was carried out using interviews and a document analysis. The effects analysis was conducted using patient surveys, focus groups (project A only) and administrative data analyses (project A only). Validated questionnaires were used for the patient surveys. Interviews and surveys were conducted in two waves, at the beginning of implementation to capture emergence, then 2 years later to capture FMG implementation. The methods used to collect and analyze the data seem to meet the general scientific standards.

In terms of learning capacities arising from the implementation analysis, both evaluation projects revealed several factors related to the policy and contexts that affected implementation. These elements were analyzed by the evaluations as obstacles and barriers to implementation. For example, the evaluations revealed that joint work between physicians and nurses, the presence of strong leadership at the FMG and regional levels and a history of collaboration among professionals were factors that contributed to the development of group practice associated with the FMG. Conversely, the implementation of an FMG composed of several sites and the presence of diffuse leadership have limited the development of such practice and interprofessional collaboration. The evaluation results also revealed that other factors, such as the number of physicians or the information systems in place in the region, affected implementation.

The method chosen for these evaluations had several implications for learning related to the effects of FMGs on services provided. The patient survey was favored by both evaluations. It is a widely used approach with many advantages for assessing health services (Gibbons *et al.* 2016). The surveys carried out made it possible to assess several effects associated with the implementation of FMGs, but left others in the shade. They highlighted a certain improvement in coordination with specialized services and certain aspects of accessibility for patients followed by a nurse. On the other hand, using questionnaires distributed to patients in the waiting room at the beginning and 2 years later, the evaluation could only reveal an effect for patients already deservedly served by FMG physicians. Given the additional resources associated with the creation of an FMG, this method offered limited potential for learning about the effect of FMGs on accessibility for people who did not already have access to primary care.

The results of the analysis of administrative data conducted by MSSS evaluators offered greater potential for learning about the effects of FMGs on population accessibility. For example, the analysis of the use of services could reveal certain impacts at group level suggesting possible consequences at the population level. The absence of significant differences in service use for patients followed in FMGs, with the exception of consultation with nurses, which increased in FMGs, suggests that nurses provide services in addition to those offered to the same patients by their physicians, without substituting for them. This hypothesis is consistent with the fact that greater access was reported only by patients who had follow-up with a nurse. These evaluation results did not allow for a more detailed assessment of how physicians transformed their practice following the introduction of FMG attributes.

Other dimensions of practice likely to shed light on the impact on the population were not investigated. For example, physicians explained that the group practice formalized by the creation of the FMG made it easier to replace one another when they were absent. Analysis of administrative data could have confirmed the presence and nature of such a potential impact on population accessibility (e.g. by analyzing the number of days worked by physicians). Interactions between the practices of nurses and physicians are key to understanding how the integration of these professionals influences practices, services offered and, ultimately, access to patients in the group and the population.

In terms of understanding the links between the implementation of FMG attributes and the production of effects, the evaluations offered variable learning capacities. In some cases, the analysis of implementation through interviews made it possible to explain effects revealed by quantitative measures. For example, the more difficult access to services reported in the survey of patients in one of the FMGs investigated seemed to be related to a change in the appointment scheduling system decided upon locally. Patients did not appreciate having to contact a regional emergency telephone service rather than the clinic's reception desk to make an appointment, thus negatively affecting one of the dimensions of access (ease of access). For other observed effects, the link with reform is less clear (Turner *et al.* 2016). Questions remain unanswered. How can we explain the improved coordination with specialized services revealed by the surveys? Is it the nurses or physicians who contribute to it, and what changes explain this variation?

In short, the analysis reveals that the evaluations focused on the implementation of FMG attributes and certain effects. There is much to be learned from the evaluations, although they were limited by the main objectives pursued (e.g. to support implementation and evaluate effects rather than to better understand how they are produced), the questions investigated (e.g. evaluation of effects and implementation) and the methods used (e.g. client survey). In the following section, we discuss the lessons learned from these findings.

6.4. Discussion

We began this chapter with the objective of assessing the potential for learning from evaluations of primary care reform. Our intention here is not to conclude on the potential of the FMG as an organizational model for primary care, but rather to assess the learning capacities resulting from the evaluations used to investigate their deployment. We have seen that the evaluations confirmed several factors affecting the deployment of this innovation, as well as its effects on services and the experience of professionals. However, the learning from the evaluations was also limited, on the one hand, by the low precision of the intervention theory and, on the other hand, by certain dimensions of the evaluations, including their objectives, the questions investigated and the methods used to answer them.

6.4.1. *A brief overview of intervention theory*

With respect to the precision of intervention theory, we saw that the policy was presented as a list of attributes and objectives, without explaining how these attributes were likely to contribute to the achievement of the objectives. The low level of precision of the policy is not specific to FMG reform. On the contrary, interventions to improve health services are frequently deployed despite the absence of an explicit intervention theory (Dixon-Woods 2014). A similar phenomenon has been observed in France, where the houses and health centers "are regularly presented in the form of lists of conditions to be met [having] […] the merit of showing the extent and diversity of the changes to be made, but they cannot claim to help the decision" (Schaller 2014, p. 511). As others have observed, the imprecision of the mechanisms involved in the desired change limits the learning from evaluations, since without this information, evaluations cannot monitor their deployment as directly (Howarth *et al.* 2016). Thus, the evaluations focused more on implementation and effects and less on the mechanisms involved in the production of effects. Moreover, the lack of precision in this primary care reform was identified by the Quebec auditor as a factor that limited the deployment and evaluation of FMGs and, consequently, the impact of the policy launched to improve access to primary care (Carter *et al.* 2016).

6.4.2. *Evaluations that support rather than question*

The evaluations were primarily aimed at supporting implementation and confirming effects. These objectives and the evaluation questions and methods derived from them had limited critical potential. For example, population access was central to this reform, as evidenced by the policy's first objective: "to give all Quebecers access to a family doctor" (MSSS 2002, p. 24). Population-based access has been little investigated. According to some people, the time required to produce effects at the population level justifies removing this dimension in the evaluation of the first years of the deployment of a new organizational form. On the other hand, the evaluations could have been more focused on the intermediate mechanisms involved before population-level effects could be captured. This situation may seem surprising, considering that the implementation of FMGs has been the only or one of the government's main means of responding to the access problems encountered by the Quebec population for more than 15 years.

While the evaluations paid little attention to population-based access, they did address several other dimensions of access (e.g. ease of access to obtain an appointment with his or her doctor or with another doctor, hours of operation and access outside of regular hours). They concluded that the FMG makes it possible to improve certain aspects of access. In short, it seems that the evaluation projects demonstrated the ability of FMGs to improve certain dimensions of access for those who are registered with them, but, on the other hand, there is nothing to indicate that a greater number of people have been able to benefit from primary care as a result of the dissemination of this organizational model (Aubin & Quesnel-Vallée 2016). This distinction is not always made. In fact, these evaluation reports are cited to support the fact that FMGs improve access, without specifying which dimensions of access are affected, thus contributing to the positive perception of this organizational form. For example, in an often quoted article on primary care in Canada, Hutchison *et al.* (2011, p. 265) state: "[…] Beaulieu and colleagues (2006) found that the integration of nurses and a linked clinical care protocol in Family Medicine Groups had a positive impact on the accessibility, coordination …"

However, the scope of the evaluation questions addressed is consistent with the context in which such reforms were adopted. There is a broad consensus on the potential of primary care reforms to contribute to improving the efficiency of health systems (Starfield 2012). The FMG policy focuses on the main attributes considered desirable (group, multidisciplinary, patient-centered practice, accessible and coordinated care, and information system) by the scientific community to improve primary care (Breton *et al.* 2011). The FMG model adopted by the MSSS has received the support of the main groups of stakeholders involved in primary care (CESSSS 2000). Physicians find additional support and resources in a model that enable them to maintain their position and salary, while nurses can develop a practice that is considered advanced. Faced with such a consensus, it seems natural that the evaluations were primarily aimed at supporting implementation and confirming the expected effects rather than questioning their potential or attempting to clarify the mechanisms involved in order to improve an organizational model already considered desirable (Dunlop & Radaelli 2018). The mixed results of the FMG policy and similar reforms revealed by researcher-initiated evaluations (see, for example, Strumpf *et al.* 2017) suggest, however, that the mechanisms involved in the production of effects would benefit from being investigated despite the presence of such consensus.

6.4.3. *Evaluations that are not well integrated into the GFM policy*

Finally, our results show that the assessments were conducted in accordance with the protocols developed. While a clear and stable methodological approach contributes to the credibility of the results, it does not allow the evaluation to be adjusted in such a way as to gradually develop an understanding of a phenomenon whose complexity cannot be anticipated at the time of launching an evaluation. For example, by observing the different roles played by nurses integrated into FMGs, the impact of these variations on physicians' practices or on the volume and quality of services offered could have been investigated further. Adjustments to the evaluations could have been made between the two measurement periods for the qualitative component, but the focus of the evaluations remained on analyzing implementation and effects rather than on revealing the underlying mechanisms. Developmental (Patton 2016) or realistic (Lacouture *et al.* 2015) evaluation approaches would allow for such adjustments considered essential to gradually refine the understanding of the mechanisms involved in such reforms.

6.4.4. *Improvements to increase learning potential in primary care reforms*

Taken together, our findings suggest three developments that could enhance the learning capacities that result from evaluations. First, further clarification of the mechanisms that explain how the attributes of an organizational model that has been implemented lead to outcomes would better guide implementation and support learning from evaluations. Second, since the complexity of large-scale reforms necessarily requires choices to be made in terms of the scope of the questions investigated, the evaluations would benefit from paying particular attention to their main objectives and the mechanisms involved, even if they are not very detailed in the intervention. Finally, integrating the evaluation into the policy would have made it possible to gradually develop learning and thus better support the decisions and actions of the MSSS.

6.5. Conclusion

We have seen that the evaluation projects studied have yielded many lessons, especially at the level of implementation and several dimensions of effects. On the other hand, the limited level of detail in the policy and the nature of the evaluations limited the learning that could be derived from the evaluations. These limitations appear to be related to factors specific to primary care reforms. The level of consensus on such reforms is often high, despite an intervention theory containing few details and mixed observed effects. In this context, it is not surprising that evaluations are more concerned with serving the policy by supporting its implementation and demonstrating its effects, rather than clarifying the mechanisms by which effects are produced (Hill & Hupe 2009). Such an orientation, on the other hand, limits the learning useful for improving, developing or even replacing policy.

This study has several limitations. It was aimed at the reflexivity arising from two evaluations mandated by the MSSS. Other analyses may have been carried out by the MSSS or in FMGs outside these. Other studies will benefit from focusing on the entire learning process by investigating both its reflective dimension and the mobilization of this learning to guide improvement. Comparisons of learning capacities related to different reforms, implemented in the same system or in different systems, may also be illuminating. Finally, the interaction between learning at the level of health professionals, organizations and systems also warrants further investigation. Despite these limitations, our results illustrate the value of focusing on the learning capacities arising from evaluations and the potential of the proposed framework to do so.

6.6. References

Aubin, É.L. and Quesnel-Vallée, A. (2016). Augmenter l'accessibilité et la qualité des services de santé de première ligne avec les Groupes de Médecine de Famille. *Health Reform Observer – Observatoire des réformes de santé*, 4(1).

Baslé, M. (2013). Méta évaluation des politiques publiques et qualité des évaluations. *Revue française d'administration publique*, 1017–1027.

Beaulieu, M.-D., Denis, J.-L., D'Amour, D., Goudreau, J., Haggerty, J., Hudon, É., Jobin, G., Lamothe, L., Gilbert, F., Guay, H., Cyr, G., Lebeau, R. (2006). Implementing family medicine groups: A challenge in the reorganization of practice and interprofessional collaboration. Doctor Sadok Besrour Chair in Family Medicine, Montreal.

Breton, M., Lévesque, J., Pineault, R., Hogg, W. (2011). L'implantation du modèle des groupes de médecine de famille au Québec : potentiel et limites pour l'accroissement de la performance des soins de santé primaires. *Pratiques et organisation des soins*, 42, 101–109.

Brouselle, A., Champagne, F., Contandriopoulos, A.P., Hartz, Z. (2009). *L'évaluation : concepts et méthodes*. Presses de l'Université de Montréal, Montreal.

Carter, R., Riverin, B., Lévesque, J.-F., Gariepy, G., Quesnel-Vallée, A. (2016). The impact of primary care reform on health system performance in Canada: A systematic review. *BMC Health Services Research*, 16, 324.

CESSSS (2000). Les solutions émergentes : rapport et recommandations. Report, Commission d'étude sur les services de santé et les services sociaux, Quebec.

Cooksy, L.J. and Caracelli, V.J. (2009). Meta-evaluation in practice. *Journal of Multidisciplinary Evaluation*, 6, 1–15.

Coryn, C.L., Noakes, L.A., Westine, C.D., Schröter, D.C. (2011). A systematic review of theory-driven evaluation practice from 1990 to 2009. *American Journal of Evaluation*, 32, 199–226.

Denis, J.-L., Brown, L., Forest, P.-G., Normandin, J.-M., Cambourieu, C., Cannizzaro, V., Préval, J. (2015). Policy capacity for health system reform. Report, Nova Scotia Health Research Foundation, Montreal, Canada.

Dixon-Woods, M. (2014). Perspectives on context: The problem of context in quality improvement. Report, The Health Foundation, London.

Dunlop, C.A. and Radaelli, C.M. (2018). The lessons of policy learning: Types, triggers, hindrances and pathologies. *Policy & Politics*, 46, 255–272.

Durlak, J.A. and DuPre, E.P. (2008). Implementation matters: A review of research on the influence of implementation on program outcomes and the factors affecting implementation. *American Journal of Community Psychology*, 41(3), 327–350.

Gibbons, E., Black, N., Fallowfield, L., Newhouse, R., Fitzpatrick, R. (2016). Patient-reported outcome measures and the evaluation of services. *Health Services and Delivery Research*, 4(16), 55–69.

Haggerty, J., Pineault, R., Beaulieu, M.-D., Brunelle, Y., Goulet, F., Rodrigue, J., Gauthier, J. (2004). Accessibility and continuity of primary care in Quebec. Report, Canadian Health Services Research Foundation, Ottawa.

Heikkila, T. and Gerlak, A.K. (2013). Building a conceptual approach to collective learning: Lessons for public policy scholars. *Policy Studies Journal*, 41, 484–512.

Hill, M. and Hupe, P. (2009). *Implementing Public Policy*. SAGE Publications, New York.

Howarth, E., Devers, K., Moore, G., O'Cathain, A., Dixon-Woods, M. (2016). Contextual issues and qualitative research. *Health Services and Delivery Research*, 4(16), 105–120.

Howlett, M. (2009). Policy analytical capacity and evidence-based policy making: Lessons from Canada. *Canadian Public Administration*, 52, 153–175.

Hutchison, B., Levesque, J.-F., Strumpf, E., Coyle, N. (2011). Primary health care in Canada: Systems in motion. *Milbank Quarterly*, 89, 256–288.

Judge, K. and Bauld, L. (2006). Learning from policy failure? Health action zones in England. *The European Journal of Public Health*, 16, 341–343.

Kringos, D.S., Boerma, W.G., Hutchinson, A., Van Der Zee, J., Groenewegen, P.P. (2010). The breadth of primary care: A systematic literature review of its core dimensions. *BMC Health Services Research*, 10, 65.

Lacouture, A., Breton, E., Guichard, A., Ridde, V. (2015). The concept of mechanism from a realist approach: A scoping review to facilitate its operationalization in public health program evaluation. *Implementation Science*, 10, 153.

Lévesque, J.-F., Pineault, R., Grimard, D., Burge, F., Haggerty, J., Hogg, W., Katz, A., Wong, S. (2012). Regarder en arrière pour mieux avancer : synthèse de l'évaluation de la réforme des soins de première ligne dans les provinces canadiennes. Report, Forum de synthèse et d'échange des connaissances sur l'impact des modèles d'organisation des soins de première ligne et de leurs contextes, Gouvernement du Québec, Quebec.

Lévesque, J.-F., Harris, M.F., Russell, G. (2013). Patient-centred access to health care: Conceptualising access at the interface of health systems and populations. *Int. J. Equity Health*, 12, 18.

Michie, S., Van Stralen, M.M., West, R. (2011). The behaviour change wheel: A new method for characterising and designing behaviour change interventions. *Implementation Science*, 6, 42.

Moore, G.F., Audrey, S., Barker, M., Bond, L., Bonell, C., Hardeman, W. (2015). Process evaluation of complex interventions: Medical Research Council guidance. *BMJ*, 350, h1258.

MSSS (2002). Groupe de médecine de famille. Summary Document, Ministère de la Santé et des Services sociaux, Quebec.

MSSS (2008). Évaluation de l'implantation et des effets des premiers groupes de médecine de famille au Québec. Report, Ministère de la Santé et des Services sociaux, Quebec.

OECD (2019). Realising the full potential of primary health care. Document de politique générale, OECD, Paris.

OMS (2018). Technical series on primary care – quality in primary health care. Report, OMS, Geneva.

Patton, M.Q. (2008). *Utilization-focused Evaluation*. SAGE Publications, Thousand Oaks.

Patton, M.Q. (2016). The state of the art and practice of developmental evaluation. *Developmental Evaluation Exemplars*, 1–24.

Perret, B. (2008). L'évaluation des politiques publiques. *Esprit*, 350, 142–159.

Posavac, E.J. (2015). *Program Evaluation: Methods and Case Studies*. Routledge, Abingdon-on-Thames.

Radaelli, C.M. (2009). Measuring policy learning: Regulatory impact assessment in Europe. *Journal of European Public Policy*, 16, 1145–1164.

Sanderson, I. (2002). Evaluation, policy learning and evidence-based policy making. *Public Administration*, 80, 1–22.

Schaller, P. (2014). Éléments pour une gestion stratégique d'une maison de santé. *Santé publique*, 26, 509–517.

Scriven, M. (2012). Evaluating evaluations: A meta-evaluation checklist [Online]. Available at: http://michaelscriven.info/images/EVALUATING_EVA-LUATIONS_8.16.11.pdf [accessed February 2021].

Starfield, B. (2012). Primary care: An increasingly important contributor to effectiveness, equity, and efficiency of health services. SESPAS Report 2012. *Gaceta Sanitaria*, 26, 20–26.

Strumpf, E., Ammi, M., Diop, M., Fiset-Laniel, J., Tousignant, P. (2017). The impact of team-based primary care on health care services utilization and costs: Quebec's family medicine groups. *Journal of Health Economics*, 55, 76–94.

Turner, S., Goulding, L., Denis, J.-L., Mcdonald, R., Fulop, N.J. (2016). Major system change: A management and organisational research perspective. *Health Services and Delivery Research*, 4(16), 85–104.

Vedung, E. (2006). Evaluation research. In *Handbook of Public Policy*, Peters, B.G., Pierre, J. (eds). SAGE Publications, London.

Wu, X., Ramesh, M., Howlett, M. (2015). Policy capacity: A conceptual framework for understanding policy competences and capabilities. *Policy and Society*, 34, 165–171.

7

Variety and Performance of Innovative Organizational Structures: The Emergence of Territorial Support Platforms[1]

7.1. Introduction

The healthcare sector, in France as in many other countries, has experienced and is still experiencing a wide range of organizational innovations aimed at providing a response to the main challenges encountered (demographic, epidemiological, economic or social). At the primary care level, current reforms are based on the "territorialization" of health and social services provision, which is expected to counterbalance the shortcomings of a historically highly centralized health system. The aim of these reforms is to increase the coherence between the services provided by the different players in each territory, and to take into account its specificities. The difficulties inherent in the care and support delivered to so-called "complex patients", characterized by polypathology and/or chronicity of pathologies, often combined with social difficulties (ageing, isolation, insecurity, etc.), are trying to be overcome by the implementation of more fluid "healthcare pathways", based on increased coordination between the different health and social professionals and structures, or even on the integration of care. This approach in terms of "healthcare pathways" results from the importance of not reducing the complexity of the patient to strict clinical criteria (polypathology, co-morbidity and chronicity) and inherent in

---

Chapter written by Matthieu SIBÉ, Sandrine CUEILLE and Tamara ROBERTS.

1 The study presented in this chapter is part of a research program funded by the French Ministry of Health – PREPS Program, 2014, No. PREPS14001103N; ClinicalTrials.gov, ID: NCT02837406, 08/18/2016.

the patient's characteristics only. Indeed, the recent literature considers that patient complexity also stems from the complexity of health determinants (societal, social and economic) and of the organizational and structural components of health systems (Manning & Gagnon 2017). Consequently, "complex healthcare pathways"[2] require the participation of numerous categories of health and social professionals and a high degree of coordination between these professionals. In order to facilitate the implementation of such pathways, French health authorities have recently promoted the development of territorialized organizational devices, such as territorial support platforms (*plateformes territoriales d'appui*, PTAs) studied in this chapter.

The development of these organizational innovations also pertains to the objective of digital transition in healthcare that is expected to support and facilitate changes in the behavior of health and social professionals toward better cooperation between them in the service of patients and population health. The use of digital technologies to meet the current challenges facing healthcare systems is not, of course, specific to France. The World Health Organization (WHO) considers them as essential drivers for better access to healthcare services[3]. Nevertheless, the use of these technologies can, depending on the context and country, take extremely varied forms. For example, concerning primary care, the British National Health Service (NHS) has promoted the development of "digital patient portals"[4]; France, for its part, has largely supported the use of these technologies by healthcare professionals and the combination of organizational and digital devices, for example within territorial professional communities of healthcare professionals (*communautés professionnelles territoriales de santé*, CPTS) or territorial support platforms (PTAs). In addition, the territorial and digital transformations of the French healthcare system have to face some specific characteristics, such as a hospital-centered model, medical hyperspecialization and the historical principles of liberal medicine. The national health strategy "Ma santé 2022"[5] aims to smooth institutional divisions in order to make a shift toward preventive health and to reorganize care around local groups bringing together healthcare players for the benefit of the patients and population health. More specifically, at the level of primary care, the development of coordinated ways of working for health professionals is encouraged (thanks to the

---

2 According to Article 74 of Law No. 2016-41 of January 26, 2016 (*Journal officiel de la République française*), "the healthcare pathway is said to be complex when the patient's state of health, disability or social situation requires the intervention of several categories of health, social or medico-social professionals".

3 See, for example, the WHO eHealth website: https://www.who.int/ehealth/en/.

4 https://www.england.nhs.uk/blog/digital-nhs/.

5 Ministère des Solidarités et de la Santé (2017). Stratégie nationale de santé 2018-2022 [Online]. Available at: https://solidarites-sante.gouv.fr/IMG/pdf/dossier_sns_2017_vdefpost-consult.pdf.

development of multi-professional health centers or of territorial health professional communities, for example), reflecting an effort to improve the structure of primary care. In so doing, the organization of primary care in France, historically in the hands of health professionals, would move closer to models developed in other countries, based on a clear definition and delimitation of the supply of primary care (European Nordic countries, Spain) or on a strict hierarchy of access to the healthcare system (the United Kingdom, the Netherlands, Australia and New Zealand) (Bourgueil *et al.* 2009).

Within the framework of the national health strategy "Ma santé 2022", the so-called "digital health territories" (*territoires de santé numériques*, TSN)[6] experiment first led to the emergence of a dual digital and organizational device structured around digital coordination tools and PTAs in five French health territories. The major challenge was to strengthen coordination between healthcare professionals in order to streamline and secure complex healthcare pathways. Then, the national rollout of PTAs was quickly covered by the 2016 law[7] and its legislative decree no. 2016-919 of July 4, 2016, which decided the generalization of PTAs and defined the procedures for implementing their missions. The implementation of these organizational and numerical devices raises many questions, including: What are the organizational characteristics of these structures? Are they effective in carrying out their missions? What are their main contingency factors, and consequently, the expected organizational characteristics of these structures? Is there a discrepancy between their observed and expected organizational characteristics? If so, does this gap correspond to a lower performance of the organization? The aim of this chapter is to shed light, through the example of the first development of PTAs in France in the 2010s, on the organizational variety of structures likely to promote innovation in patient care and support, and to discuss possible differences in the performance of these structures according to their organizational characteristics.

The chapter is structured as follows. Section 7.2 provides an overview on recent research on innovative organizational forms in the healthcare sector and sets out the empirical context of the research. Section 7.3 describes the conceptual framework of the research. Section 7.4 explains how the empirical analysis was conducted and presents the results. Finally, section 7.5 paves the way for recommendations on the evaluation of organizational arrangements aimed at ensuring the coordination of healthcare professionals and facilitating the implementation of complex healthcare pathways.

---

6 The TSN program was launched in 2012–2013 by the French Ministry of Health in order to adapt the health system, and particularly primary care medicine, thanks to a digital and organizational transformation of healthcare pathways.

7 Law No. 2016-41 of January 26, 2016 (*Journal officiel de la République française*).

7.2. Context of the study

This section first presents a synthesis of the recent academic literature in social sciences, aimed at analyzing the organizational forms likely to respond to the specificities of the care and support provided to complex patients (section 7.2.1). Section 7.2.2 is specifically dedicated to the presentation of PTAs. Finally, the empirical context in which the study presented in this chapter was carried out is described (section 7.2.3).

7.2.1. *Organizational forms for the care and support to complex patients: an overview of the literature*

Numerous studies, based on different theoretical frameworks, have attempted to identify organizational forms that could enable healthcare structures to provide coordinated care to complex patients and to better understand how to produce organizational innovations that could improve their care.

Networks, composed of various healthcare professionals and structures, have been widely promoted in many countries as a means of generating innovation and creating changes in the way health problems are addressed (Bilodeau *et al.* 2003). Networks have long been studied as a hybrid form of organization of exchanges, between the market and the hierarchy (or organization), that would be optimal regarding the level of transaction costs when, overall, exchanges between partners are characterized by a medium level of asset specificity, uncertainty and frequency. The advantages of such hybrid structures over hierarchical structures pertain to the reduction in the costs induced by bureaucracy organizations (especially control costs) and increased adaptability (Williamson 1991). When belonging to formalized networks, healthcare structures can benefit from privileged relationships with a wide range of professionals, which are the basis for increased coordination between those involved in care and support, while maintaining their legal independence. Important issues, such as the quality of collaboration between healthcare professionals and structures, and the ability to produce integrated care have been largely investigated in the academic literature (Contandriopoulos *et al.* 2001; Fleury *et al.* 2002; Brossard & White 2016; Marchand *et al.* 2019). In the past decades, healthcare networks have been implemented in many countries. With the benefit of hindsight, it appears that difficulties resulting from the complexity of these organizations and shortcomings in outcomes may hinder networks' ability to produce systemic changes regarding the way care is organized. Studies led to recommendations concerning the management of networks in healthcare and the implementation of team management practices (Fleury *et al.* 2018), as well as the development of support functions for coordination and the integration of digital technologies (French Ministry of Health 2012).

Recently, much research has focused on the types of organizational structures, devices or arrangements that could lead to innovation in highly institutionalized sectors, such as health or social services (see, for example, Touati *et al.* 2016; Grenier & Denis 2017). Outside the health sector, studies have also identified various forms of organizations or arrangements likely to promote innovation, such as "experimental spaces" within the framework of institutionalized fields (Cartel *et al.* 2018), "creative collectives" in the case of cities (Simon 2009), "inter-organizational communities of practice" that allow several organizations to share good practices and knowledge with each other and facilitate coordination between the different stakeholders in a given industry (Létourneau *et al.* 2010), "virtual teams" as groups of people or communities linked by the use of information technologies (Furst *et al.* 1999). Another stream of research on entrepreneurial ecosystems, widely analyzed in the entrepreneurship literature (see, for example, Isenberg 2011; Spigel 2016), focuses on the relationships that the entrepreneurial structure must maintain with its various stakeholders and the main interrelated components of its environment in order to be successful, and more specifically to produce innovations. This approach could also be useful for analyzing the linkages between healthcare providers and for identifying conditions that could produce innovative approaches to address the current challenges of this sector.

7.2.2. Territorial support platforms: a new organizational arrangement in the French healthcare system

The development of telemedicine and the use of various digital tools (connected applications, e-health technologies, etc.) as well as the territorialization of health and social services provision are two key orientations of the current French health policies that aim to ensure more effective and efficient care for complex patients simultaneously facing a wide range of health and social problems. Thus, after an experimental phase, the French health authorities decided in 2016 to deploy throughout the country a new system based on a dual organizational and digital device, relying on PTAs and digital coordination tools. The aim of this system is to support professionals in coordinating care and setting up personalized care plans, to ensure better mobilization of the health and social professionals and support systems in each territory and to help patients in their orientation within the healthcare system. PTAs must thus contribute to the integration of care, and in particular to the achievement of reciprocal integration (Contandriopoulos *et al.* 2001), which is necessary when patients must simultaneously benefit from care and support provided by several healthcare professionals or structures, and which therefore implies a strong interdependence between these professionals. In addition, PTAs constitute an organizational device that is both integrative and collaborative. Indeed, PTAs first rely on a so-called "internal" team, composed of doctors, nurses, social workers, psychologists, etc., acting as coordinators, which is dedicated to helping general practitioners organize coordinated health services for their complex patients. Secondly, PTAs benefit from a network of health professionals and structures that they can call upon to facilitate each patient's healthcare pathway and provide adequate care to complex patients. Thus, PTAs rely on both "internal" and "external" members. As very young organizational structures, the functioning of PTAs raises many questions, including whether they are able to fulfill their mission effectively and efficiently.

7.2.3. *Context of the study, expected empirical observations on organizational forms and performance of PTAs*

The research was conducted during the experimental phase of PTAs, which provides an opportunity to examine how such an organizational innovation was adopted (or adapted) by local professionals responsible for designing the first PTA models. More specifically, the research allows for the analysis of different organizational arrangements that emerged during this experimental phase. It also paves the way for reflection on the evaluation of organizational innovations aimed at strengthening the coordination of healthcare professionals and facilitating the implementation of healthcare pathways for complex patients.

More specifically, the analysis proposed in this chapter is based on an empirical study conducted as part of a large research program on digital health territories (TSNs) launched during the experimental phase of PTAs[8]. The results presented here are based on an in-depth analysis of the five PTAs that were created during this experimental phase. Data were collected through semi-structured interviews with PTAs coordinators, PTAs referring doctors and varied healthcare professionals belonging to the patient's "circle of care"[9], as well as through a direct observation of each PTA over several days in order to identify key elements of their functioning. Table 7.1 details the data collection protocol. By doing so, the research team analyzed the context in which each PTA was created and how it has been structured, and was able to identify its main organizational characteristics.

8 The authors participated in the TSN evaluation protocol (Saillour *et al.* 2017) and one of them was in charge of the empirical study of the five PTAs.

9 All the professionals who ensure the health and medico-social care of the patient. According to the *Association canadienne de protection médicale*, "the 'circle of care' is the group of professionals who require certain information to take care of a patient", which refers to the flow of information and the patient's consent to share information about him or her with his or her physician and other healthcare professionals. This terminology is also used in the context of palliative care, which requires an interprofessional healthcare team (Canadian Hospice Palliative Care Association 2013).

In addition, a multidimensional model for measuring the performance of PTAs was developed by the authors (see section 7.4.2.1), making it possible to analyze the organizational characteristics of PTAs in relation to their level of performance.

Data collection method	Scope	Profiles of interviewed people
Semi-structured interviews (SSI) with professionals of 5 PTAs	23 SSIs	Administrative directors (2) or medical directors (1) or executive coordinators (1), management assistants (1), regional coordinators (1), PTA deployment coordinators, platform assistants (2), call center switchboard operator (1), coordinating doctors (2), coordinating nurses (5), coordinating social workers (6), coordinating psychologist (1)
Interviews with patients referred to one of the 5 PTAs	16 patient interviews (2 interviews with 8 patients)	–
Interviews with professionals belonging to the "circle of care" of patients referred to one of the 5 PTAs	31 interviews	PTA coordinators (4), general practitioners (6), social worker (1), pharmacists (2), physiotherapists (2), nurses (3), municipal social services administrative officers (2), ambulance driver (1), psychologist (1), patient care givers (2), regional director of a national cancer association (1), hospital executives (2), home service network coordinator (1), pediatric network coordinator (1), pneumologist (1), speech therapist (1)
Direct observation of each PTA (for several days)	Observation of several intervention situations, team meetings, multi-professional consultations, multidimensional evaluation visits at patient's home, meetings with external health structures	–

Table 7.1. *Data collection protocol*

7.3. Conceptual framework

The study is based on the use of the "structural contingency" conceptual framework, the main elements of which are recalled in section 7.3.1. Particular attention is paid to the organizational model of adhocracy, the characteristics of which are considered to be favorable for enabling innovation and carrying out complex tasks in dynamic environments (section 7.3.2).

7.3.1. *Analytical framework and concepts from structural contingency theory*

The research is based on structural contingency theory, according to which increased performance can be explained by better organizational congruence to external (e.g. complexity or dynamism of the environment) and internal (e.g. age of the structure and technological sophistication of the production process) contingency factors (Figure 7.1). The popular concept of congruence is frequently used to predict the performance of organizational structures according to internal and external characteristics.

In their process-oriented view of organizations, Nadler and Tushman (1984) consider congruence as the relative degree of coherence (fit) that exists between inputs (e.g. the environment, resources, history or strategy of the organization) and organizational components (individual competencies, tasks, formal and informal organizational arrangements). There would therefore be no unique better way to organize, but different forms of organization resulting from adjustments to internal and external contingency parameters. The organization problem then becomes: "How to find effective combinations of organizational components that allow congruent adjustments between them?" (Nadler & Tushman 1984).

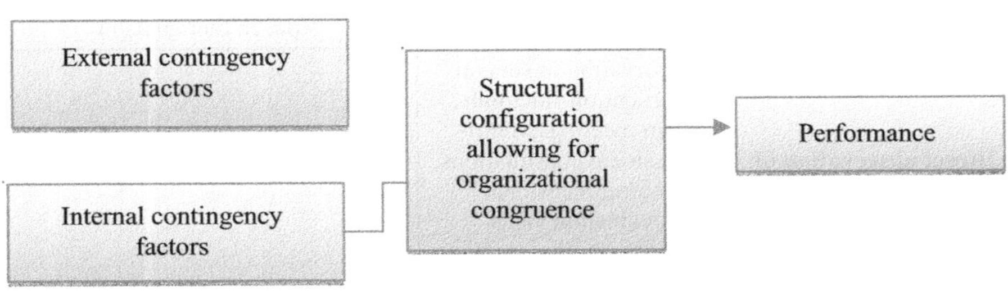

Figure 7.1. *Contingency factors, organizational congruence and performance. For a color version of this figure, see www.iste.co.uk/grenier/frontiers.zip*

7.3.2. *The adhocratic structural configuration: an innovative organizational form to carry out complex tasks in dynamic environments*

Structural contingency theory states that organizational components and internal/external contingency factors tend to align into coherent sets, called "structural configurations". The most famous classification distinguishes seven organizational configurations (Mintzberg 1989), each associated with one main coordinating mechanism, one key element of the organization, one type of decentralization, a specified category of age and size of the organization, a certain degree of complexity and stability of the environment, and a certain level of complexity of the technology system (Table 7.2).

The configurative typology can provide a kind of "organizational simulator" based on the estimated congruence between internal and external parameters, and between structural and situational elements. This typology also makes it possible to explain the past or future trajectories of organizations.

Thus, theoretically and generally speaking, organizations facing changing environmental conditions and performing complex tasks are expected to move away from the traditional bureaucracy model (which is dominant in healthcare structures), and develop the characteristics of adhocracies or innovative organizations (Mintzberg 1989, 1993).

Adhocracies are defined as flexible organizations, combining multidisciplinary and interdisciplinary skills, capable of adapting to the needs and constraints of the tasks to be carried out and of successfully producing innovations. Mutual adjustment is preferred to other types of coordination between members of the organization and support functions play a dominant role in the organization. In addition, there is little distinction made between administrative and operational work. The term *ad hoc* indicates that members of these organizations work in informal project groups that enjoy considerable autonomy from the procedures and hierarchical relationships that exist in most other organizational structures (Waterman 1993). The development of a culture of adhocracy (Cameron & Quinn 1999) should also improve the effectiveness of organization when flexibility, innovation and fulfillment of the organization's missions (ahead of members' interests) are required.

According to the formal definition of their role, PTAs must implement a support program for healthcare professionals in order to facilitate collaboration between varied health and social professionals and structures, and ultimately smooth the trajectories of complex patients. The implementation of this mission relies, on the one hand, on the key role of a coordination team composed of multidisciplinary experts; it requires, on the other hand, a great capacity to adapt to the specificities of each situation, and therefore the produce innovative solutions oriented toward the care and support of each patient.

Configurations	Structural elements		Situational elements		
	Main mechanism of coordination	**Main part of the organization**	**Age and size of organization**	**Environment**	**Technology**
Entrepreneurial/simple Structure	Direct supervision	Strategic apex	Rather young and small	Simple and dynamic	Simple
Machine bureaucracy	Standardization of the work process	Technostructure	Rather old and big	Simple and stable	Low complexity
Professional bureaucracy	Standardization of skills	Operating core	Variable	Complex and stable	Low complexity
Divisionalized form	Standardization of production	Middle line	Rather old and big	Rather simple and stable	Variable according to units
Innovative/adhocracy	Mutual adjustment	Support staff	Rather young and varied size	Complex and dynamic	Frequent complexity
Missionary organization	Standardization of standards	Ideology	*	*	*
Political organization	None	None	*	*	*

*: not applicable.

Table 7.2. *Characteristics of the seven structural configurations according to Mintzberg (1989)*

These elements, when confronted with the analysis of the literature on organizational configurations, suggest that PTAs should develop an organizational form that presents the main features of adhocracy. The empirical study presented below aims to test this proposition and to analyze the relationship between the organizational characteristics of PTAs and their performance level.

7.4. Empirical analysis

This section aims to report on the structuring of the empirical approach and to explain the main contributions of the analyses carried out. Firstly, the qualitative data collected make it possible to highlight various situational elements, internal and external contingency factors, and to characterize their intensity for each PTA (section 7.4.1). This first step leads to the characterization of the *expected* organizational configuration for each PTA, with regard to the situational elements identified. Secondly, a comparison of the structural factors and the level of performance is carried out for each of the PTAs studied (section 7.4.2). This second step is based on an evaluation of the performance of the five PTAs. As with any organization performing complex tasks with varied stakeholders to be satisfied, a multidimensional approach of performance is adopted, reflecting the PTA's ability to satisfy key players (healthcare professionals and structures) and to cover the main health needs of patients and families on its territory.

7.4.1. *Analysis of contingency factors (situational elements) and expected organizational form of PTAs*

7.4.1.1. *Analysis of internal contingency factors*

Thanks to the data on the five PTAs that was collected, it is possible to depict precisely four internal contingency factors (Table 7.3): the way the PTA was created and its age; the size (workforce) and composition of the PTA team (number of members and competences); the roles and strategies played by the PTA (scope of missions carried out – either oriented solely toward healthcare professionals or also toward patients); and the existence of a digital coordination tool (implementation of a single software program for all professionals).

Since the legislative decree that led to the creation of PTAs was published in July 2016, the five PTAs studied were logically quite young at the time of the study (first quarter 2018). With the exception of PTA 1, which had anticipated the decree, the other four PTAs were less than 2 years old at the time of data collection. PTA 5 was the most recent with barely 1 year of existence. Nevertheless, the empirical study suggests that the emergence of the five experimental PTAs was the result of two major structuring patterns. The first one formally corresponds to the *ex nihilo* creation of a PTA structure, in which no pre-existing structures in the territory were integrated. The second is based on the integration of an existing organizational structure. This integration could be a merger of existing healthcare networks into a PTA, as is the case for PTA 2. Integration could also be based on the integration of the PTA system into one of the existing coordination networks in the territory, as in the case of PTA 3. This variety of structuring modes reflects the capacity of the operating professionals to produce organizational innovations within the general framework prescribed by the regulatory authorities. It also means that the age of the PTA does not perfectly reflect the presence, sometimes longstanding, of coordination structures in the territory. Thus, some PTAs may build on old coordination networks.

Regarding the workforce, PTAs are usually composed of a small management team and a central coordination team. The latter invariably relies on a duo of a nurse and a social worker; only some PTAs also benefit from the presence of a doctor. These skills may be supplemented by other health and social services experts, or by administrative professionals. PTAs 1 and 4 can also benefit from the work of a territorial coordinator. The administration team and the basic coordination team constitute the first perimeter of the PTA organization. In the five PTAs that were studied, the size of the latter varied from one to five (minimum 3 FTE[10] in PTA 5; maximum 15.4 FTE in PTA 1). The central PTA coordination team is complemented by professionals from pre-existing health networks who have been integrated as "internal members". The number of integrated networks and their level of integration likely determine the PTA's ability to meet its support missions in the territory. In addition, some of the health and social structures and pre-existing networks are also PTA components, but act as "external members", which define a third organizational level. The last level of analysis is the PTA environment, where patients, general practitioners, physiotherapists, independent nurses, health and social structures, regulatory authorities, etc., are located.

The strategy of the PTAs is formally defined by the legal definition of their support role for healthcare professionals, which includes three main missions: information and guidance for healthcare professionals (mission no. 1), organizational support for the coordination of "complex pathways" (mission no. 2), and support for the sharing of good professional practices concerning safety and quality of care (mission no. 3). The five PTAs that were studied report on these missions, but comply more or less perfectly with them, sometimes focusing on one or two of them (such as PTAs 2, 4 and 5). Some of the PTAs carry out secondary missions that are directly oriented toward patients, and become "service providers" (e.g. assistance for administrative formalities) for the latter (PTAs 2, 3 and 4).

10 Full-time equivalent.

Internal contingency factors	Definition	PTA 1	PTA 2	PTA 3	PTA 4	PTA 5
History of the PTA	Origin and creation of the PTA	Totally new structure Age of PTA: > 2 years old	Integration of existing network(s) Age of PTA: 1 year < x < 2 years	Integration of existing network(s) Age of PTA: < 1 year	Totally new structure Age of PTA: 1 year < x < 2 years	Totally new structure Age of PTA: 1 year < x < 2 years
Size of PTA (workforce)	"Internal" PTA team (composition)	Executive coordinator, nurses, social workers, doctors, territorial coordinator PTA size: 15.4 FTE[(b)]	Director, executive assistant, call center assistant, assistant coordinator, nurse, social worker, psychologist, occupational therapist PTA Size: 7.6 FTE	Director, territorial animation officer, assistant, nurse, social worker, doctor, psychologist PTA Size: 10.9 FTE	Medical director, executive assistant, nurses, social workers, doctors, territorial coordinator PTA Size: 5 FTE	Executive coordinator, call center assistant, nurse, social worker PTA Size: 3 FTE
PTA strategy (activities)	Scope of missions[(a)] carried out by the PTA	Equal development of the 3 missions	Uneven development of the 3 missions: mission no. 2 most developed	Equal development of the 3 missions	Uneven development of the 3 missions: mission no. 2 most developed	Uneven development of the 3 missions: mission no. 1 most developed

Table 7.3. *Analysis of internal contingency factors*

Internal contingency factors	Definition	PTA 1	PTA 2	PTA 3	PTA 4	PTA 5
PTA strategy (relationships with patients)	Direct interactions with patients	Yes (phone calls)	Yes	Yes	Yes	No
Technology	Digital tool to support coordination between different health and social professionals	Unique software to coordinate the patients' health pathways Files created by the coordination assistant and completed by all PTA coordinators	Duplication of software programs Files created by the coordination assistant but poorly completed by PTA coordinators	Duplication of software programs Files created by the coordination assistant but poorly completed by PTA coordinators	Unique software to coordinate patients' health pathways Duplication with other communication modes Partial use of functionalities Files created by the coordination assistant and completed by all PTA coordinators	No specific software to coordinate patient's health pathways

Notes:

(a) – mission no. 1: information and guidance for health professionals;

– mission no. 2: organizational support for the coordination of complex pathways;

– mission no. 3: support for the sharing of professional best practices regarding safety and quality of care.

(b) Full-time equivalent.

Table 7.3 (continued). *Analysis of internal contingency factors*

With regard to the technology, various contextual elements shed light on the variety and complexity of the technical coordination system at work in the PTAs at the time the study was carried out. PTAs were created in conjunction with the deployment of TSNs, which resulted in the development of digital coordination tools or platforms for all healthcare professionals in the same territory. Moreover, the adoption of a common coordination tool in a given PTA results from the way it was created, and proves more difficult in PTAs that are built on pre-existing networks and had their own digital tools. The variety of digital tools and business software programs in the five PTAs reflects the complexity of the technical coordination system. Indeed, varied situations were observed with regard to the technical coordination system implemented in the PTA: PTAs 1 and 3 use a digital coordination platform shared by all of their "internal" and "external" members, in addition to other communication tools, particularly in the case of PTA 3; PTAs 2 and 4 also use a digital coordination platform, but in duplication with existing communication software programs (in connection with the network-PTA transition), which can have an impact on the appropriation of coordination practices. Finally, PTA 5 does not offer any specific digital solution.

7.4.1.2. *Analysis of external contingency factors*

The empirical data make it possible to contrast three external contingency factors (Table 7.4): the density of healthcare professionals and structures in the territory; the needs of targeted patients; and the strategic orientation formulated by the regional regulatory authorities regarding primary care coordination.

The PTAs studied are confronted with varied territorial issues, resulting mainly from the more or less high density of health and social services and from the geographical characteristics of the territory (urban, semi-rural, with or without problems of accessibility to certain parts of the territory). For example, PTA 1 is located in a semi-rural area with a low density of population and healthcare professionals and structures, with cases of geographic isolation, which often makes it more difficult to coordinate the patient's healthcare pathway.

The characteristics of the target patients are an additional element in the complexity of PTAs' environment. In general, PTAs focus on pathologies or populations identified as priorities by regional regulatory authorities, and seek to streamline the complex healthcare pathways of patients suffering from at least one chronic disease. In the five PTAs studied, dependent elderly people are among the beneficiaries. However, some PTAs were diversifying their supported population, whether in terms of age or pathology: psychiatric disorders, addictions, oncological care, etc. Overall, the five PTAs all deal with complex needs and situations (diversity of interventions, patients and pathologies), this complexity of patients being combined with the specific characteristics of each territory.

External contingency factors	Definition	PTA 1	PTA 2	PTA 3	PTA 4	PTA 5
Characteristics of the territory	Demographic characteristics of the territory Density of healthcare professionals in the territory	Semi-rural Areas with low density of population and of healthcare professionals and structures Cases of geographic isolation	Urban High population density and health professionals and structures	Semi-rural Areas with low density of population and of healthcare professionals and structures Cases of geographic isolation	Contrasted territory Areas with low density of population and of healthcare professionals and structures Cases of geographic isolation	Urban High density of population and of healthcare professionals and structures
Characteristics of the patients	Target population and/or main associated pathologies	Elderly dependent patients, young patients suffering from a rare disease or psychiatric disorders	Elderly dependent patients, patients with oncology care, patients with psychiatric disorders and social problems	Elderly dependent patients, patients with polypathology or benefiting from oncological or palliative care, patients with chronic diseases, disabled people, patients with social problems	Elderly dependent patients, young patients living with chronic diseases, disabled children, patients benefiting from care in oncology or nephrology	Elderly dependent patients, young patients living with psychiatric disorders, disabled persons

Table 7.4. *Analysis of external contingency factors*

External contingency factors	Definition	PTA 1	PTA 2	PTA 3	PTA 4	PTA 5
Strategic orientation given by the regional regulatory authorities (ARS) concerning the implementation of the PTA	Main objective given to the PTA Change management characteristics	Digital convergence Constructed change (voluntary and progressive)	Digital and organizational convergence, promotion of a single operator on the territory Prescribed change (imposed and progressive)	Digital and organizational convergence, promotion of a single operator on the territory Constructed change (voluntary and progressive)	Digital convergence Constructed change (voluntary and progressive)	Convergence of practices Adaptive change (voluntary and abrupt)

Table 7.4 (continued). *Analysis of external contingency factors*

Finally, the strategic orientation formulated by the regional regulatory authorities regarding primary care coordination is not exactly the same in all territories, even if the objective of a greater convergence among the players in order to improve the organization of healthcare pathways is systematically present. The way to achieve this convergence differs from one PTA to another: digital convergence through the deployment of a single digital tool (PTAs 1 and 4), organizational and digital convergence through the implementation of a single coordinating operator (PTAs 2 and 3) or just convergence of care practices (PTA 5). As a result, the management of change (voluntary or imposed) and the temporality (gradual or abrupt) of the PTA implementation are different. The nature of the change can thus be linked to the typology defined by Autissier and Moutot (2012): most often, the change is constructed, voluntary and progressive (PTAs 1, 3 and 4); in PTA 2, the prescribed change leads to the progressive integration of stakeholders; finally, in PTA 5, the change is rather adaptive, voluntary, but abrupt.

7.4.1.3. *Synthesis of the situational elements, expected organizational form of PTAs*

To summarize the situational elements, PTAs are young or very young organizations (<2 years old except for PTA 1), made of a multi-level structure with a central coordinating team composed of administrative and health professionals ($3 < n < 15$), with very diverse total sizes. Digital technology oriented toward the coordination of patients' healthcare pathways plays a major role in this structure. A frequent complexity results from a lack of standardization of the digital devices: use of a single business software (the digital coordination tool) in PTAs 1 and 4 (which can create problems of use, as this tool is not necessarily adapted to the management of a structure); juxtaposition of the digital coordination tool and business software in PTAs 2 and 3 (that result from pre-existing networks and still use existing business software to ensure administrative management); absence of specific business software in PTA 5. The history and strategy of PTAs are in line with a flexible and innovative organizational form to improve the coordination of care for complex patients. A variety in the implementation of the organization's formal missions and in its structuring modes is also observed: different levels of compliance with the three missions defined by the regulatory authorities (concentration on one or two missions in PTAs 2, 4 and 5; extension of certain missions in PTAs 2, 3 and 4); creation of PTAs as totally new structures (PTAs 1, 4 and 5) or by integrating existing healthcare networks (PTAs 2 and 3). The newness of the organization and the orientation toward innovation directed to patients' care improvement are two major characteristics of the situational elements of the PTAs that make adhocracy the *expected* organizational form of these structures (Figure 7.2).

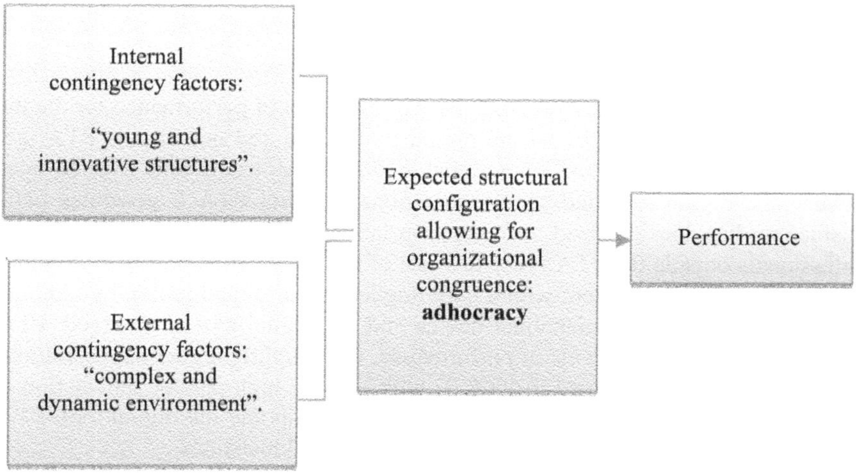

Figure 7.2. *Expected organizational form of PTAs after situational analysis. For a color version of this figure, see www.iste.co.uk/grenier/frontiers.zip*

7.4.2. *Organizational congruence and PTAs performance*

This second stage of the empirical approach aims to interpret possible differences in performance between the five PTAs studied, with respect to their level of organizational congruence. To do so, a multidimensional assessment of PTAs performance is achieved (section 7.4.2.1). Then, the congruence between the situational elements (previously analyzed in section 7.4.1) and the observed structural elements is estimated for each of the PTAs (section 7.4.2.2). Finally, an interpretation of these results is proposed (section 7.4.2.3).

7.4.2.1. *Analysis of PTAs performance*

On the basis of the data available at the time of collection, different performance indicators for PTAs were selected. In terms of performance *vis-à-vis* external stakeholders, two indicators are evaluated: appropriation and degree of use of the digital PTA tool by healthcare professionals outside the PTA (used as an indicator of coordination success)[11] ; and patient satisfaction (used as an indicator of the quality of care and of the organization of the healthcare pathway). An internal performance dimension is also taken into account: the quality of the fit between the

11 The data were collected at the same time as the digital tools were deployed, which may explain the appropriation still in progress and the still fragmented use of these tools in the PTAs. This situation does not call into question the relevance of a comparison between their levels of appropriation and use between the five PTAs.

organizational system and the digital PTA tool (used as an indicator of the organizational effectiveness of the PTA).

The results suggest that PTA 1 achieves a high level of performance for the three selected indicators: good use of the digital tool inside and outside the PTA, good patient satisfaction with the operational coordination team, and a good match between the digital tool and the organizational system. PTA 2 generates patient satisfaction, but does not lead to the appropriation of the digital tool by healthcare professionals outside the PTA (very low use of the PTA's digital tool at the time of the study, which is consistent with a high duplication of digital tools). In addition, a poor fit between the organizational device and the digital tool is observed. PTA 3 and PTA 4 have similar levels of performance, with slightly higher appropriation of the digital tool than observed in PTA 2, high or very high patient satisfaction and medium quality of fit between the organizational set-up and the digital tool. PTA 5 is characterized by low levels of performance in most dimensions.

7.4.2.2. *Analysis of the level of organizational congruence of PTAs*

The organizational congruence of the PTAs is estimated on the basis of the two key structural elements of adhocracy, which constitute the expected organizational form of the PTAs, taking into account their situational elements (see section 7.3.2): on the one hand, mutual adjustment as a coordination mechanism; on the other hand, the level of integration of the PTAs' operational team, conditioning the quality of their support mission. This last structural element can be assessed through the quality of collaboration between the "internal" and "external" levels of the PTAs.

The organizational congruence analysis shows that the five PTAs studied rely on the use of mutual adjustment and promote horizontal communications, as is the case in adhocratic configurations, except for PTA 5, for which no observations in this sense could be made. The weekly multi-professional team meeting is the main coordination instrument for all core teams in PTAs 1 to 4. The topics covered are relatively similar across all PTAs: use of digital tools, review of cases, management of adverse events, reflection on professional practices and evolution of partnerships. These multi-professional meetings are not so much a place for making care decisions as a space for reflection and exchange about patients' needs. They function as a collective of experts or a project team, where health professionals compare their points of view to find constructive solutions. The five PTAs also improve the coordination of care by connecting the professionals of the circle of care. At their initiative or at the initiative of patients or professionals, the PTAs organize multi-professional meetings to remove barriers between professionals and institutions, which often do not communicate otherwise. Thus, PTAs help to break with the professional logic organized in silos or "organ pipes". In a way, PTAs serve as a link between professionals, who can provide a neutral and fresh look at a situation, allowing all the professionals to take the necessary distance and resolve complex situations. Finally, these meetings often provide an opportunity to decide on a plan of action and to (re)activate the professional network around the patient. Three of the five PTAs also organize home visits to assess the complexity of the patient's situation in a multidimensional way. On these occasions, the PTA coordinator usually meets with the closest circle of care (family general practitioner and homecare nurse). PTA 1, which does not make home visits, arranges telephone meetings not only to maintain this link with the patient as the final beneficiary, but also to build trust with external PTA professionals. The quality of the mutual adjustment seems to be closely related to the ability of each PTA to build good collaboration between the "internal members" integrated into the operational team and the "external members" of the PTA. Analysis of the data shows some contrast on this point between the five PTAs studied. Professionals in PTAs 1, 2 and 4 report good relationships with the "external members", as reflected by their participation in the PTA Board of Directors.

The second key structural element of the adhocracy is the importance of support functions. In the case of PTAs, the entire organization is dedicated to this support function, oriented toward their primary external stakeholder, the health professionals, even though the five PTAs were unevenly fulfilling their formal missions. The level of integration of pre-existing networks in the territory may be a first indication of PTAs' capacity to mobilize a wide variety of coordination resources and to manage great complexity. In this respect, PTAs 1 and 3, and to a lesser extent PTA 2, seem organized to fulfill this mission with their operational team which integrates several existing players with different skills and resources (hospitals, palliative care units, geriatric units, oncology network, homecare service, Alzheimer's information and liaison center, etc.). On the other hand, PTAs 4 and 5 have a less integrated operational team, which suggests that the capacity of their internal support staff may need to be further developed.

Finally, the results make it possible to contrast the five PTAs studied as follows. PTAs 1 and 3 seem to present the best organizational congruence, with a high level of mutual adjustment and strong integration of support staff; PTA 2 is in an intermediate situation with a high level of mutual adjustment and average integration; PTA 4 also presents a high level of mutual adjustment but seems even less integrated than PTA 2, which distances it from the characteristics of adhocracy; finally, PTA 5 presents poor organizational congruence, with a low level of integration and little mutual adjustment, and is quite distant from the characteristics of adhocracy.

7.4.2.3. *Interpretation of results*

Built as complex organizations, the five PTAs studied are multi-level structures. They rely on an operational coordination team, composed of a core administration and coordination team, and on "decentralized internal members", that are complemented by external healthcare professionals and structures, in order to optimize the access to the resources and competences available in the territory for the benefit of care and support to complex patients. This complex organization can be an advantage for attracting resources and producing innovative solutions, but can be a disadvantage for structuring coordination and achieving a high level of cooperation between actors.

Four out of the five PTAs studied have organizational characteristics close or relatively close to adhocracy (PTAs 1, 2, 3 and, to a lesser extent, PTA 4), as originally defined by Mintzberg. Their ability to comply with the adhocratic form depends on their capacity to integrate healthcare networks, structures and professionals in the territory, on the quality of the mutual adjustment, and on the degree of collaboration between their members. They are structured to promote organizational agility and to cope with the complexity of their environment. One of the contributions of this study is to identify, through the PTAs studied, several degrees of achievement of the adhocratic configuration.

Finally, it is possible to link the ability of the PTAs to implement an adhocratic organizational model to their level of performance. The analysis carried out reveals that the more PTAs conform to the characteristics of the adhocratic model, the higher their performance is, as shown in the case of PTA 1, and conversely, at the other end of the continuum, that of PTA 5.

7.5. Conclusion

The results of our study make it possible to grasp, shortly after their creation and in a still experimental phase, the variety of organizational forms implemented within the PTAs, and to depict, more specifically, an "adhocratic variety" among them. They also suggest that the performance of PTAs seems to be higher the closer their organizational characteristics are to those of adhocracies.

The deployment of PTAs is now effective in all French territories. As stated in the national health strategy "Ma santé 2022", the objective is that "the isolated private medical practice – that is, the medical practice by a health professional alone in his or her office – [will] become the exception by 2022". The creation of primary care teams under the impetus of CPTS (*communautés professionnelles territoriales de santé*), provided for in the law of 2016[12], is now emerging more actively. At the same time, support functions are structured around DACs (*dispositifs d'appui à la coordination*, coordination support systems), defined in the law of 2019[13], the purpose of which is to bring together all the coordination expertise of a territory: MAIA (*méthode d'action pour l'intégration des services d'aides et de soins dans le champ de l'autonomie*, action method for the integration of support and care services in the field of autonomy), PTAs and territorial healthcare networks. The current integration of the pre-existing tools, systems, organizational arrangements and skills for the coordination of healthcare pathways makes it necessary to build a methodology for evaluating their outcomes. The first lessons drawn from this study pertain to the importance of adhocratic characteristics in the good functioning of the PTAs, which could be part of the "points of vigilance" to be taken into account in the evaluation protocols for these integrated support systems (such as in current DACs). It would thus be relevant to check whether these integrated support systems continue to invent solutions to best meet the expectations and needs of complex patients, or whether they eventually standardize healthcare pathways, at the risk of further bureaucratization of the primary care system and loss of the advantages inherent in hybrid organizational forms.

Finally, it is important to ensure that the will to reform the organization of primary care by increasing the number of tools and devices (not to mention those used specifically in the medico-social field) does not nip their innovative capacities in the bud. The structuring effort, if necessary, should not mask the general ambition to propose an organizational model that is sufficiently flexible and responsive to meet the complexity of situations encountered by patients, to satisfy the conditions in which healthcare professionals work, and to contribute to the health of populations.

7.6. Acknowledgments

The authors would like to thank Corinne Grenier and Philippe Mossé for proofreading this chapter and for their comments and suggestions for improvement.

7.7. References

Autissier, D. and Moutot, J.M. (2003). *Pratiques de la conduite du changement. Comment passer du discours à l'action ?* Dunod, Paris.

12 Law No. 2016-41 of January 26, 2016 (*Journal officiel de la République française*).

13 Article 23 of Law No. 2019-774 of July 24, 2019 (*Journal officiel de la République française*).

Bilodeau, A., Lapierre, S., Marchand, Y. (2003). Le partenariat : comment ça marche. Mieux s'outiller pour réussir. Direction de la santé publique, Régie régionale de la santé et des services sociaux de Montréal-Centre, Quebec.

Bourgueil, Y., Marek, A., Mousquès, J. (2009). Trois modèles types d'organisation des soins primaires en Europe, au Canada, en Australie et en Nouvelle-Zélande. *Questions d'économie de la santé*, 141, 1–6.

Cameron, K.S. and Quinn, R.E. (2011). *Diagnosing and Changing Organizational Culture: Based on the Competing Values Framework*. John Wiley & Sons, New York.

Canadian Hospice Palliative Care Association (2013). *A Model of Hospice Palliative Care: Based on National Norms of Practice and Principles*. Canadian Hospice Palliative Care Association, Ottawa.

Cartel, M., Boxenbaum, E., Aggeri, F. (2018). Just for fun! How experimental spaces stimulate innovation in institutionalized fields. *Organization Studies*, 40(1), 65–92.

Contandriopoulos, A.P., Denis, J.L., Touati, N., Rodriguez, R. (2001). Intégration des soins : dimensions et mise en œuvre. *Ruptures*, 8(2), 38–52.

Fleury, M.J., Mercier, C., Denis, J.L. (2002). Regional planning implementation and its impact on integration of a mental health care network. *The International Journal of Health Planning and Management*, 17(4), 315–332.

Fleury, M.J., Grenier, G., Bamvita, J.M., Vallée, C., Farand, L., Chiocchio, F. (2018). Évaluation du Plan d'action en santé mentale (2005–2015) : intégration et performance des réseaux de services. *Santé mentale au Québec*, 43(1), 15–38.

Furst, S., Blackburn, R., Rosen, B. (1999). Virtual team effectiveness: A proposed research agenda. *Information Systems Journal*, 9(4), 249–269.

Grenier, C. and Denis, J.L. (2017). S'organiser pour innover : espaces d'innovation et transformation des organisations et du champ de l'intervention publique. *Politiques et management public*, 34(3–4), 191.

Isenberg, D. (2011). The entrepreneurship ecosystem strategy as a new paradigm for economic policy: Principles for cultivating entrepreneurship. *Presentation at The Institute of International and European Affairs*, Dublin.

Létourneau, P., Beaudoin, J., Shabah, Y., Girard, M. (2010). Comment gérer des communautés de pratique interorganisationnelles ? *Gestion*, 35(4), 64–72.

Manning, E. and Gagnon, M. (2017). The complex patient: A concept clarification. *Nursing and Health Sciences*, 19, 13–21.

Ministère français chargé de la Santé, Direction générale de l'offre de soins (2012). Améliorer la coordination des soins : comment faire évoluer les réseaux de santé ? [Online]. Available at: https://solidarites-sante.gouv.fr/IMG/pdf/Guide_reseaux_de_sante-2.pdf.

Mintzberg, H. (1989). The structuring of organizations. In *Readings in Strategic Management*, Asch, D., Bowman, C. (eds). Palgrave Macmillan, London.

Mintzberg, H. (1993). *Structure in Fives: Designing Effective Organizations*. Prentice-Hall, Upper Saddle River.

Nadler, D.A. and Tushman, M.L. (1980). A model for diagnosing organizational behavior. *Organizational Dynamics*, 9(2), 35–51.

Saillour-Glénisson, F., Duhamel, S., Fourneyron, E., Huiart, L., Joseph, J.P., Langlois, E., Pincemail, S., Ramel, V., Renaud, T., Roberts, T. *et al.* (2017). Protocol of a controlled before-after evaluation of a national health information technology-based program to improve healthcare coordination and access to information. *BMC Health Services Research*, 17(1), 297.

Simon, L. (2009). Underground, upperground et middle-ground : les collectifs créatifs et la capacité créative de la ville. *Management international*, 13, 37–51.

Spigel, B. (2017). The relational organization of entrepreneurial ecosystems. *Entrepreneurship Theory and Practice*, 41(1), 49–72.

Touati, N., Denis, J.-L., Grenier, C., Smits, P. (2019). Implementing spaces to favor the emergence of ecologies of complex innovation in the public sector: An empirical analysis. *Administration & Society*, 51(3), 463–490.

Waterman, R.H. (1993). *Adhocracy*. W.W. Norton & Company, New York.

Williamson, O.E. (1991). Comparative economic organization: The analysis of discrete structural alternatives. *Administrative Science Quarterly*, 36(2), 269–296.

PART 3

Reflective Insights on Organizational Innovations in Healthcare

Introduction to Part 3

The first two parts of this book have shown that thinking about altering frontiers through organizational innovations in healthcare organizations requires an in-depth study of the subject under investigation: moving from the individual to the collective and thinking about the management and governance of these organizations.

This third part defends the idea that a reflexive and critical look at current organizations and at the innovations developed constitutes a complementary way of enriching reflection (Hibbert 2013). Reflexivity produces results on a triple level. First, it offers the individual the possibility of taking a step back from his or her own actions, of taking stock of the activity he or she has carried out, of his or her state of progress, of his or her successes and of the limits he or she has encountered. Then, it allows the action to be re-started and to decide, according to the assessment that has been drawn up beforehand, what the most relevant next steps will be. Finally, this individual reflexivity can become collective by involving several people in the organization and thus has an impact on the teams and the organization as a whole. Reflexivity is first and foremost an individual positioning, which can be adopted collectively and which not only transforms individual behavior but also, potentially, the functioning of the entire organization (Palpacuer *et al.* 2015).

To produce its full effects, reflexivity requires certain conditions to be met (Verhezen 2010). First, at the level of the individual, it implies that employees have the necessary skills for this reflexivity. Like know-how, reflexivity can be learned. Then, it must be supported by the organization. Reflexivity can here be of great benefit to the organization. It can allow for innovation, new models to be proposed and new modes of organization. It can enable work to be carried out better, faster and, above all, differently. However, it does take time: reflexivity about one's own activity implies that the employee is not directly producing. Although reflexivity is an investment whose cost-effectiveness can quickly become very strong (it can save much more time than it costs), an investment is initially needed. Reflexivity must also be supported by tools that allow it, recognize it and value it. Indicators and evaluation techniques are thus central to reporting on what has been done and what could be done in the future. More broadly, in order to be effective and to develop, reflexivity must be based on a true culture that values error, sees it as normal, as a source of learning and not as a load that needs to be eradicated (Verhezen 2010).

This third part of the book is devoted to putting into perspective the organizational innovations presented in the first two parts. It concludes this book on altered frontiers through organizational innovations by showing how reflexivity allows us to think about the strengths and weaknesses of organizational innovations – and thus the means of disseminating them.

The first two chapters of this part emphasize that a renewed vision of evaluation constitutes a major lever for the development, valorization and diffusion of organizational innovations. The low level of use of innovative evaluation methods explains why, until now, these organizational innovations have been little known and remain very limited in scope.

Chapter 8, proposed by Jessica Gheller, Christian Bourret and Gérard Mick, deals with the case of interface platforms that organize cooperation on the ground (PTA, PAERPA, CPTS, MSP[1], CLIC, etc.). The authors show that the experience of the stakeholders involved in the operation of these territorialized care networks plays a major role in the dissemination – often invisible – of innovations. The results of this analysis show the relevance of a renewed approach to evaluation that is able, for example, to recognize, value and support the development of phenomena that are difficult to perceive, such as the experience of stakeholders in the territory.

Chapter 9, proposed by Corinne Grenier and Christine Dutrieux, highlights the role that absorptive capacity plays in the diffusion of organizational innovations in healthcare systems. Absorptive capacity corresponds to the degree to which an organization has the capacity to take ownership of "good ideas that come from outside". Taking examples from several research fields, this chapter identifies three factors that can limit this absorptive capacity. First, an organization may have difficulty appropriating innovations when everything else is pushing it toward reproduction and

---

1 PTA: territorial platform for support of complex healthcare pathways (*plateforme territoriale d'appui*); PAERPA: experimentation "Health pathway of elderly people at risk of autonomy loss" (*parcours de santé des aînés*); CPTS: territorial healthcare communities (*Communautés Professionnelles Territoriales de Santé*); MSP: multidisciplinary primary care center (*Maison de Santé Pluridisciplinaire*), CLIC: Territorial information and coordination centers for seniors (*Centres Locaux d'Information et de Coordination*).

permanence. Second, an organization may be reluctant to explore new ideas and knowledge. It may favor those that are already familiar to its members. Finally, organizations may find it difficult to get internal stakeholders to accept innovations that challenge their practices. For each of these difficulties, this chapter proposes recommendations to overcome them.

Finally, in Chapter 10, Hugo Bertillot argues for greater attention to the indicators – particularly quality indicators – that have been multiplied in healthcare systems in recent years. Quality indicators are a genuine organizational innovation. They do not simply measure the presence of this or that situation. They sometimes radically transform professional practices. It is from this perspective that the various stakeholders in healthcare systems must look at them in order to truly grasp their effects. This contribution therefore ends with a very clear plea for healthcare system stakeholders to take control of the indicators used, otherwise their professional practices may well be profoundly transformed by them.

References

Hibbert, P. (2013). Approaching reflexivity through reflection: Issues for critical management education. *Journal of Management Education*, 37(6), 803–827.

Palpacuer, F., Taskin, L., Balas, N. (2015). Quelle est la place du terrain dans les recherches critiques en management ? *Économies et sociétés (série K)*, 4(2), 251–269.

Verhezen, P. (2010). Giving voice in a culture of silence. From a culture of compliance to a culture of integrity. *Journal of Business Ethics*, 96(2), 187–206.

8

Proposals for New Approaches to Contributory Evaluation of Healthcare Pathways from Interface Organizations

8.1. Introduction

Recent legislative initiatives in France, particularly in the context of the law on the organization and transformation of the healthcare system[1], position organizational innovation as one of the main levers for improving the healthcare system, based on the deployment of new forms of territorial cooperation, such as support structures for complex healthcare pathways[2]. As the questions raised by the field of innovation, particularly in territories, intrinsically linked to those of evaluation (Godet *et al.* 2010), the evaluations of public policies conducted in France seek to identify the levers of innovation and to identify the most effective ways of improving the healthcare system.

Chapter written by Jessica GHELLER, Christian BOURRET and Gérard MICK.

1 Law No. 2019-774 of July 24, 2019 on the organization and transformation of the healthcare system.

2 At the request of health, social and medico-social professionals, support structures for healthcare pathway coordination ensure a global response to the demands of professionals, in conjunction with the attending physician (reception, situation analysis, orientation, referral, access to health resources, monitoring and support for situations, and planning of the healthcare pathway); contribute to answers regarding needs and wishes of individuals and their caregivers (reception, identification, information, advice, orientation, referral and support); participate in territorial coordination aimed at structuring healthcare pathways. See: https://www.legifrance.gouv. fr/eli/loi/2019/7/24/SSAX1900401L/jo/article_23 [Consulted 9 September 2019].

The aim of this study is to make recommendations for the extension and generalization of existing research. This chapter therefore focuses on the dimension of experience in the development aid processes of territorial organizations. It deals with the links between the experience acquired by the stakeholders involved in support structures for healthcare pathway coordination and the dynamics of the emergence of spaces conducive to the dissemination of organizational innovations in healthcare systems. In order to make an original contribution to the collective reflection of this book, we propose a relational and interactionist approach. After the presentation of the theoretical framework used, we will show, through the descriptive analysis of five territorial dynamics of local collaboration initiated in support structures for healthcare pathway coordination, how taking into account the dimension of the acquired experience of collective stakeholders in the territories allows for a better understanding of the invisible phenomena of diffusion of organizational innovations in healthcare.

8.2. Context and research questions

8.2.1. *Background*

Over the past 30 years or so, the organizations at the interface between hospitals, general practitioners and homecare professionals have gradually developed, with a strong social and organizational innovation dimension concerning the co-production of services with patients and the reduction of social and territorial inequalities in healthcare (Bourret 2016).

The successive reforms carried out since the 1990s have led to the creation of a plurality of organizational innovations, which now coexist in the territories. Among others, *Healthcare networks* were experimented with as early as 1996, and then perpetuated in 2002; the *Territorial information and coordination centers for seniors* (*Centres locaux d'information et de coordination*, CLIC) created in 2001; then the Method of Action for Integration of Care and Support Services for Older People, (Méthode d'action pour l'intégration des services d'aide et de soins dans le champ de l'autonomie, MAIA) as early as 2011, following various experiments conducted in 2008 (Ministère de la Santé et des Sports 2009) and 2010 (CNSA 2010). More recently, territorial support coordination was implemented in the framework of PAERPA experimentation (Health pathway of elderly people at risk of autonomy loss). These innovations, *resulting from the evolution of pre-existing local system*, now coexist in a certain number of territories, and are now merging within "new" structure bringing together all their missions of coordination and integration of aid and care services[3].

Recent legislative orientations take advantage of the existence of interface organizations to support a national strategy to alter the frontiers within the healthcare system, the development of coordination of healthcare pathways and cooperation between medical, domiciliary care and social services and professionals, integrating the massive development of information systems beyond the hospital framework alone, and the use of digital health services aimed at strengthening communication between hospitals, general practitioners and homecare professionals. These orientations are notably reflected in the structuring of new forms of organizational innovation, deployed for example in the structuring of primary healthcare services[4]. These are mainly multidisciplinary group practice and primary healthcare communities (CPTS), accompanied by the advent of cooperation protocols between health professionals (HPST law), experiments with digital health territories (TSN) and experiments with collectives of innovative stakeholders (article 51 of the Social Security financing bill, 2018).

However, the development models implemented in the territories, and the positioning granted to coordination systems, depend, on the one hand, on the appropriation of public policies by the regional health agencies (regional level of French state for healthcare organization and regulation) and, on the other hand, on the initiative of healthcare system stakeholders at the territorial level. Consequently, the evaluation of organizational transformations in health territories constitutes a knowledge tool at their disposal to uncover and understand the often invisible logics at work within these systems, supporting the dissemination of organizational innovations.

The *Haut Conseil pour l'Avenir de l'Assurance Maladie* (HCAAM)[5] highlights the importance of implementing evaluation methods as an aid to the development of territories emerging from all stakeholders (professionals, institutions and administrations), and functioning thanks to the existence of "experience feedback loops" mobilizing the experience acquired by the stakeholders in the field and effectively involving them in an iterative logic.

---

3 Article 72 of the LMSS Act.

4 Article 36 of Law No. 2009-879 of July 21, 2009 on hospital reform and relating to patients, health and territories [Online]. Available at: https://www.legifrance.gouv.fr/eli/loi/2009/7/21/SASX0822640L/jo/article_36 [Accessed 23 September 2019].

5 HCAAM (2018). Contribution à la transformation du système de santé. Report.

8.2.2. *Positioning for the method*

This research is part of an approach to the evolution of the French healthcare system based on the role of interface organizations to overcome compartmentalization, promote the development of "healthcare democracy" and build trust between all partners, including patients (Bourret 2010).

It also insists on the notion of complex health pathways which, in a care context marked in particular by uncertainty, inaccuracy and informational incompleteness, makes it necessary to share and exchange meaningful and contextualized information (Mick *et al.* 2018).

Finally, this research is based on the notion of coordination, integrated care and assistance services as a means of accompanying the evolution of aid and care system by articulating the corresponding specific structures created in the past according to a logic of "integrative innovation" that takes full account of the context, capitalizing on the existing system and making the most of it to develop new systems, with a concern for added value in the conduct of actions (Bloch & Hénaut 2014).

We therefore believe that organizational innovations should be evaluated according to a contributory approach that integrates the experience, into the healthcare system, of the stakeholders developed within pre-existing territorial organizations.

This chapter focuses more particularly on the experience acquired by groups of stakeholders historically established in territories, as one of the levers to be taken into account in order to understand the invisible processes of organizational change in terms of diffusion (within territories of practice) and generalization (to new territories) of organizational innovations promoted by public policies.

This approach is based in particular on a doctoral thesis work (in progress) in information and communication sciences, carried out in the framework of a partnership agreement with the National Federation of Healthcare Networks (Union Nationale des Réseaux de Santé, UNR.Santé), and developed from a constructivist perspective, with back and forth between theory and practice in the field, in a perspective of "engaging communication" (Bernard 2018).

This chapter therefore proposes to bring to the discussion elements of understanding relating to the way in which the experience acquired by collective stakeholders in the territories can be a vector for change and improvement of territorial organizations for health.

The question here is twofold: (1) How can the experience of pre-existing territorial organizations be taken into account in understanding the dynamics of change in structured healthcare system at the territorial level? (2) What dissemination processes can be made visible by taking into account the field of experience of stakeholder groups? In such a perspective, we postulate that the systems constituting the diffusion of organizational innovations are optimized in territories capitalizing on the experience acquired from the support structures for healthcare pathway coordination, historically established and imbedded in existing relationships and interactions.

8.2.3. *Methodology*

Constructivist approaches to innovation show that the phenomena of diffusion of innovations also result from the diffusion of knowledge in collective spaces, within which the social and organizational dimensions of knowledge are decisive (Gastaldi *et al.* 2017).

This chapter presents the results of the investigations carried out concerning the description of the "achievements" of stakeholders involved in the support structures for healthcare pathway coordination, i.e. the general representations they have of their roles, positions and practices, the experience they have of them and their visions of the studied environment (Mucchielli & Noy 2005).

The support structures for healthcare pathway coordination studied were chosen according to three main criteria, namely, their strong territorial roots, a longstanding presence in the areas where they operate, and organizational methods that integrate forms of cooperation between stakeholders, aimed at reducing the compartmentalization between support and care services.

This study was carried out over a period of 4 years in various collective spaces throughout France, representing 17 support structures for healthcare pathway coordination, spread over eight major regions and involving the equivalent of 231 salaried professionals.

An analysis grid was developed from the categories defined by the constructivist method of contextualization through the fields of experience and interaction (Mucchielli *et al.* 2005).

The study carried out here concerned precisely the inventory of the experience acquired by social stakeholders in their spatial contexts of intervention (the "acquired" or "already there"). It was a question of studying their interactional practices, their positioning and their uses of sociotechnical devices.

Thus, the method sought to link different elements, namely, the "stakeholders", the "contexts" and the "sociotechnical devices", in order to account for both formal and informal dimensions of the dissemination processes studied.

The implementation of this approach was achieved by an analysis carried out as close as possible to the system of relevance of the social stakeholders in the situation, namely, that of the stories of practices and actions of the groups of stakeholders studied.

Various techniques were used to collect raw data in the field, namely, semi-directive interviews with the heads of coordination systems as resource persons[6] in the field (Linard 1996). This was a combination of participatory observation, long-term observation and field surveys. The collection of raw data focused, on the one hand, on the communicational elements of the stakeholders in a situation of animation of territorial cooperation (production of all kinds, concrete achievements, handling of technical objects, behaviors and actions, various writings, speeches, words, etc.), and, on the other hand, on the relevant contexts in which these behaviors make sense for the stakeholders concerned.

8.3. Framework for analyzing the processes of diffusion of organizational innovations: definition and principles (conceptual framework)

We propose to consider the support structures for healthcare pathway coordination as spaces of territorial intelligence defined as information and communication systems, supporting the diffusion of organizational innovations by contributing to the transformation of social practices over time, proceeding from their previous forms while acquiring new properties[7]. These specific spaces are composed of a set of professional communities carrying out collective activities through the sharing of practices and actions on the same territory. Based on the notion of "modeled memory", these spaces of territorial intelligence constitute a readable result of complex processes of learning, prescription and transmission.

The collective activities of these spaces are part of "daily ordinary innovation", whose importance has been highlighted by Alter (2015), who also insists on the role

6 The notion of "resource person" refers here to the "expert" stage proposed in the work of H.L. Dreyfus, and taken up by Linard (1996, p. 31), cited by (Mucchielli & Noy 2005, p. 210).

7 Borrowing here the notion of evolutionary system, notably developed within the disciplines interested in the study of networks in their geographical dimension and in a perspective of interdisciplinarity with communicational approaches.

of the "secant marginals" (Alter 2012), i.e. forms of dissent in creativity and innovation. The dynamics of innovation supported by these spaces of territorial intelligence must be supported by logics of invention, daily creativity and the development of cooperation in order to solve difficulties not foreseen by the system (Dejours 2012).

In this perspective, the analytical framework takes a particular look at the processes of interaction, creation and hybridization of knowledge as vectors of organizational innovation. The approach adopted in this study therefore invites us to consider the dissemination of innovations through the study of relational contexts, focusing on the dimension of trust, the quality of interpersonal and inter-institutional interactions, and the construction of shared meaning.

First, we analyze the importance of the relational and communicational properties of coordination platforms and devices as a springboard for the successful dissemination of organizational innovations, in the face of resistance, particularly from the professionals, motivated by the perception of a threat to existing habits and practices (Vedel 2010).

The analysis then focuses on the systems that make up these spaces of territorial intelligence with regard to the experience acquired by the coordination systems, as an element of "maturity" of territorial organizations and thus a determining factor in the deployment of organizational innovations in healthcare.

Finally, the analysis takes into account the collective dimension of the acquired experience, understood in terms of networks and interactions between stakeholders, encompassing both formal and informal dimensions of existing territorial organizations.

For us, the aim of the analytical framework is therefore to mobilize new evaluation methods in order to make visible the phenomena of diffusion of innovations at work within territories, and thus improve understanding of the role of building a true "collective intelligence" between stakeholders, emphasizing that "we often think we are cooperating when all we are doing is communicating", and finally by promoting a "cooperative know-how" (Zara 2008).

8.4. Empirical illustrations of the innovation diffusion processes supported by coordination platforms

This section presents the empirical observations made and describes the field of experience acquired, the "already there" of the stakeholders concerned, their daily practices in given situations, their world views and their realities. The analysis categories "stakeholders", "contexts" and "devices" are used in reference to the method of contextualization by the fields of experience and interaction (Mucchielli & Noy 2005).

8.4.1. *A community of "expert" stakeholders, resulting from dynamic processes of territorial construction*

The participant observation highlighted different stages of "maturity" in the experience of support structures for healthcare pathway coordination, ranging from that of "novice stakeholders", newly created with recently formed teams, to that of "expert" systems corresponding to systems made up of teams already in place.

According to the research objectives, focused on the study of the links between experiences and dissemination processes, we have chosen to focus on the analyses related to the description of the experience acquired by the expert stakeholders:

– history of a support structures for healthcare pathway coordination from a gerontological network:

> History means that there have been cooperations on the territory for years: 2000 the healthcare network, 2004 the CLIC, 2009 the platform, 2011 the MAIA. The partners have been collaborating for decades. Including the birth of the health network that was born from the collaboration between the general practitioners and the local hospital, which thanks to this has had beds in day hospitalization. Again, this leaves its mark, because this collaboration is set in stone because of that [...]. The current situation is that we are at the same time CLIC, a gerontological network, MAIA, a respite platform, and an assessor evaluate for CARSAT (French pension fund for workers), and that we have positions for mission leaders to improve the quality of public home care services. [...] So now it is a single legal and administrative entity, with a revised board of directors, which makes room for all the stakeholders in the territory [...]. (Director of a support structure for healthcare pathway coordination)

– history of a support structure for healthcare pathway coordination originating from a hospital:

> We were first a healthcare network run by an association, then by a healthcare cooperation group [...]. What is important is that we were from the outset situated in the dynamics of the work. We were really in a permanent quality approach, since each of the group's themes has a primary healthcare/hospital monitoring committee and experts who

> meet three times a year to check what we do, what we produce, how it is evolving and where there is redundancy, because the supply landscape is changing. […] In this area all care and assistance service is in the group. (Doctor in charge of a support structure for healthcare pathway coordination)

– history of a support structure for healthcare pathway coordination organized as a healthcare network for the elderly:

> On our territory, the gerontological network, which has existed since 2005, had been working in the field for many years, accompanying primary care professionals. It has been promoted by the stakeholders (including primary care stakeholders) in order to copy the system with the "Elderly-disabled persons" service of the departmental council, which is a CLIC. Then, our territory was part of the first wave of experimentation of the PAERPA experimentation, launched in 2013 and operational since October 2014, with a territorial extension in 2016. Based on the modeling of the method with elderly people, the stakeholders within the system are now expanding their missions to those of a support structure for healthcare pathway coordination. (Doctor in charge of a support structure for healthcare pathway coordination)

– history of a support structure for healthcare pathway coordination resulting from by primary care professionals:

> The development of our platform dates back to the 1980s. […] This development focused on the challenge of developing the health project in order to provide a collective by building an intersectoral health and social organization through work on professional practices. […] Initially, we worked informally, based on the needs of the attending physician through field work with the CCAS (city centers for social action), the social workers of the retirement and CARSAT (French pension fund for workers), the town hall services, mutualist clinics, health professionals in the area, social workers from the town and the departmental council, MAIA), CLIC, CCAS (city centers for social action), and healthcare networks. […] Thanks to this work, these meetings concerned the implementation of health pathways for the territory's healthcare networks. Then, the networks worked on the healthcare pathways through meetings between primary care, the hospital, the MSP and the Regional Union Representing Health Professionals. Today, the networks are merging within a territorial platform for support of complex healthcare pathways and an

> organizational innovation project concerning the complex diseases of children in a situation of obesity has been proposed and accepted at the CPTS of the territory. (General practitioner coordinator of a territorial platform for support of complex healthcare pathways)

We observe, first of all, that each "expert" coordination structure comes from a singular cultural ecosystem, whether it is a general practitioner, a hospital, a healthcare network for the elderly or a CLIC.

We observe how, in each of the ecosystems considered, collective stakeholders emerge as bearers of a specific identity. They take on the mission of developing spaces for sharing a common vision by building a system of interaction with other stakeholders. It is therefore a question of certain social stakeholders who, endowed with a particular intentionality, develop in an informal way, an identity based on the stakes of construction with the other stakeholders of the dynamics of transformation of an organizational environment, which is shared by the same token.

Secondly, the singular histories presented above show that the capacities for action and projects of these "expert" territorial coordination systems are the result of long-term experience in specific territorial ecosystems.

To understand the processes resulting from the experience gained from coordination structures, it is necessary to link the nature of the projects of the stakeholders, the contexts of the behaviors and the sociotechnical systems mobilized. It is a question of taking into account the general framework of stakeholders' intentions within their contexts of relevance, in order to bring out the meaning of their behaviors.

We are therefore now focusing on describing the processes enabling the dissemination of organizational innovations within the territories where the coordination structures and integrated systems operate.

8.4.2. *Territory of practices as a framework for the intelligibility of processes for disseminating organizational innovations*

The observations made show that the general intentionality of the coordination systems resides mainly in the capacity to carry out actions and projects for the territorial development of care and assistance services in their intervention areas. The aim of these systems is to contribute to an integration, over time, of the relationships between the different skills and services of the healthcare and homecare sectors. This dynamic of transformation of local organizations concerning care and assistance services is built up by the implementation of actions and projects that facilitate attendance, exchanges, mutual knowledge, affinities and the imitation of practices, thereby creating a context conducive to the dissemination of organizational innovations. The aim of these systems is to organize their functioning and develop their actions with the aim of contributing to the quality of relations between stakeholders through the constitution of a system of relations and knowledge oriented toward the development of healthcare services on the territory.

8.4.2.1. *Example of a territorial platform for support of complex healthcare pathways evolved from a healthcare network for the elderly*

> [...] Concretely, there are two levels of our work, one level on individual support [...]; and there is a collective level, both on collective actions for users (conference for diabetic users for example), and the other collective element is the improvement of the system. In other words, how can we [...] integrate the system at the territorial level? And this is played out in terms of the paths and links that we can have with the healthcare institutions, with the hospital, on strategies with the institutions, for the reception of homecare professional, in temporary reception or to improve the entries in place permanent [...]. It is the basic work of getting to know the partners among themselves. That is to say, how we can serve as a link between all the stakeholders in the territory and thus enable them to identify more with each other, and [...] facilitate exchanges and collaborations between stakeholders. [...] There is work on the knowledge of the territory's service offer, mapping and display of the offer that is done through our intermediary and in connection with CLIC. In short, there is in-depth work on interstructural knowledge. (Director of a territorial platform for support of complex healthcare pathways)

The spatial context of reference of the "expert" coordination devices is here a space of territorial intelligence, whose organizational construction is based on the interweaving of actions and projects at different relational scales mobilizing the quality of interpersonal and inter-institutional interactions in the same way as cooperation between professionals around complex situations.

The progressive implementation of these relations induced similarities, producing homogeneous groups of stakeholders and organizational affiliations defined as networks or groups of stakeholders, platforms or devices according to the reference term. The reference ecosystem of the experience acquired by the coordination devices thus formed a system of relations linking the intervention territory.

The spatial context of relevance is therefore based on a "relative" conception of territory (as opposed to health territories that can be assimilated to "fixed" territories), and proves to be an essential reference for understanding the specificities of the experience acquired in coordination systems.

8.4.2.2. *Example of a territorial platform for support of complex healthcare pathways resulting from primary care*

> [The] actions are implemented in different parts of the territory, on different paths and with different stakeholders, on different financing. And all of this contributes to facilitating the work of general practitioners, [...] especially to provide support outside of consultations and in patients' homes. [...] Various applications of this method have been carried out, the construction of an intersectional health and social coordination at the service of the general practitioner is an example, in connection with the medico-social networks, thanks to field work with the CCAS (city centers for social action), the social workers of CARSAT (French pension fund for workers), the town hall services, mutualist clinics and the healthcare professionals of the territory. These meetings concerned the implementation of a healthcare pathway for the territorial platform for support of complex healthcare pathways of the territory and work on the continuity of patient care for children in a situation of obesity (General practitioner coordinator of a territorial platform for support of complex healthcare pathways)

Going beyond the formal dimension of the legal structures relating to coordination and integration in healthcare, we can see that the construction dynamics thus illustrated have as a common characteristic the creation of change processes, leading to the implementation of connections between a diversity of stakeholders involved in aid, care and information, orientation and coordination. These processes are concretized by sustainable and cumulative interactional practices between the stakeholders and the coordination system, giving the coordination systems global automatisms of operation.

8.4.3. *Learning process*

The construction of a shared meaning between professionals in a situation is observed during the conduct of coordination actions in response to a problematic situation to be solved. In this case, the processes of diffusion of innovations are the result of collective professional learning in situation, comparable to *systemic* emergences. The intentionality of coordination systems is the creation and hybridization of knowledge of professionals confronted with a problem, in order to share reference contexts, to build a common understanding of the situation and to modify their behavior according to the knowledge thus collectively produced.

8.4.3.1. *Collective professional learning*

The professional processes deployed by the teams of the coordination structures were the result of an analysis and the production of a framework of intelligibility (comparable to a shared meaning).

The processes thus observed were linked to the diffusion of organizational innovations in that they preceded a multi-professional decision-making process, which can also mobilize an inter-institutional decision. All of the decision-making resulting from these situational practices visibly contributed to the processes of diffusing organizational innovations in healthcare. The challenges related to the dissemination of these innovations were related to the production of a framework of trust shared between the stakeholders in the healthcare system, integrating the dimensions of the norms, values and identities of the person being cared for and his or her family and friends. Furthermore, the approach of problem solving through situational practices based on a companionship logic raised the question of interpersonal and inter-institutional trust. The behaviors of the stakeholders were then modified, producing innovations in their own practices and institutional frameworks, whose norms and rules governing access to help and care were questioned.

8.4.3.1.1. Example of coordination around complex situations

Thus, a director of a territorial platform for support of complex healthcare pathways summarized the meaning of the interventions carried out in a situation:

> One of our working methods is to re-examine the needs and to put them into context [...], because in many situations, we are not going to respond to the demand, [...] we are going to digest this demand, we are going to analyze to find out what is not identified.

The deepening of the understanding of the process involved leads to the identification, among the employees conducting these situation analyses, of the different contexts of relevance from the point of view of the stakeholders concerned, including the patient. We were in the presence of an effort to contextualize the problems from a "multi-actor" point of view; that is to say, a process of collective construction of a reference context, going beyond the initial contexts of understanding of each professional.

Thus, a support coordinator from the same system explained the meaning of his intervention:

> The information shared by each professional is projected in an organizational and decision-making environment specific to their parent organizations. It therefore proves to be uncertain, its relevance being conditioned by the non-exhaustiveness of the evaluations, the lack of consultation and cooperation between professionals from various services and institutions: the professional is lost, he does not understand.

Or again: "We look at the complexity of the situation, which poses a problem [...]. There is no standard definition: it is what is dysfunctional, it is the difficulties of a professional".

In the case of this situational practice, the process of collective construction of a shared meaning had the particularity of integrating the patient and his or her entourage as stakeholders of the situation to be resolved.

One employee pointed out that:

> professionals often no longer see the person, the life project [...], because they are mired in their difficulties. [...] The starting point is the explicit needs expressed by a person [...]. Our intervention is to take stock with the patients in a collaborative manner, to enable them to regain control of what they knew how to do.

The process at work then made it possible to identify the relevant contexts for each of the stakeholders involved in complex situations, integrating the points of view of patients and their entourage and consequently the norms and values of the latter, who therefore entered into dialog with the norms and values of healthcare and social professionals, as well as those of their referral structures.

A physician working with the territorial platform for support of complex healthcare pathways discussed this point as follows:

> The determinants of the inflection points of the healthcare pathway are multiple, such as the patient's health behavior before any contact with the care and assistance services, the expression of a complaint during examinations, the patient's representation of his identity at the time of diagnosis, the loneliness of a patient at home following a particular episode of care [...]. For the caregivers, they lead to changes in content, material, and therefore in the direction of the healthcare pathway.

8.4.3.2. *Organizational learning*

Within the spaces of territorial intelligence developed by the territorial platform for support of complex healthcare pathways, innovations spread through organizational learning processes (knowing or experiential knowledge), engaging informal knowledge sharing perspectives. The mobilized operating modes led to an organizational learning process built by professionals in the framework of their practices and in their own organization (social construction). These were modes of learning organized within networks of stakeholders, with a view to producing and formalizing tacit knowledge that did not yet exist (expansive learning) and the associated operating modes.

Communities of practices and actions were thus structured with the aim of developing shared resources as collective norms, which could later be used to solve problems in daily practice. This organizational learning process was based, on the one hand, on the mobilization of knowledge of skills of each of the stakeholders in the healthcare pathways and, on the other hand, on the integration of this expertise by each of the stakeholders in their concrete place of professional practice.

8.4.3.2.1. Example of intersectoral coordination

Although not very visible because it was mostly informal, this organizational learning process was observed in each of the territories studied. The following *verbatim* provides a concrete illustration of a process that was developed from the contributions of professionals in action and their direct experience of the problems encountered in the organization of the care and assistance system (formative approach):

> The method used by the coordination platform since the 1980s uses Piaget's constructivist pedagogical approach. The underlying challenge in developing a health project is to produce the collective by building intersectoral health and social organizations through work on professional practices. [...] The case analysis method is mainly used, in order to collectively construct responses adapted to the problems of general practitioners. It is a question of people knowing each other to produce a collective. It is a question of carrying out consultation times around complex situations between general practitioners, social workers from the town and the departmental council, the MAIA, the CLICs, the CCAS (city centers for social action), the health networks. Thanks to this work and the sharing of cell phone numbers, general practitioners know who to refer to and vice versa for situations that were once inextricable, but are now simple. (General practitioner, coordinator of territorial platform for support of complex healthcare pathways)

8.4.4. *Process of building collective standards*

While the processes of elaborating a shared meaning were identifiable at the level of individual situations (micro) and were part of systemic emergence dynamics, the processes of building collective norms were identifiable at the level of interactions between organizations (meso). This second type of process relates to the dynamics of the implementation of a collective norm and its negotiation. The observations carried out led to differentiate processes of collective construction of norms by the approaches of organizational prescription and transmission.

8.4.4.1. *Organizational prescription process for innovation*

The purpose of coordination systems is to enable the sharing of collective values, vision and goals. This collective functioning in fact aims to produce frameworks for the development of the organization's ideology, i.e. the choices and choices necessary for its foundations and the expression of a vision of the future. The territorial platform for support of complex healthcare pathways thus implemented specific activities relating to the integration of the professional community, including political-organizational activities, which contributed to the organization of a space of territorial intelligence through the definition of a collective structuring as well as operational and strategic decision-making[2].

8.4.4.1.1. Example of political-organizational activities

The organizational prescription process for innovation was also followed in each of the territories studied. The following *verbatim* report helps to illustrate its development, which is based on the contributions of the professionals and services represented and *a posteriori* of the problems encountered by the organization of the care and assistance system (summative approach):

> We were first a healthcare network run by an association, then by a health cooperation group, [...] what's important in this is that we are really in a permanent quality approach, which is done permanently since each of the themes, of the group have a primary care/hospital monitoring committee with experts who meet three times a year to check what is being done, what is being produced, the evolution, the redundancies, because the supply landscape is changing [...]. Over the last ten years, we have set up a monitoring committee for each of the themes, three times a year, to ensure that the system evolves. [...] the monitoring committees will be representative of the major stakeholders in the care of this type of population. [...]. It is also an opportunity to analyze new needs or dysfunctions that may arise between stakeholders. This is what we are looking for in cooperations, on the lack of representation of each other's worlds [...]. What comes out of all these monitoring committees is taken up again in the framework of the select committee with the decision-makers [...]. At the end of the day it depends on a decision by the hospital director or a president of the pharmacists' association, and so the select committee meets every six

weeks, and from time to time when there are real sticking points, it is [the role of the medical director] to bring up a sticking point during the monitoring committee, so that a director can make a decision, and also in terms of evaluation. (Hospital doctor, medical director of a territorial platform for support of complex healthcare pathways)

8.4.4.2. *Process of transmitting organizational experience*

The territorial platforms for support of complex healthcare pathways studied here offer examples of transmission processes that are part of the invisible logic of cooperation. The analysis of the genesis and history of these organizations allows us to identify the existence of cognitive devices as supports of transmission processes, which appear to us to be capable of supporting the replicability of organizational innovations through the transmission of the experience acquired to other territories. The experience of coordination devices is materialized by a network of different heterogeneous elements that form a whole: discourses, institutions, legislative framework, physical spaces, administrative rules, ideas, etc. Considering the coordination devices as organized and finalized sets of intellectual objects, articulated among themselves and distributed in space and time for the purpose of knowledge production, they play a role of instrumentalization of the thinking and action capacities of communities of practice (the individual's thinking being dependent on the tools of the organization in general). Based on the learning and prescription processes mentioned above, they are set up by territorial organizations to promote in particular the processes of "diffusion of ideas" (organizational learning) and "organization and readability" (training). It can be observed that the transmission processes are therefore part of a larger collective of practices, holding an "immaterial knowledge capital" that is perpetuated over time, via cognitive devices (documents, databases, software, knowledge repositories, etc.).

8.4.4.2.1. The professional standard as a transmission lever

Informal interviews and documentary research on the genesis and history of two territorial platforms for support of complex healthcare pathways showed that, in addition to the organizational culture of the territory, the transmission processes could also rely on the presence of intellectual devices such as "learned medical societies". A backing, or a very close but informal link, with learned societies in the medical field, provided the territorial intelligence spaces with a capacity to capitalize on the knowledge produced over a long period of time, particularly in the context of the production of a repository recognized by the medical discipline. Thus, we have identified several examples of close links between the academic spheres and the coordinating bodies.

One example is a system for coordinating healthcare pathways, for which the local establishment of a learned society in geriatrics had been decisive for the conservation and dissemination of knowledge. This context of production of professional standards allowed this territory to be the bearer of more recent national organizational innovations, following the example of the national experiment PAERPA. Indeed, in 2005, a group of 15 healthcare networks for the elderly was formed within a regional college of geriatricians based on the regional learned society. Numerous works have been carried out in close collaboration with the geriatricians of this learned society, in particular the deployment of joint health projects, carried out with liberal professionals, experts and the social and medico-social sector, such as the "Oral health and nutrition of the elderly", "Frail elderly and alcohol misuse" and "Caregiver health" programs. Research, harmonization of professional practices, evaluation and information sharing, such as the implementation of a common "standardized geriatric evaluation" and an "emergency card" were also shared.

8.4.4.2.2. Approaches to improving professional practices as a driver of transmission

Cognitive devices related to training practices were an invisible element in the structuring of the transmission processes present within the coordination platforms, supporting the dissemination of organizational innovations. These structures were each time the result of an enlarged community of practices, integrating new territorial stakeholders to share knowledge. These inter-mediation stakeholders could be either an association created on an *ad hoc* basis, a university, or the legal structure carrying the coordination system.

This strategy of transmission within territorial intelligence spaces is based on a logic of strong contextualization of interactions between stakeholders and strong personalization of knowledge, centered on individual expertise, tacit knowledge and an attachment to the quality of relations between stakeholders of the community (training in small groups, tutoring, companionship and proximity research). In this perspective, a coordination system member explained that

> training [is] a challenge to ensure a "territorial quality approach" in the service of skills development [...] for a territorial dynamic that is still in the process of being structured. This new activity of the association also represents a perspective of diffusion and transmission of our work and our "state of mind" of territorial animation, support to healthcare pathways and shared governance [...].

The role of actions to improve professional practices (continuous professional training and development) as a cognitive, immaterial and invisible device allows for the legibility and sequencing of acquired experiential knowledge. The coordinating physician of a territorial platform for support of complex healthcare pathways explained that:

> it is a question of carrying out meetings of consultation and case analysis around complex situations on the method of case analyses, between the attending general practitioners, social workers of the town and the departmental council, the MAIA, the CLICs, the CCAS (city centers for social action), the health networks. [...] These actions can therefore be financed by [continuing education systems for health professionals] or the financing of public health missions. All the work on homecare professionals' articulations has been done under the aegis of an independent training organization.

The specific forms of training implemented in the territories observed represent a lever to support the dissemination of organizational innovations. In each of the territories studied, we observe the motivation of the cognitive training system, under various practical modalities. Each time, the platforms must proceed with the dissemination of the acquired experiences.

8.5. Conclusion

8.5.1. *Lessons*

The field study enabled highlighting the experience acquired by pre-existing territorial organizations, as an informal dimension, going beyond their simple legal structure, to be defined on the scale of a territorial system of relations, mediation and intermediation between stakeholders. The specificity of an intervention at different relational scales (institutions, professionals, patients/persons and their entourage) allows the existence of spaces conducive to the dissemination of organizational innovations, through relationships and flows (information, knowledge, practices and instruments). The processes of diffusion of organizational innovations can therefore be thought within the framework of territorial intelligence spaces. The analysis shows that while each territory had developed its own model of cooperation according to its representations, the already existing cooperations and the specificities of its environment, it was possible to identify common (invariant) processes allowing a framework of comprehension of these spaces of territorial intelligence to be defined. These collective spaces or ecosystems resulted from: (1) professional and organizational learning processes through the rebalancing of knowledge and the reconfiguration of professional practices in a situation of multi-professional coordination; (2) of prescription processes through organizational adjustment and in a situation of structuring collective activities; and (3) of transmission processes by organizing, modulating and reconfiguring knowledge within the framework of cognitive devices within territories.

8.5.2. *Perspectives*

The perspectives at the end of the study presented here concern the practical and methodological contributions for the stakeholders in the field.

From a methodological point of view, the contextualization approach is a scientific approach to collecting data from a constructivist posture, i.e. from the viewpoints of the stakeholders in the situation. It thus offers the observer the possibility of understanding the meaning of a situation for the stakeholders carrying out a specific project, confronted with the arrival of new organizational devices, and involved in a collective action situated in more or less normative organizational contexts. The proposed approach presents such a method through the dimension of the field of acquired experience, which is held by the historical stakeholders of the integration of services in spatial and cultural contexts that are each time distinct.

From a practical point of view, the method opens up perspectives for databases for the capitalization of experiences with a view to their replicability, which remain difficult to animate. It would be a matter of renewing the way we look at coordination structures in order to better integrate the invisible and qualitative dimension of the processes of developing shared meaning – associated with situational and organizational learning processes on the one hand, and with the processes of developing collective standards on the other hand – and of organizational transmission.

From a societal point of view, these new evaluative perspectives could constitute an opportunity for the evaluation of public policies, based on evaluation elements such as learning, prescription and transmission processes, which are less traditional than other evaluation items, but which carry dynamics for the stakeholders in the field themselves, making it possible to go beyond the conception of evaluation as a value judgment, often quantitative, made by an external observer.

All in all, the originality and the interest of the method seem to us to lie in taking into account an in-depth analysis of what already exists, the "already there", which is not common in the framework of methodological organizations for the evaluation of coordination and integration structures, which usually focus on the "here and now". The analytical framework thus constituted will have to be completed, in a second stage, by the proposal of a framework for understanding the limits and tensions encountered by coordination systems in relation to the replicability of organizational innovations in new areas of intervention.

Furthermore, the results presented, based on an analysis of "expert" coordination systems, could eventually constitute a reference for analyzing the stages of development of the experience of coordination systems (along a continuum from "novice" to "expert" stages); the aim being to enrich the tools already available for carrying out an "inventory" prior to any project to support organizational change or the replicability of innovative experiences in new contexts.

8.6. Acknowledgments

The authors would like to thank the professionals of all the coordination support structures and platforms, the regional healthcare network federations and unions for conducting the interviews and observations in each of their areas of intervention, as well as UNR.Santé.

8.7. References

Alter, N. (2012). *La force de la différence : itinéraires de patrons atypiques*. PUF, Paris.

Alter, N. (2015). *L'innovation ordinaire*. PUF, Paris.

Bernard, F. (2018). Pour une communication engageante, vers un développement durable. In *Développement durable : une communication qui se démarque*, Tremblay, S., D'Almeida, N., Libaert, T. (eds). Presses de l'Université du Québec, Quebec.

Bloch, M.-A. and Hénaut, L. (2014). *Coordination et parcours : la dynamique du monde sanitaire, social et médico-social*. Dunod, Paris.

Bourret, C. (2010). Évaluation et communication des nouvelles organisations d'interface : le cas des réseaux de santé. *Communication et organisation*, 38, 77–88 [Online]. Available at: https://doi.org/10.4000/communicationorganisa-tion.1411.

Bourret, C. (2015). Éléments de réflexions autour du positionnement et des domaines d'actions de l'intelligence économique. In *Organisations digitales : individus, santé, déontologie en contexte numérique*, Gardère, E., Le Moënne, C. (eds). L'Harmattan, Paris.

Bourret, C. (2016). Nouveaux métiers d'intermédiation dans les organisations d'interface en santé. *I2D – Information, données & documents*, 53(3), 32–33 [Online]. Available at: https://www.cairn.info/revue-i2d-information-donnees-et-documents-2016-3-page-32.htm.

CNSA (2010). Impacts de la coordination sur l'état de santé, les pratiques professionnelles et le recours aux services pour les personnes âgées dépendantes à domicile : évaluation du modèle d'intégration des services COPA (coordination personnes âgées) sur le 16ème arrondissement de Paris sous le nom de réseau gérontologique "Ancrage". Final report [Online]. Available at: https://www.cnsa.fr/documentation/007-de_stampa-rapport-final.pdf [accessed 9 September 2019].

Dejours, C. (2012). *L'évaluation du travail à l'épreuve du réel*. Quæ, Versailles.

Gastaldi, L., Krohmer, C., Paraponaris, C. (2017). *Activités et collectifs : approches cognitives et organisationnelles*. Presses universitaires de Provence, Aix-en-Provence.

Godet, M., Durance, P., Mousli, M. (2010). *Libérer l'innovation dans les territoires*. La Documentation française, Paris.

Linard, M. (1996). *Des machines et des hommes : apprendre avec les nouvelles technologies*. L'Harmattan, Paris/Montreal.

Mick, G., Debellis, M., Weissmann, M., Saby, M., Genthon, A. (2018). Coordination between professionals: A public health issue. In *Health Efficiency. How Can Engineering Be a Player in Health Organization?* Sarazin, M. (ed.). ISTE Press, London, and Elsevier, Oxford.

Ministère de la Santé et des Sports (2009). Intégration des services aux personnes âgées : la recherche au service de l'action. PRISMA France report [Online]. Available at: https://www.ladocumentationfrancaise.fr/var/storage/rapports-publics/094000078.pdf [accessed 9 September 2019].

Mucchielli, A. and Noy, C. (2005). *Approches constructivistes, étude des communications*. Armand Colin, Paris.

Vedel, I. (2010). Un modèle français d'intégration des services pour les personnes âgées fragiles : de l'innovation de sa conception à son implantation. PhD Thesis, Université de Reims Champagne-Ardenne, Reims [Online]. Available at: http://ebureau.univ-reims.fr/slide/files/quotas/SCD/theses/sante/2008REIMM209.pdf.

Vedel, I., Stampa, M.D., Ankri, J., Henrard, J.-C. (2005). Le changement à l'œuvre dans un dispositif local de soins et d'aide à partir d'un projet de réseau gérontologique ville-hôpital (Commentaire). *Sciences sociales et santé*, 23(2), 103–114 [Online]. Available at: www.persee.fr/doc/sosan_0294-0337_2005_num_23_2_1653.

Zara, O. (2008). *Le management de l'intelligence collective : vers une nouvelle gouvernance*, 2nd edition. M21, Paris.

9

Innovation and Absorptive Capacity of Organizations in the Healthcare Field

9.1. Introduction: absorbing to innovate

When it comes to innovation and the ability of organizations to innovate, it is now the paradigm of open or collaborative innovation that offers interesting perspectives for maneuvering in today's complex and turbulent environments. To put it bluntly, it is a matter of considering that "good ideas come from elsewhere", i.e. from other sectors of action or other entities than just the organization that wishes to renew its portfolio of interventions or the management models of its teams. Consequently, innovation is less and less the business of a single player, but of a set of partners contributing to it, at different stages of the long trajectory that stretches from the emergence of a new idea to its concrete deployment with the target audiences.

However, this assertion becomes an oxymoron when we look at organizations, naturally enclosed in their routines and cultures, and in particular healthcare organizations, reputed to be professional bureaucracies (Glouberman & Mintzberg 2001), pluralist (Denis *et al.* 2001) and compartmentalized in their sector of intervention. Therefore, developing the capacity to innovate requires developing the ability to open up to ideas and knowledge that are present outside the organization's boundaries, then to adopt and deploy them in new services or new organizational or management models. We thus question the *absorptive capacity* of organizations, understood as a set of organizational routines and processes through which the organization acquires and mobilizes external knowledge to produce a dynamic

Chapter written by Corinne GRENIER and Christine DUTRIEUX.

organizational capacity (Zahra & George 2002). Following a presentation of this concept, we will draw attention to three critical elements of the absorption process through various illustrations.

9.2. Context and questions: the challenge of openness

When we look at the life of organizations in the health field, we cannot help but be astonished by the variety of discourses and practices related to change and innovation, which often reason like "nothing changes!" or "impossible to transform!".

These organizations have the particularity of being first and foremost professional bureaucracies (Glouberman & Mintzberg 2001) in which the codification of knowledge is important, creating different forms of rigidity, perfectly adapted to predefined and routine situations, but not very conducive to change. This model also makes it possible to identify the sphere that holds legitimacy, i.e. the "professionals", those who intervene with the people being cared for (or users) (doctors, nurses, social workers, etc.). However, this traditional source of legitimacy has been contested in recent years by the "managerialization" of these organizations and the piloting of management tools by "experts". Thus, these bureaucratic organizations take more the form of pluralist organizations (Denis *et al.* 2001), characterized by a plurality of actors (managers, healthcare professionals, caregivers and public stakeholders) with often unaligned interests, with a distribution of their powers at numerous levels of responsibility or intervention, making it difficult to deploy any innovative initiative upward, or any strategic policy downward. As a result, any initiative for change or innovation may prove difficult to carry out, or even be blocked at any level of such an organization.

In the same manner, when directors and managers of these healthcare or homecare services are questioned[1] about the difficulties in innovating, they often use the image of a confrontation of worlds within their pluralistic organization to explain these difficulties (Boltanski & Thévenot 1991; Boltanski & Chiapello 2005). The work of Orvain and Angelé-Halgand (2011) sheds light on the imprint of the domestic, civic and industrial worlds on the logics of action of organizations in the healthcare field. These partitions of legitimacy are not conducive to innovation, and it is important for directors and managers to break down these conventions to support the elaboration of compromises for the common good (Boltanski & Thévenot 1991).

---

1 As part of an "Innovation management" course of the MSAIS specialized master, KEDGE Business School.

Through these different points of view, we will soon understand how much innovation is a real challenge for organizations in the healthcare field, especially when we look at open and collaborative innovations. Innovation is considered open when it is fueled by ideas, knowledge, models, etc., that come from outside the boundaries of structures. In addition to this usual definition, we also consider that the approach of a service or department that wants to open up to other internal entities in order to develop a new offer or intervention constitutes, in healthcare organizations that are very often hierarchical and compartmentalized, a real challenge that the open innovation paradigm makes it possible to grasp. Open innovation can be seen as a collaborative innovation, based on the identification and networking of various stakeholders (and entities of various kinds, including the patient or user) who contribute to all or part of the steps in an innovation process.

Current and future transformations in the healthcare field call for innovations characterized in this way. The emergence of new needs or the taking into account of hitherto (partially) ignored groups (elderly disabled people, users in great social and economic precariousness, in social and medical emergencies), the objective of reducing inequalities in health and access to healthcare services. The interest in further developing preventive medicine and health promotion, or the importation of new technologies (AI, the Internet), is forcing the cooperation of individuals who were not used to working together until now, to imagine solutions "at the boundaries" of many fields of expertise. In the same way, the reorganization of the offer of services around health (or even life) trajectories obliges many stakeholders to cooperate and to imagine integration mechanisms and multidisciplinary interventions. This collaborative economy (Arena 2018) is also a knowledge economy, in which the circulation of knowledge, expertise, ideas, beliefs, values, etc., becomes critical.

However, the challenge of how to respond is important, since the previous characteristics of organizations reveal how much more disruptive, or unrecognized, or not perceived as relevant, what comes from outside their boundaries will be perceived as disruptive. However, at the risk of devaluing or impoverishing any intervention, it is only by interweaving expertise from different fields in an innovative way that professionals (and users, patients) will be able to imagine and deploy relevant responses. Nevertheless, each sphere must be able to identify, appropriate and deploy such knowledge from outside.

We propose to renew the way in which we look at innovation in healthcare organizations through a theoretical framework that is still little explored in this context, that of organizational absorptive capacity (OAC; Cohen & Levinthal 1990). They allow us to analyze how organizations can break away from or question their usual routines and norms in order to open up to the outside world, identify, assimilate and deploy a novelty.

9.3. Theoretical framework: the notion of organizational absorption capacity

Cohen and Levinthal (1990) have shown how an organization's strategy or its potential for innovation is nourished by knowledge and ideas that are external to it, provided that the organization is able to absorb this newness[2]. They define OAC as the ability of an organization to acquire new knowledge, assimilate it and apply it in innovative projects. This OAC offers a relevant perspective "to explain how reconfigurations of resources and skills are developed to enable organizations to cope with changes in their environment and to innovate" (Van der Yeught 2017, p. 143), and thus enable organizations to develop innovative solutions.

OAC occurs through four processes (Zahra & George 2002), namely, the acquisition, assimilation, transformation and exploitation of new ideas and knowledge in the development of an activity or project:

– *Acquisition* refers to the organization's ability to recognize, value and acquire the external knowledge it considers necessary for its activity. It is facilitated by various factors such as: usual practices of openness to the environment (when, for example, the organization is a member of a cooperation network or a collective to offer a more global response; when the organization also encourages its employees to participate in external conferences or working groups that confront them with other practices and ways of thinking about the intervention); varied professional trajectories (and sometimes outside the sector), and also the motivation to gather new knowledge. For example, the work of Noblet and Simon (2008) underlines the crucial role of the leader in creating a context for interaction, scanning the environment and eliciting a diversity of viewpoints for the acquisition of new knowledge.

– *Assimilation* refers to the organization's routines that enable it to understand, analyze and interpret external (or new) knowledge (Szulanski 1996). Facilitating factors are: encouraging the circulation of knowledge between those who will have acquired new knowledge (acquisition stage) and those (sometimes different) who may be interested in using it; encouraging discussion around this new information to highlight the "distance" (potential source of change) from habits; collectively questioning the values carried by the strategic project (or institutional project) in

2 Absorption capacity can be studied at an organizational level or at an individual level. Although we do not consider these two levels to be watertight, this chapter chooses to focus on the organization and its capacity to absorb what comes from outside.

progress in the light of the newly acquired information. Other practices show that this assimilation will be all the richer the more stakeholders have debated and begun to imagine new projects in "spaces" that protect them from their usual ways of thinking or behaving (Grenier & Denis 2017).

– *Transformation* is the ability to develop new routines to facilitate the combination of the acquired stock of knowledge with newly identified and analyzed knowledge. This result is the product of a "bisociation" (Koestler 2011).

– *Exploitation* describes the ability to mobilize and apply this renewed stock to achieve objectives that the organization has set for the development of new goods, new processes or new forms of organization.

These last two phases are facilitated by the use of innovative, collaborative methods, often considered agile (because they involve the client or user) project management to deploy the new product.

More generally, Daghfous (2004) has identified a few other principles that facilitate OAC: recognize the right to make mistakes, encourage experimentation and evaluation (to make new practices visible and stabilize them, to mobilize all teams around proven results), present change as the normal driving force in the life of organizations, increase the diversity of employee profiles, encourage connections between the organization's various departments and services, circulate all information, be attentive and know how to interpret in an original way (outside of the usual routines and patterns) the pressures of the environment, the expectations and needs of the target audiences, etc.

For the authors, it is a question of questioning (organizational) routines, defined as "repetitive and recognizable patterns of interdependent actions involving several actors" (Feldman & Pentland 2003, p. 96), and considered to be an important element in structuring organizational behavior. Absorbing is thus based on a process of questioning and possible transformations of the organization's routines which, in order to innovate, must be able to forge new ones, based on knowledge and ideas found outside its boundaries. More generally, absorptive capacity is seen not only as a set of formal rules, procedures, manuals, organizational charts and indicators, but also as being based on beliefs, informal knowledge, and elements of corporate culture and identity (Zahra & George 2002).

Finally, it should be noted that the four processes of an OAC process do not necessarily form four steps that would take place in a particular order (Todorova & Durisin 2007); indeed, they should not be understood as watertight steps between them (possible overlap) (Dali 2008). Nevertheless, these authors admit that absorption capacity is based on the distinction between potential OAC (acquisition and assimilation) and actual OAC (transformation and exploitation) (Zahra & Georges 2002).

A review of the recent literature as well as the support of healthcare organization directors and the doctoral work conducted by one of the co-authors[3] lead us to identify three pitfalls or difficulties that limit or even block the organization's ability to absorb novelty from beyond its boundaries.

First of all, when we take a closer look at organizational routines, we must distinguish three forms (Durand 2006): operational (routine executed automatically), generic (object of improvement through a continuous learning process) and research (supporting new combinations of rules and information with a view to innovation). In this way, routines root the organization between stability and change. However, it is much more operational and generic routines that dominate. Miller (1992) had already evoked, through his metaphor of the myth of Icarus, the extent to which organizations are more inclined to pursue trajectories that have proven their worth in the past than to venture along new paths that are always perceived as risky. All the more so since an obvious strategic art encourages organizations to exploit their core competencies in order to continue to develop their differentiating base (Mignon 2009). We thus formulate a first pitfall: how to get an organization into an absorption process?

A second pitfall is related to what is called "path dependency", i.e. OAC depends on knowledge already acquired (Imbert & Chauvet 2012; Van der Yeught 2017), which was not much emphasized in the initial work. To overcome this limitation, Imbert and Chauvet (2012) questioned the ability to absorb novelty according to the proximity between knowledge already acquired and knowledge to be acquired or according to the quality of the relationships that an individual can establish with the outside world. Other work advocates ambidextrous organizational arrangements (O'Reilly & Tushman 2004) to isolate (differentiate) services that use acquired skills from those that need to explore new knowledge. Beyond these solutions, we formulate this second pitfall as follows: how can we encourage a distance in the exploration of new ideas and knowledge in relation to the stock acquired? We will examine this through the "quality" of what is acquired.

Finally, there is a certain "comfort" for the stakeholders to remain anchored in the process of exploring new knowledge without taking the risk, or daring, to transform it into concrete projects. These organizations "risk bearing the costs without reaping the associated competitive advantages" (Mignon 2009, p. 82). Thus,

3 Doctoral Thesis conducted by Christine Dutrieux and entitled: L'articulation des capacités d'absorption organisationnelles avec les conventions de compromis: le cas d'un établissement de formation en travail social, Aix Marseille University.

the transition from a potential capacity (to acquire and assimilate) to an actual capacity (to exploit and transform) is not as "automatic" as many studies suggest. We thus ask: how can we move from *potential* to *realized* capacity?

9.4. Responses to the three OAC pitfalls: illustrations

We illustrate our point with examples from research conducted by the authors of this chapter, from research conducted by directors of healthcare organizations that the authors mentor during their training, and from examples in the literature.

9.4.1. *Entering the absorption process*

While the absorption of ideas and knowledge from outside the boundaries of the organization supports its capacity for innovation, this process is not an unanticipated or random approach, as also valued when looking at the capabilities or characteristics of the organization that can imagine and deploy novelty. Thus, in this manner, researchers are exploring organizational and managerial innovations, such as "spaces" that protect stakeholders from usual routines and norms, in order to strengthen the organization's potential to innovate (Bucher & Langley 2016; Grenier & Denis 2017).

On the contrary, OAC is a proactive approach to identify problems and then assimilate and exploit external ideas and knowledge. Some questions then arise about what can trigger this approach (notion of triggers for Easterby-Smith *et al.* 2008) in organizations that are naturally anchored in their certainties, moving at best toward some incremental changes (Grenier 2019). If we refer to theories on institutional innovation, a "jolt" (Munir 2005) is often at the origin of an entry into a transformation process. This jolt may be political, regulatory, cognitive or relational in nature, and for example:

– a sudden event, such as the urgency to respond to the competition, an injunction to transform an organization following an external evaluation highlighting poor performance in a quality of service, or on financial indicators;

– on the contrary, an awareness of the need to innovate in a context of slow but inexorable change in the healthcare landscape.

However, these "facts" are never objective events; they must be perceived, understood, assimilated, even constructed ("enacted") as such, to have this capacity to trigger an entry into an OAC process.

So, how can we encourage social entrepreneurs, managers of small businesses in the healthcare field, to listen to the ideas of others, to enrich their development project? These entrepreneurs are generally unmotivated to change their habits and engage in collective approaches – which would nevertheless help them identify new avenues of exploration for innovation (Maus & Sammut 2017) – locked in the belief in their own abilities, used to acting and deciding alone; for them, any outside idea is perceived more as a threat than an opportunity (Cooper & Saral 2013). Thus, how can they be encouraged to listen to the ideas of others, to enrich their development project?

Interesting experiments are based on a methodological organization to bring such actors into a process of acquiring ideas or external knowledge, such as the organization in a very short time (half a day) of a workshop of interaction of entrepreneurs to help them explore new development paths for their company through the deployment of a codesign approach capable of inspiring the design process of innovation. The "jolt" here is twofold: to bring entrepreneurs to learn from the ideas of others and to use an original approach (of codesign) to do so. The absorption was thus of two kinds: substantive and procedural.

A different way of entering an absorption approach is offered by Harvey *et al.* (2015) who studied how three hospitals under the authority of the NHS (National Health Service, Great Britain) reacted to a similar announcement of rapid improvement in their performance indicators, under threat of sanctions. The emphasis here is on the role of the stakeholders in these organizations in accepting this announcement, and in being (or not being) in a position to initiate a process of change in order to comply with the injunctions. In particular, we contrast the differentiated-differentiated behavior of two of the three cases studied:

– case A: the first hospital was a small, poorly structured organization that had not set up a specific department (or function) dedicated to knowledge management. It operated in relative isolation within its territory (few partnerships, for example). When the NHS established in its report its very poor level of performance and the urgency to initiate changes, top management reacted first of all by denying this information and the situation thus described, by an attitude of external bias (NHS report) and internal prejudice (*vis-à-vis* the healthcare teams, who are aware of this low level of performance and want to change their practice). It then refused to work with the team of external consultants appointed by the NHS. However, the NHS seized the opportunity to fill vacancies to bring new stakeholders into the organization who facilitated the start of a change process. The absorption of external knowledge was thus carried by these new professionals, supported by authority, which itself had issued the order to change;

– Case B: when the NHS report was sent, all the teams were "devastated" and agreed to work with the external consultants. The director set up a process of visits to other hospitals and partners, supported by procedures to systematically and strategically collect information (acquisition phase) in order to better understand the reasons for the poor performance of his structure (assimilation phase).

These two cases reveal two ways in which external knowledge is acquired: by new employees bringing their own experience and repertoire into the organization (case A), and by working with external partners to bring these new cognitive elements back into the organization (case B). They also underline the importance of organizational factors or characteristics (already acquired) that are favorable to triggering an absorption process (and more generally to supporting its development): organizational culture, particularly with regard to organizational learning, the strategic attention of top management to be alert to environmental changes, the existence of processes and structural elements (specific services or functions, for example) dedicated to knowledge management (capitalization, circulation in particular). It then appears that OAC is cumulative, and the more an organization has in the past become accustomed to feeding itself with external information and ideas, the more it will be able to take into account any new event in order to build an appropriate response.

Finally, case A reveals that a "shock" in itself is not enough to trigger an absorption process. On the contrary, in case B, this shock is "translated" and is carried structurally and politically by the general management, whose relational and tactical routines will be implemented. This director, a nurse with initial training (and therefore recognized as legitimate by the nursing staff) appointed several new directors to play the role of relaying her message and the imperative she carried (i.e. an internal network of translators and facilitators). This modality of relaying, i.e., of disseminating a capacity to absorb, came to take the form (in case C not presented here) (Harvey *et al.* 2015) of a dedicated team set up by management as a driving force of change. It was multi-professional in its composition, and thus capable of understanding and dialoguing with all parts of a healthcare organization, understanding this in a cognitive dimension (apprehension of the diversity of medical, care and managerial expertise) and in a political dimension (apprehension of the places of power in such an organization that we have described as pluralist).

9.4.2. *The quality of what is absorbed*

It is not enough to observe that new "information" penetrates the organization to conclude that there is an absorptive capacity. The latter must be questioned in terms of the strategic project or the issues that the organization intends to address. And one way to analyze this is to question the nature and relevance of what is being absorbed, particularly because health organizations are often rightly referred to as "institutions", i.e. relatively closed worlds. "I was astonished to see that the sector's withdrawal into itself was still so pervasive [...]. The medico-social sector is a very conservative sector", notes the director general of a foundation of managers of establishments for the elderly and disabled in southwestern France[4]. We propose several variations of this general questioning around the "what to absorb".

Berta *et al.* (2010) study the adoption of a good practice guide by seven homecare organizations in Ontario, Canada. Beyond the information and tools offered by this guide, it is what we call the "opening of the black box" that these authors highlight. Absorbing consists of identifying, discussing and adopting the principles of the guide – which are based on the principles of evidence-based medicine, or evidence-based practices – that challenge the usual routines within these structures and lead them to consider or evaluate what they consider to be their good practices. The authors then show how a translation process was used to absorb the essence of this guide, without which the recommendations presented in it would have been implemented in a poorly implemented manner. A first result of Berta *et al.* (2010) is based on the key role of leaders in supporting this process of appropriation, leaders that can be the management of these organizations, and also, and more broadly, the main "professions" (with their own employees with whom they work on a daily basis) in these complex healthcare organizations. A critical phase in this process of appropriation was then to develop familiarity with this type of guide, both in terms of: (1) awareness – i.e., the ability to locate relevant information; (2) the guide format itself – i.e., a set of recommendations to be followed formulated by others – and the principles of the guide – which is mentioned earlier; and (3) agreement within the structures to use it.

It is for the authors with this triple condition, through a process of translation, that professionals have managed to recognize a value to the guide, in connection with the strategy of home service structures. According to Rogers' (2010) model of diffusion of innovation, this strategy is more a strategy of differentiation for the first adopters of a novelty (here the guide) and more a strategy of similarity (or institutional isomorphism) for the followers. A complementary understanding of these complex processes is provided by Easterby-Smith *et al.* (2008) who study the boundaries embedded in new knowledge that must be overcome during an absorption process. They mobilize Carlile's analysis framework (2004) to study the three facets:

– syntactic boundary: transfer of "words" (or even acronyms) from one world to another, so as to avoid any misunderstanding;

4 Quoted in her professional thesis work of the Specialized Mastère MSAIS, KEDGE Business School, in partnership with IRTS Nouvelle-Aquitaine (IRTS, Institut Régional en Travail Social, Regional Institute for Social Work).

– semantic boundary: translation dealing with the different meanings and representations that the different professional worlds perceive through the new knowledge to be acquired;

– pragmatic boundary: transformation necessary to overcome the political interests that these worlds have in wanting, or not wanting, to acquire new knowledge.

During the absorption process initiated by a hospital's general management in the face of declining performance problems, it is first of all syntactic work that is observed on the knowledge and experience provided by newly appointed department heads; each of these department heads benefits from a network of relationships with high-performing hospitals (Easterby-Smith *et al.* 2008). Then, the creation of multidisciplinary groups and meetings enabled healthcare professionals and managers to cross semantic and pragmatic boundaries.

When OAC is studied in situations of innovation, we consider that the "what to absorb" must question the (cognitive) distance between the routines of the organization and the new knowledge or ideas it wants to bring into it. Indeed, we consider that innovation very often involves being inspired by ideas and practices developed in other professional fields. Is it still necessary that the stakeholders are able to identify "what comes from afar" (acquisition phase) and then to know how to encourage collective analysis (assimilation phase)? We report on the original approach initiated by the Erik and Odette Bocké Foundation and analyzed by its managing director in Box 9.1[5].

The Foundation manages residential establishments for dependent elderly people and disabled people (EHPAD[6]) in the southwest of France. It is a solid management structure, well established in its territory. However, after a period of crisis and restructuring, its Board of Directors decided in 2013 to redirect its development strategy in a different direction: to develop the professions, work more in a network, and be more identified by the guardians as an entrepreneurial operator on its territory. Thus, an association was acquired to increase the Foundation's capacity for intervention. However, this acquisition was made by reaffirming

5 Example taken from the professional thesis of Alexandra Penin-Guérineau, Executive Director of the Erik and Odette Bocké Foundation, as part of the MSAIS Specialized Mastère's degree, Bordeaux 2017–2018. The Foundation is legally an association (under French private law) that acts in the public healthcare field and is strongly regulated by the regulatory arsenal of the supervisory authorities at the national level (Minister of Health, Social Cohesion, Finance, etc.) or at the local level (regional health agency and departmental council).

6 EHPADs are medico-social establishments regulated by a law of January 2002, and operating under the dual supervision of the regional health agencies and the departmental councils. The same applies to the various medico-social establishments that receive or accompany disabled persons (children or adults) in France.

the Foundation's traditional values, despite changes in the environment to which it remained less receptive (opening up to its territory in order to develop the care of beneficiaries) and carried by a very hierarchical and top-down management (the directors of the establishments being more managers, not very strategic, careful to apply the protocols set by the administrative headquarters). Aware of the limits of this managerial model, in 2017 the Executive Director initiated a vast process of change to bring the directors toward greater autonomy, the ability to take innovative initiatives and to open up to their environment.

It transformed some meetings into creativity seminars by asking its managers to draw inspiration from other models and practices: Cirque du Soleil (this organization has revisited its core business by reconsidering its employees, no longer as athletes but as artists); the University Hospital Center of Strasbourg (a public hospital that has innovated not only in terms of care and technicality, but also in terms of support, based on the concept of hospitality). During these seminars, managers were given documentation on these examples and were encouraged to imagine similar side steps for their establishments. The seminars were appreciated and participation was rich and open. A few lessons were learned by the Managing Director from these initial experiences: taking great care in setting up the discussion space to encourage conviviality, respect for each person's word, and feeling that one does not take one's place in a usual working environment; preparing the seminar carefully (anticipate reactions so as to be able to respond and avoid any arguments, list a few techniques to encourage speaking that is never natural, etc.); guiding the reading and appropriation of documents by employees before the seminar began.

Box 9.1. *Drawing on exotic worlds to transform an organization*[7]

9.4.3. *The transition from potential to realized*

The literature (Zahra & Georges 2002) distinguishes between potential capacities (acquisition and assimilation) and realized capacities (transformation and exploitation). The two so-called potential phases generally take the form of project groups that progressively learn to work together, seek external information and collectively debate it in order to give it meaning and question the organization's methods. In this way, mutual trust and a common language for change gradually emerge. The next two phases consist of deploying the knowledge thus "digested" into new projects. Although little discussed in the literature, we have observed how delicate this passage between a potential OAC and an actual OAC is and how never automatic, as Dutrieux (forthcoming) and the example presented in Box 9.2 reveal.

7 This example is taken from (Grenier 2019).

The general management of the social work educational institution, a pluralistic organization, has taken the measure of the important transformations in its environment, namely, the field of training and research in social intervention. These transformations concern both the evolution of the professional training landscape and its consideration in terms of the offer of training as well as those related to new pedagogical modalities (e-learning, so-called "reverse" class giving learners more room to build their learning, etc.). To lead this transformation, it has launched or encouraged various transformation projects, including one focusing on the deployment of new digital teaching methods and another specific to Local Social Development (LSD[8]) to initially boost an internal dynamic by setting up collective projects and by developing the theme in training courses.

These two transformation projects (digital and LSD) are not of the same nature. The first is mainly aimed at the production of digital training and the second has more of an institutional and organizational dimension. For each project, a volunteer pilot is appointed and its legitimacy is acquired through its professional experience. Interdepartmental cross-functionality is sought for each group, made up of employees from both the educational and administrative divisions. After a rapid and concentrated training period, for all members of the digital group, the transition from potential to actualization was achieved very quickly through the individual creation by each member of the group of an e-learning training course. Conversely, the LSD group, which also benefited from training time for all its members, then "installed" the potential phase by creating common sense, notably by calling itself the "LSD Collective" and by a reflexivity brought about by the integration of students into the group. However, the transition to the realization stage was slower: group members had difficulty translating the new routines created during the assimilation phase into projects. It was more a "pressure" from outside the group, exerted by the institute's management, that led to the creation of two collective solidarity projects led by employees and students.

Thus, the process of group absorption is present in both cases but is implemented differently by the pilots.

For Dutrieux (forthcoming), consolidating the ability to move from potential to realized in these two groups translates differently depending on the pilot's integration of related organizational capacities within them (Van den Bosch *et al.* 1999; Noblet & Simon 2010).

Box 9.2. *The absorptive capacity of a social work training institution based on a study of two projects*

8 Local social development is a global approach of intervention that allows the capacity of people and groups to act on their environment to be developed, in order to encourage responsibility, the involvement of people in the solutions to their daily problems, the promotion of autonomy and citizenship.

Jansen *et al.* (2005) show that coordination, socialization and formalization capacities have effects on potential and achievement. Thus, capacities are exercised differently in the groups studied, particularly through a phenomenon of "bisociation" in the transformation phase (Zahra & Georges 2002), which is only present in the LSD group and produces a different realization for the organization. This phenomenon begins in the potential phase, through socialization mechanisms exercised by a collective interpretation of the shared reality, commonly called "common sense". A reflexivity between employee and student members, reinforced by the pilot's coordination capacity, produces new organizational routines. Nevertheless, reflexivity must also be exercised between the organization and the group through coordination mechanisms, such as regular management meetings, which ensure close monitoring of the progress of transformation projects. Sometimes, this passage comes up against the fact that the stakeholders who are comfortable questioning organizational routines (assimilation) are not necessarily those who wish to or are in charge of possible concrete deployments. Dutrieux (forthcoming) then draws inspiration from the work of Argyris (2003, p. 15), who defines actionable knowledge as being

> not only the knowledge that the world of practice demands; it is also the knowledge that serves to create it […]. From this perspective, action is not just about discovering new ideas and developing new policies; it is also about implementing those ideas and policies and evaluating their effectiveness.

The reflective dimension of actionable knowledge (Argyris 2003) makes it possible to overcome defensive routines that are detrimental to the development of organizational absorption capacities.

For example, Bucher and Langley (2016) analyze the deployment of public health projects through the mechanism of the strategic community, defined as a

> temporary structure for inter-organizational collaboration, composed of professionals, first-level managers, general practitioners, medical specialists, representatives of community organizations, etc., whose mandate is to generate, put into practice and evaluate new ideas regarding the organization of inter-organizational work. (Roy *et al.* 2011, p. 5)

This community is made up of two bodies, one in charge of promoting reflexive work in order to generate ideas by grasping new concepts that challenge established routines (reflexive space), and the other in charge of validating these ideas by deploying them in projects that must find their place in existing routines (experimentation space). Touati and Maillet (2017) deployed this analytical framework to study the deployment of innovations in sexual health practices in Montreal. While the reflexive space allowed for the production of new ideas and concrete proposals for action, their concrete deployment in experimentation did not withstand a major external change. For the authors, there will have been a lack of stakeholders who could make the link between these two spaces.

9.5. Conclusion

We have explored different experiences carried by healthcare organizations to overcome the three difficulties or pitfalls that can limit OAC: the entry into the absorption process, the "quality" of what is absorbed and the transition from the potential to the realized. The renewal offered by the perspective of absorptive capacities to rethink organizational innovation leads to the development of new ways of operating in a more collaborative and open manner, integrating ideas and stakeholders who still too often remain on the periphery of the institutionalized boundaries of these organizations. The examples developed thus enrich the literature on OAC by emphasizing the political dimension of the absorption process, understood in three ways:

1) by aligning (or enriching) the strategy of organizations;

2) by leaders and directors taking into account the stakes of knowledge management and common sense (Weick 1995), in a context where organizations are required to evolve;

3) by the development of new profiles of stakeholders, who, like the Broker and the "boundary actor", develop skills to make the institutional and cognitive silos of the healthcare field interact.

This chapter does not exhaust the forms of knowledge enhancement with respect to OAC in this field. The current stakes in many countries of a reorganization of resources in territories (or living basins) encourage organizations (and researchers) to analyze the extent to which their territory of action can be a lever for strengthening their capacity to open up and assimilate new ideas and knowledge. This then leads us to question the extent to which a territory of action can be conducive to different forms of proximity (geographical, cognitive, social and institutional) for Le Nadant *et al.* (2018), or of opportunities (Horvath & Dechamp 2016), when "creative collaborations are often based on intuition, a chance encounter, an opportunity seized together" (Horvath & Dechamp 2016, p. 155).

9.6. References

Arena, L. (2018). Économie collaborative, formes d'organisations et de travail – opportunités et risques d'un pseudo-nouveau paradigme en management. Quelles régulations pour l'économie collaborative ? *HALSHS*, May.

Argyris, C. (2003). *Savoir pour agir : surmonter les obstacles à l'apprentissage organisationnel.* Dunod, Paris.

Berta, W., Teare, G., Gilbart, E., Ginsburg, L., Lemieux-Charles, L., Davis, D., Rappolt, S. (2010). Spanning the know-do gap: Understanding knowledge application and capacity in long-term care homes. *Social Science & Medicine*, 70, 1326–1334.

Boltanski, L. and Chiapello, E. (2005). *Le nouvel esprit du capitalisme.* Gallimard, Paris.

Boltanski, L. and Thévenot, L. (1991). *De la justification : les économies de la grandeur.* Gallimard, Paris.

Bucher, S. and Langley, A. (2016). The interplay of reflective and experimental spaces in interrupting and reorienting routine dynamics. *Organization Science*, 27(3), 594–613.

Carlile, P. (2004). Transferring, translating and transforming: An integrative framework for managing knowledge across boundaries. *Organization Science*, 15(5), 55–568.

Cohen, W.M. and Levinthal, D.A. (1990). Absorptive capacity: A new perspective on learning and innovation. *Administrative Science Quarterly*, 35(1), 128–152.

Cooper, D.J. and Saral, K.J. (2013). Entrepreneurship and team participation: An experimental study. *European Economic Review*, 59, 126–140.

Daghfous, A. (2004). Organizational learning, knowledge and technology transfer: A case study. *The Learning Organization*, 11(1), 67–83.

Dali, K. (2008). Trois essais sur le concept de capacité d'absorption, leçons du cas Arcelor-Mittal dans les consortia de R&D en automobile. PhD Thesis, Université de Reims Champagne-Ardenne, Reims.

Denis, J.L., Lamothe, L., Langley, A. (2001). The dynamics of collective leadership and strategic change in pluralistic organizations. *Academy of Management Journal*, 44(4), 809–837.

Durand, R. (2006). *Organizational Evolution and Strategic Management.* SAGE Publications, Thousand Oaks.

Dutrieux, C. (forthcoming). L'articulation des capacités d'absorption organisationnelles avec les conventions de compromis : le cas d'un établissement de formation en travail social. Thesis, Aix-Marseille Université, Laboratoire CERGAM, Aix-Marseille.

Easterby-Smith, M., Graça, M., Antonacopoulou, E., Ferdinand, J. (2008). Absorptive capacity: A process perspective. *Management Learning*, 39, 483–501.

Feldman, M. and Pentland, B. (2003). Reconceptualizing organizational routines as a source of flexibility and change. *Administrative Science Quarterly*, 48, 94–118.

Glouberman, S. and Mintzberg, H. (2001). Managing the care of health and the cure of disease. Part I: Differentiation. Part II: Integration. *Health Care Management Review*, 26(1), 56–69, 70–84.

Grenier, C. (2019). Le changement et les processus transformationnels en milieux organisationnels publics. In *Gestion du changement en contexte et milieu organisationnel publics*, Mazouz, B., Gagnon, S. (eds). Presses de l'Université du Québec, Quebec.

Grenier, C. and Denis, J.L. (2017). S'organiser pour innover : espaces d'innovation et transformation des organisations et du champ de l'intervention publique. *Politique et management public*, 34, 191–206.

Harvey, G., Jas, P., Walshe, K. (2015). Analysing organisational context: Case studies on the contribution of absorptive capacity theory to understanding inter-organisational variation in performance improvement. *BMJ Quality & Safety*, 24(1), 48–55.

Horvath, I. and Dechamp, G. (2016). Quand les pouvoirs publics favorisent la proximité pour stimuler la créativité du territoire. *Gestion et management public*, 4(4), 139–155.

Imbert, G. and Chauvet, V. (2012). De la capacité d'absorption à la capacité d'insémination. *Revue française de gestion*, 221, 111–127.

Jansen, J.P., Van den Bosch, F.A., Volberta, H.W. (2005). Managing potential and realized absorptive capacity: How do organizational antecedents matter? *Academy of Management Journal*, 48(6), 999–1015.

Koestler, A. (2011). *Le cri d'Archimède : l'art de la découverte et la découverte de l'art*. Les Belles Lettres, Paris.

Le Nadant, A.L., Marinos, C., Krauss, G. (2018). Les espaces de coworking : le rôle des proximités dans les dynamiques collaboratives. *Revue française de gestion*, 272, 121–137.

Maus, A. and Sammut, S. (2017). Les structures d'accompagnement, des entreprises comme les autres. Contribution de la théorie des capacités dynamiques. *Gestion 2000*, 34, 203–206.

Mignon, S. (2009). La pérennité organisationnelle : un cadre d'analyse. *Revue française de gestion*, 192, 73–89.

Miller, D. (1992). *Le paradoxe d'Icare : comment les entreprises se tuent à réussir*. Presses universitaires de Laval, Quebec.

Munir, K. (2005). The social construction of events: A study of institutional change in the photographic field. *Organization Studies*, 26(1), 93–112.

Noblet, J.-P. and Simon, E. (2010). La capacité d'absorption, un état de l'art. *Management & Avenir*, 5(35), 33–50.

O'Reilly, C. and Tushman, M. (2004). The ambidextrous organization. *Harvard Business Review*, April, 74–81.

Orvain, J. and Angele-Halgand, N. (2011). Les manufactures de santé : l'art du compromis entre domesticité et industrie. *Sciences sociales et santé*, 29(1), 5–27.

Penin-Guérineau, A. (2018). Comment impulser une nouvelle dynamique au sein de la Fondation Erik et Odette Bocké : par quelle méthode rendre la structure plus innovante et plus ouverte en soutenant le développement de sa capacité à absorber des connaissances et des idées nouvelles ? MSAIS Thesis, KEDGE Business School.

Rogers, E. (2010). *Diffusion of Innovations*. Simon and Schuster, New York.

Roy, M., Audet, M., Gosselin, A.B., Lortie P., Fortier, L. (2011). La communauté stratégique : une approche pour développer la collaboration interorganisationnelle. Report, Fondation canadienne de la recherche sur les services de santé, Ottawa.

Todorova, G. and Durisin, B. (2007). Absorptive capacity: Valuing a reconceptualization. *Academy of Management Review*, 32(3), 774–786.

Touati, N. and Maillet, L. (2017). Soutenir l'émergence d'une écologie d'espaces d'innovation grâce à des communautés stratégiques : leçons d'une expérience au Québec. *Revue politiques et management public*, 34(3), 247–266.

Van Den Bosch, F.A.J., Van Wijk, R., Volberda, H.W. (2003). Absorptive capacity: Antecedents, models, and outcomes. In *Handbook of Organizational Learning and Knowledge Management*, Easterby-Smith, M., Lyles, M.A. (eds). Blackwell, Oxford.

Van der Yeught, C. (2017). Comment un intermédiaire en tourisme durable insémine des capacités dynamiques d'innovation responsable chez ses bénéficiaires. *Management & Avenir*, 91, 141–161.

Walshe, K., Harvey, G., Jas, P. (eds) (2010). *From Knowing to Doing: Connecting Knowledge and Performance in Public Services*. Cambridge University Press, Cambridge.

Weick, K.E. (1995). *Sensemaking in Organizations*. SAGE Publications, London.

Zahra, S.A. and George, G. (2002). Absorptive capacity: A review, reconceptualization, and extension. *Academy of Management Review*, 27(2), 185–203.

10

Quality Management in Hospitals: The Two Faces of Rationalization Through Indicators

10.1. Introduction: are quality indicators a managerial innovation?

Contemporary public action is marked by the proliferation of management, evaluation and comparison instruments. Presented as "innovations" by their promoters, these management tools claim to deploy new methods for optimizing organizations, improving the efficiency of professional activities or service quality. Hospitals, in particular, have been affected for several decades by reforms designed to optimize their organization and regulation (Pierru 2007), by the deployment of management techniques from the commercial sector (Belorgey 2010), by activity-based pricing instruments (Juven 2015) and by systems for assessing the quality of care (Castel & Robelet 2009). Based to a large extent on the commitment of professionals, the dynamic around quality has been sedimented in various systems: certification of healthcare institutions by the French High Authority for Health (*Haute Autorité de santé*, HAS), reference systems for practice and evaluation of professional practices. This chapter focuses on one of the most striking innovations in the field of quality assessment: comparative indicators which, since the end of the 2000s, have been integrated into the certification procedure and made public at national level.

By mobilizing an approach at the crossroads of the sociology of public action, organizations and management, this chapter deconstructs this managerial innovation in order to analyze its effects in healthcare institutions. In section 10.2, we will outline the context of the emergence of these systems from the end of the 1990s and

Chapter written by Hugo BERTILLOT.

the issues they raise. Then, in section 10.3, we will explain the theoretical question of the relationship between management tools and rationalization dynamics in professional organizations, while showing how we have worked on it in our empirical approach. The results will be presented in sections 10.4 and 10.5, which will analyze the two faces – professional and managerial – of the rationalization dynamics induced by quality indicators in hospitals, before being the subject of a concluding discussion (section 10.6).

10.2. Context and issues

Before understanding how these quality indicators can affect healthcare institutions, it is necessary to briefly review their history. The aim here is not to propose an in-depth analysis of the sociogenesis of quality indicators, which is dealt with elsewhere (Bertillot 2016), but to sketch out the context in which they emerged in order to better understand some of their characteristics.

10.2.1. *An institutional response in the context of a confidence crisis*

In the second half of the 1990s, the question of measuring hospital quality gradually emerged as a public issue in France, under the cross-influence of several social dynamics, foremost among which was the militancy of the association Le Lien, representing the victims of nosocomial infections, and the publication of the first hospital blacklists and rankings. These publications have led to clear-cut positions on the part of hostile federations and representatives of professionals, who have denounced in chorus their methodology deemed unreliable and their effects in terms of stigmatization of hospitals or medical services.

Faced with these approaches, which were considered brutal, administrative and political leaders, who were themselves blamed for their inability to evaluate and control the quality of healthcare institutions, began to look for a more legitimate quality assessment system, developed under the aegis of the State, capable of providing patients with rankings based on information collected in hospitals and clinics. At the turn of the 2000s, this development work took the form of institutional support for the handful of expert researchers in management or public health who were familiar with medico-administrative databases. During the 2000s, this expertise in metrology was gradually structured to develop quality indicators, through a methodology leading to a panel of about 10 indicators considered acceptable to health professionals, generalized from 2005 on at the national level. Since then, these quality indicators have gained the support of hospital federations and certain medical learned societies. Displayed on the institutional Websites of the Ministry of Health and the HAS, on hospital webpages, they are also included in hospital rankings published in the press. Most often, they are also visible in the form of posters in the administrative reception areas of institutions.

10.2.2. *From cautious indicators to equivocal uses*

Most of these indicators are process indicators, which do not measure the results of care, but rather the organization of the quality management policy or the traceability of care based on information collected in administrative documents (particularly the patient record). For example, the indicator called the "Composite Index of Activities for the Control of Nosocomial Infections" (*indice composite des activités de lutte contre les infections nosocomiales*, ICALIN) assesses the organization of local policy, the human resources deployed and the actions implemented for the prevention of nosocomial infections. The Patient Record Keeping (*tenue du dossier patient*, TDP) indicator assesses the TDP by noting the presence of a number of pieces of information or documents in the file (admission document, entry medical examination, discharge treatment writing, prescription timestamp, etc.). Other measures are more like resource indicators, as is the case with the indicator entitled "consumption index of hydroalcoholic solutions" (*indice de consommation des solutions hydroalcooliques*, ICSHA), which evaluates the volume of hydroalcoholic solutions purchased in comparison with a target set according to the characteristics and activity of each establishment.

While a few indicators are closer to outcome indicators in the sense that they measure the traceability of practices recommended in the guidelines of learned societies concerning specific pathologies (such as the management of myocardial infarction in its acute phase), none are constructed to evaluate the results of care in terms of mortality, unlike the criteria mobilized by the first hospital blacklists. These indicators measure quality at the level of the healthcare establishment rather than at the level of hospital departments or practitioners, so as not to directly implicate individuals or teams, as was the case with the blacklists published in the press at the end of the 1990s. The conditions of data collection give an important place to professionals: most of these indicators require specific work to verify criteria from randomly selected samples of patient records.

These quality indicators are distinguished by the ambiguity of their social uses. They have been constructed to equip three types of uses that are not mutually exclusive and that can serve the objectives of the different stakeholders involved in the process of their construction. First of all, they are presented as an instrument for regulating the hospital system. At the national level, since 2009, the indicators have been integrated into the HAS certification process for establishments, with the aim of reinforcing its objectivity. They can also be used by regional healthcare agencies in their management contracts with hospitals as a decision-making tool and an incentive to improve service. The use of indicators in performance-based payment mechanisms has been tested since mid-2010. The quality indicators are then presented as an internal driver for quality improvement at the level of the establishments, which can be used by all stakeholders involved in this area: directors in charge of quality, individuals in charge of quality and risk management, doctors and healthcare nurses and healthcare professionals participating in the various quality-related committees. Finally, these indicators are designed to provide valid information about quality to any patient who has to choose a hospital, according to a principle of democracy and transparency: a ministerial Website was created in 2006 to publicly display this information, which is also made available by all the establishments and included in most of the hospital rankings.

10.3. Management tools and organizational rationalization dynamics

These indicators are part of the long history of hospital rationalization projects. They allow us to question the links between management tools and organizational rationalization dynamics.

10.3.1. *What rationalization of professional organizations?*

While they have come to generate strong national mobilization, the ability of indicators to transform hospitals is far from self-evident. One might even consider that healthcare institutions present a context that is *a priori* unfavorable to the implementation of this type of device, notably because of the traditionally strong autonomy of the medical profession (Hassenteufel 1997), the esoteric and difficult to codify character of medical know-how (Bezès *et al.* 2011, p. 310) and the specific characteristics of professional bureaucracies in which external control devices are traditionally highly contested (Power 2005, p. 108). This questioning is similar to that highlighted by the literature that has focused on rationalization and standardization approaches in industry (Segrestin 1996), in the broader field of "professional services" (Gadrey 1994), or in the medical world (Timmermans & Berg 2003; Castel & Robelet 2009). All this research underlines, more or less explicitly, the relationship between quality systems and Weberian dynamics for rationalizing social activities: standards, certifications or quality management tools are likely to drive the development of formalization, calculability and predictability within organizations. This rationalization may also be accompanied by renewed bureaucratic forms and reaffirmed hierarchical control.

A central tension runs through this literature. On the one hand, the deployment of quality assessment systems would be similar to a *professional rationalization* process, which would lead to "rationalizing medicine without standardizing it"

(Castel & Robelet 2009), leaving significant room for maneuver to professionals. Such professional approaches seek to improve the efficiency of healthcare practices, notably by equipping professional judgment with new knowledge, new tools and new ways of reasoning. They are common in "professional services", for which the "industrialization" of work and organizations seems all the more unlikely since professionals have mastered the routine activity (Gadrey 1994). On the other hand, it is an *industrial* or *neomanagerial rationalization* that is highlighted in research on *New Public Management* in the healthcare sector (Belorgey 2010; Mas *et al.* 2011). The deployment of performance assessment instruments, under the aegis of a state that has become "neoliberal", would have the consequence of putting professionals under greater pressure from neomanagerial power and increased economic competition, threatening professional autonomy. Such managerial approaches can be driven by the rise of industrial criteria for judging performance, based on quantitative managerial instruments, putting increased pressure on professionals through the evaluation of work productivity or customer satisfaction. To what extent are quality indicators involved in rationalization processes of both types?

10.3.2. *Investigating rationalization induced by quality indicators*

In this chapter, we would like to contribute to these reflections on the basis of an empirical investigation, based on a thesis devoted to the transformation processes that quality indicators induce in the hospital sector (Bertillot 2014). Anchored in the sociology of organized action (Musselin 2005) and the sociology of management, the approach mobilized took the instrumental and cognitive dimension of these indicators into account. The methodology consisted of capturing the indicators *in vivo* within four institutions chosen to be comparable while presenting various contexts. Among the common characteristics of the establishments: an average size (between 200 and 300 beds) and standard activities in medicine, surgery and obstetrics corresponding to the situation of many French establishments. The singular characteristics of the surveyed establishments made it possible to mix the status, geographical situations and regional institutional contexts. For the sake of clarity, we will refer to the different establishments with capital letters (Public Hospital, Private Clinics 1 and 2 and Private Hospital of Collective Interest), so as to avoid any confusion with more general statements about the "public hospital", for example. We conducted four interview campaigns involving a presence on site for a few weeks. In total, just over 90 interviews were conducted between 2009 and 2011 with hospital stakeholders, with a mix of hierarchical levels and professional affiliations. These stakeholders were questioned about their perceptions of the quality policy in general and the measurement systems in particular, and about the way in which they mobilize them (or not) in their activities. Particular attention was placed on the perceptions of the situation in institutions, professional activities and relationships in organizations.

These interviews were supplemented by a smaller number of observations, informal discussions and documentary analyses. Sections 10.4 and 10.5 present the results of the survey, successively questioning the professional and managerial dimensions of the rationalization induced by the indicators.

10.4. A dynamic of professional rationalization?

The formalization, standardization and monitoring of activities, through writing and evaluation devices, are classic aspects of professional rationalization approaches (Gadrey 1994). In its scholarly form, the hospital quality assessment is part of a more rationalized approach to practices, designed to equip professional judgment with new knowledge, new tools and new modes of reasoning. Indicators are part of this movement.

10.4.1. *Standardization of professional practices*

Firstly, the indicators are part of the vast movement to standardize professional practices in hospitals, through the formalization of protocols and a certain homogenization of practices. Other studies have shown that this standardization constitutes a resource for professionals: it has made it possible to organize care, codify complex situations, mark out practices and simplify work, without reducing the autonomy of professional judgment (Castel & Merle 2002).

While numerical evaluation approaches have the power to institute and standardize the categories they claim to describe (Desrosières 2014), the criteria measured by the various quality indicators come from a set of rules established in interaction with certain medical learned societies. By assessing the compliance of local practices with professional standards, the indicators are likely to strengthen the latter's hold. For example, indicators that standardize hygiene practices and the prevention of nosocomial infections have strong effects in terms of standardization. Institutions have formalized their policies for preventing nosocomial infections by recruiting operational hygiene teams and setting up nosocomial infection control committees, which have encouraged caregivers to stop wearing jewelry that could carry germs, and to change handwashing practices and care kits. This major trend is recognized as a progress in patient care by most professionals.

Indicators from the Ministry of Health's Nosocomial Infection Control Dashboard played a role in giving strength to professional recommendations. At the Public Hospital, the Medical Officer of Health and the hospital's Nurse Health Officer have been working since 2003 to convince surgeons and anesthesiologists in the operating room to change their hand disinfection practices. The aim is to ensure the local application of a recommendation of the French Society of Hospital Hygiene (*société française d'hygiène hospitalière*) published in 2001, which establishes the superiority of hand disinfection with hydro-alcoholic solutions over surgical hand washing with Bétadine. Hydro-alcoholic disinfection is less restrictive; it is also considered to be more effective, and therefore likely to limit the risk of infection. However, getting operating room professionals to adhere to it has proven to be difficult. Having been accustomed to different hand washing procedures for years, it took time for them to convert to this new practice. It was the publication of the hospital's "bad" score on the ICSHA (ICSHA Indicator of Hydroalcoholic Solution Consumption) that changed the team's practices:

> As far as hydro-alcoholic solutions are concerned, we were fed up with them! We had been taught to wash our hands for years, so we had to stop using the product like that ... The former nurses, they had a hard time. So in 2006, when we told them that the indicators were not good at all in terms of quality, it moved them! (Nurse, hygiene referent, anesthesia unit, operating theater, public hospital)

Mobilized alongside other systems, the indicators also allow for local objectification of infections, and thus for the institution of their prevention as a proper and legitimate professional activity. By providing data and equipping the intellectual methods by which professionals can reflect on risks, these indicators are similar to cognitive tools that enable forms of learning. The Surgical Site Infection Surveillance (SURVISO) indicator has prompted surgeons and anesthesiologists to increasingly report and monitor their nosocomial infection rates by type of surgical procedure. Getting into the habit of reporting infections has not been easy to accept. While surgeons have been particularly reluctant, with a few years of hindsight, operating room professionals consider that the monitoring of these two indicators has shed light on the frequency of nosocomial infections. Although practices did not change overnight with regard to infections, the measurement of their rates was, at the end of the 2000s, considered to be one of the relevant criteria for evaluating the quality of professional work in the operating theater. The indicators thus contribute to a cognitive type of professional rationalization, involving the formalization of problem-solving procedures and the use of a repertoire of validated routines to prevent healthcare-associated infections.

10.4.2. *Traceability of hospital activities*

Secondly, the indicators are closely related to the traceability of medical practices, which is an important aspect of the rationalization initiatives deployed by professionals. Other studies have shown how formalized medical protocols can become structural tools for coordinating care (Timmermans & Berg 2003). It is no coincidence that record evaluation has been placed at the heart of quality indicators: indicators of patient record keeping, anesthetic record keeping and pain traceability play a leading role here, by measuring the rate of patient records judged to be "in line" with institutional expectations, based on the evaluation of criteria for the traceability of certain information. Many professionals consider that this dynamic, beyond its burdensome dimension, can constitute a form of progress in practice.

On the one hand, certain aspects of healthcare activities that have long been considered peripheral to healthcare activities become more important when their written record in the patient record is subject to a targeted evaluation by an indicator. Through a mechanism well identified in the literature, "commensuration" reinforces and transforms the attention paid to the information evaluated (Espeland & Sauder 2007). What is measured becomes more important in the eyes of professionals, who recognize the value of these practices that were previously too often neglected. For example, the rigorous and precise writing of drug prescriptions is assessed through the patient record keeping indicator. However, for a long time, the traceability of prescriptions has been neglected in favor of other more noble dimensions of the medical activity. Over the last 10 years or so, a more rigorous traceability of prescriptions has been progressively imposed in the four healthcare establishments. Healthcare professionals perceive this evolution as an undeniable improvement in practice. This is also the case for the quantified evaluation of pain by caregivers. The fact that the pain assessment process has been mapped out has resulted in the systematization of this assessment practice:

> Before, we used to ask, but it was less systematic. Now that we trace, we measure pain as we measure tension, in fact. Every time we take a turn, we ask the patient if they're in pain, and if they're in pain, we give them medication. For me, as a nurse, that's one of the really important things! (Internal Medicine Nurse, Private Community Hospital)

On the other hand, this traceability is a necessary condition for the safety of the healthcare chain between the different professionals who collaborate in the care. The main quality indicators, through traceability, evaluate the sharing of information during hospitalization, which proves to be a crucial issue. Based on their daily experience, practitioners are well aware that many care problems stem less from a lack of qualification in care acts than from a flaw in the interfaces between the different professionals who must cooperate in care. The traceability of information is crucial for coordination between professionals within a healthcare service. It is a guarantee of legibility and predictability in the handover between teams. In some extreme cases, this information is as essential as the opportunity to resuscitate a patient in a cardiology department which, if it proves to be missing, can be the cause of serious failures:

> The first thing ICU does is try to determine whether or not resuscitation is necessary. However, it is a very brief moment, and if the doctors who are supposed to take care of this patient are not there when the question arises ... If nothing is written on the file, the ICU can do a lot of mistakes! So these indicators, it has consequences! They allow the transmission of information to evolve. That's what makes them interesting. (Cardiologist, private hospital of collective interest)

Finally, the coordination of the care work with the outside world depends on the proper traceability of the information in the patient file, and its timely transmission to the attending physicians or downstream institutions.

Of course, professionals did not wait for the quality indicators to coordinate, through notes, notebooks, phone calls or informal exchanges, which are still often preferred. However, the current evolution toward a systematization, a formalization, a codification of this traceability, plays in the direction of a rationalization of the coordination of the work of care. If these instruments have a certain amount of support from professionals, it is because this rationalization offers greater comfort, security and, finally, predictability in the practice of professional work. All the more so as this introduction of traceability comes to protect those who play the game, while those who resist it can be blamed at the slightest problem.

10.4.3. *The local rooting of evidence-based medicine*

Finally, the indicators contribute to a more locally rooted *evidence-based* approach to medicine. This long-term movement became increasingly prevalent in the last decades of the 20th century, alongside – and often to the detriment of – more empirical approaches to the medical "art", which have not completely disappeared (Timmermans & Berg 2003). Linked to various other devices, indicators become the vectors of this dynamic.

On the one hand, the indicators contribute to the development of a more quantitative evaluation of professional practices. While for a long time the quality policy in hospitals was based on a very *qualitative* approach to evaluation, the physicians who are nowadays involved in the evaluation of professional practices are getting into the habit of measuring certain aspects of their activities, which they choose independently and according to the problems they encounter in their daily activities. For example, the resuscitation physicians of the *Hôpital privé d'intérêt collectif* have chosen to work on a concrete problem, which is not directly evaluated by official national indicators, but which has strong affinities with their philosophy of measurement and traceability: the management of intra-hospital cardiac arrest, which requires the intervention of resuscitators in the other departments of the hospital. First and foremost, it was a question of evaluating the relevance of this type of emergency intervention, which the institution's resuscitators experience on average once every 2 weeks. This intervention is characterized by a very high failure rate. It is therefore as disruptive as it is demoralizing for the resuscitators. The resuscitators invented their own evaluation grid and two practitioners from the department audited all the files concerned over a period of 1 year, in order to calculate the survival rate. This evaluation work not only made it possible to "deduce" mortality, but it also quickly revealed major shortcomings in the traceability of information:

> We didn't even have the layout! It's delirious. SAMU (French ambulance service) brings you a cardiac arrest patient, they have the [cardiological] charts, they know how long it lasted. And us, it was written "cardiac arrest", and nothing else! It's catastrophic … I don't mean to say that the treatment was not good, but the traceability was nil! And it's all the same arguments to know how far we go in recovery: if the arrest lasted 2 minutes, it's not the same as if it lasted 10 minutes. We realized that, sometimes, we stopped after 2 minutes of resuscitation, without any noted argumentation. I don't mind stopping after 2 minutes, but you have to be able to explain! It is necessary to say "OK, but they're 90 years old", there you go, reasonable things. (Resuscitating doctor, Private hospital of collective interest)

Following this evaluation, presented as a revelation by this doctor, the department considerably modified the intervention protocol, providing for an assessment sheet to specifically trace the management, with a care assistant participating in the intervention exclusively to trace the information and to retrieve an electrocardiogram printout. While resuscitators do not expect a reduction in mortality from these changes, the assessment was useful in addressing these traceability issues and confirming the value of continuing these management procedures. This example shows that this type of quantitative evaluation of practitioners, far from being limited to process or resource analyses, is now coming to touch on issues at the heart of management, through the analysis of activities directly related to the life and death of patients.

On the other hand, the indicators contribute to a more formalized approach to care. By conveying new reasoning within hospitals, they have their own effect on the cognition of professionals, and contribute to the transition from an approach centered on the individual benefit of practices for the patient to a more systemic and collective approach. The composite index of good antibiotic use contributes, for example, to transform antibiotic prescription practices. In the context of a national policy that seeks to limit consumption, this indicator measures the level of commitment of the healthcare institution to a strategy for optimizing antibiotic effectiveness. In recent years, institutions have been measuring their consumption. For practitioners, reducing the volume of antibiotics prescribed implies ceasing to think solely in terms of individual benefit for a single patient (maximizing the chances of avoiding an infection), in order to integrate a risk that is collective in nature (avoiding the emergence of resistant germs). By comparing infection rates and changes in antibiotic consumption, it is possible to develop an epidemiological reasoning at the local level.

In short, the study of the local effects of quality evaluation instruments allows us to defend the thesis of a *professional* dynamic of hospital transformation. Using a set of devices, more and more professionals have learned to formalize, codify and evaluate their activities in an increasing way. Although indicators are not the only vectors of this rationalization, they contribute to it through converging effects in the establishments. Is it appropriate, however, to state that quality indicators contribute to the *essentially* professional rationalization of the hospital? In our opinion, this thesis needs to be qualified. Professional uses are deployed within the limits of a constraining bureaucratic framework. Although professional autonomy has not disappeared, it has become intertwined with forms of control that are at least partly beyond the control of professionals.

10.5. A dynamic of managerial rationalization?

The place of the "industrial figure" in the conception of quality assessment (Castel & Robelet 2009) raises the question of the managerial dimension of hospital rationalization. According to Gadrey (1994, pp. 174–178), the industrialization of professional services should not be understood only in the strong sense of task standardization and process automation, to the detriment of professional autonomy. In its weak variant, it corresponds more to the development of industrial criteria for judging performance, based on quantitative instruments, which are likely to put increased pressure on professionals through the evaluation of their work. To what extent do quality indicators contribute to such a dynamic?

10.5.1. *Control and competition*

As metrological instruments with a certain robustness, quality indicators produce measurements that are compared and displayed publicly. They thus resemble "neo-liberal quantification", which is likely to put pressure on professional organizations, as described by Desrosières (2014).

On the one hand, they contribute to strengthening the control exercised by public institutions by making professional organizations more *auditable* (Power 2005), i.e. more describable, analyzable and controllable. By inducing increased traceability of activities, the indicators make professionals more accountable to patients and regulatory authorities. This doctor from the Department of Medial Information describes his perception of the rise of asymmetrical bureaucratic control well:

> The public authorities, health agencies, they have all the data! They see the hospital from every angle, you have the quality tips, the program for the mediatization of information systems, the annual statistics of health establishments [...] you have everything! They do an extraction of these things. These people, it's their job, so then when they inspect the hospitals, they're going to give this to hypercompetent people, they're going to come in and say: "We have all the hospital data." And if behind, in the hospital, we don't have the time to be able to appropriate the tools and to be able to discuss ... We are not on the same scale! Behind, indeed, there is the whole steamroller of the State, the General Inspectorate of Social Affairs or others, efficient people, at the level, who know how to analyze the figures, and opposite you have a small establishment that tries to get by ... (Physician from the Medical Information Department, Private Hospital of Collective Interest)

It is not necessary to adhere to the principles of quality indicators for them to induce a form of self-discipline: it is enough to anticipate the monitoring to which they contribute to find a reason to comply with them. As soon as an administrative sanction is conceivable, quality indicators have the capacity to define the standard that must be approached and the area of non-compliance that must be avoided.

On the other hand, the quality indicators contribute to a discreet competition between establishments. With the deployment of activity-based pricing, new regional "objectives and means contracts" and the increase in the number of hospital mergers, it is difficult to deny that a general competitive bidding process has been in place in French healthcare institutions since the early 2000s. Quality indicators contribute to this dynamic by helping, alongside other systems, to root comparative practices within healthcare institutions. Incorporated into hospital rankings since the end of the 2000s, they have a very clear disciplinary effect on managers and certain professionals in the institutions most exposed to competition. This urologist, although he does not mince his words in criticizing the rankings, clearly explains the importance of appearing among the "best" in the results of indicators related to nosocomial infections:

> When these rankings came out 10 years ago, we all laughed ... But the problem is that you have to deal with it! It comes out every two months

> ... And the patients bring it to the consultation, don't they? [...] Well, now when we appear in these bullshit rankings, we're in a pretty good position in nosocomial care. It's an important element for the public, and overall we've succeeded, we've gone from C, we've moved on to A. The result is that now, in the rankings, even if the criteria are what they are, we don't have to worry about the column "prevention of nosocomial infections"! (Urologist, Private hospital of collective interest)

However, this evolution is not neutral: in return, these rankings, which include these indicators, contribute to an increased perception of the competition that is being established between institutions. They are now part of the elements that are taken into account in the competitive analysis. While comparing oneself to other professionals or other institutions is obviously not new, indicators contribute to changing the situation by anchoring these comparisons in more formalized and rationalized information systems.

Through their disciplinary power, quality indicators are able to subtly transform the way stakeholders categorize their activities and make sense of the social world around them. Willingly or unwillingly, professionals are now getting resigned to the rise of external forms of control over their activities.

10.5.2. *Rationalization and bureaucratization*

The dynamic of rationalization of social activities not only leads to increased efficiency, but it is also accompanied by increased social control and a colder, more rigid and impersonal form of rational legal domination that weighs on individuals. Social stakeholders are as if trapped in a bureaucratic "iron cage" (Weber 1921). Indicators participate in this movement in two ways.

On the one hand, their deployment is concomitant with a more brutal economic rationalization dynamic over the last 15 years. Three of the four establishments we surveyed were strongly affected by the implementation of activity-based pricing. The deployment of measures concerning the safety of care, risk management, quality and standardization of practices can be interpreted as the counterpart of this vast movement to control expenditure. Many professionals grasp this implicit link between two forms of rationalization in their daily activities. They emphasize that the reduction in average length of stay, the acceleration of patient turnover, the deployment of medico-economic coding and the intensification of work make it necessary to take steps to formalize and codify medical activities, to organize continuity of care and to standardize practices, without which the search for productivity could only have harmful consequences on the care process. If traceability is a way of organizing continuity of care made necessary by the intensification of work and the reduction of informal coordination time, it also makes it possible to transfer the medico-legal responsibility for the risks linked to the economic pressures weighing on the establishments to local professional actors.

On the other hand, the traceability of care activities, which is costly in time and energy, is experienced as a real burden by some professionals. While doctors are the first to denounce a drift away from their core profession, they often manage to relieve themselves of their administrative tasks by having them carried out by their medical secretaries, department managers or nursing staff, who are more exposed to the intensification of work induced by the increasing use of the written word. In particular, these professionals regret a form of dehumanization of care work, linked to the rise of this so-called "administrative" time, to the detriment of time spent with patients. For them, the informal dimensions of the work (listening, contact, empathy and reassurance) are an integral part of a quality healthcare activity. With the indicators, they regret that the auditable aspects of care are *de facto* highlighted in the eyes of all, to the detriment of the informal aspects deprived of this visibility. This general feeling is particularly acute in the cancer department of the *Hôpital privé d'intérêt collectif*. The nurse who works in palliative care coordination lives her activity as a strong personal commitment to accompanying people at the end of life. It is with suspicion that she considers the effects of the traceability of pain assessment in the patient record, valued by the indicator:

> It is "written" … But in my opinion, you make a cross, you put a pain at 7, you mark the prescription, you have done your job! But what does that evaluate in terms of the quality of your work? You can't say that you've done your job *well*. […] A patient who twists himself in pain and who says "Madam, I'm in pain", it calls out to me in the same way! [laughter]. There is a relationship, and you realize that staying 5 minutes, when you leave the room, it hurts less … By bringing a little something about listening and being present, the pain is sometimes more bearable …. (Experienced nurse, cancerology, Private Community Hospital)

The rise of written objectification and quantification is thus accompanied by an intensification of work, a form of depersonalization of the care relationship and growing bureaucratic rigidity.

10.5.3. *A certain disenchantment with the hospital world*

Quality indicators contribute to a more general disenchantment of many stakeholders with their professional activities. This disenchantment can be seen first of all in the feeling of an indictment of the skills and motivations of professionals, which many stakeholders testify to. Professionals regret the generalized suspicion that reigns in terms of safety as well as in terms of the productivity of care work. Other professionals establish a clear link between the "quantified" quality evaluation process and the feeling that their skills are being called into question, or that they are not being recognized:

> I don't like being computerized! [laughter]. These people who make statistics, I think they're wasting their time! [...] All these people who come to see how we do things, they sincerely believe that it's to make things work better. I'm willing to do that. But we've had training, and we know how to work! (Experienced nurse, Private Clinic 1)

More generally, it is the feeling of no longer being able to fully control the evolution of requirements in the content of the practices around the care that characterizes the perception of many professionals.

This disenchantment is not unrelated to the various medico-legal cases that have been visible in the media over the last 20 years or so, and it also takes the form of a strong sense of insecurity in the day-to-day practice of professional activities, which is particularly prevalent among practitioners practicing high-risk specialties such as anesthesia or surgery, as well as among nurses exposed to medication errors. In a general context of work intensification, increasing recourse to temporary work, task shifting and increased traceability constraints, many professionals report anxiety in the face of a medico-legal risk that they feel is increasing. They feel they are taking risks and feel threatened by the possibility of an accident.

Finally, this disenchantment takes the form, which is well shared by the various professional groups, of a loss of meaning in healthcare activities, for individuals who no longer "recognize themselves" in these anxiety-provoking developments in the hospital sector. Some professionals use harsh terms to describe the evolution of their work context, attributing it to a form of "industrialization" of care:

> Since we've been told about quality, we're just not into quality anymore! We're in the slaughtering business. In profitability. But it's not just here, eh? We're in the society of profit, and of the CAC 40! Our work has evolved very badly [sour laughter]. [...] It's since we started talking about "clients" instead of "patients". It happened like that, following the two accreditations. (Nurse, Surgery Department, Private Clinic 1)

If such references to the industry's "counter-model" are numerous in the interviews, it is because they are a way for the professionals to report on this host of changes in which they are caught up and no longer recognize themselves. At the same time, they make it possible to underline the specificities of the hospital sector and the dangers of what they perceive as an absurd hospital-company model. If this disenchantment is far from being linked solely to the generalization of quality indicators, the latter are directly involved in it, in their links with traceability, auditability and bureaucratic control.

In short, to a certain extent, the study of the local effects of quality indicators allows us to defend the thesis of a *managerial* dynamic of hospital transformation. Through their effects of quantification, equivalence and transparency, they do not only constitute resources for certain professionals able to reappropriate the measures. At the same time, they also carry a form of exogenous control over hospital professionals, many of whom feel trapped by the deployment of an "iron cage" of measures and constraints that weigh on them.

10.6. Conclusion: rationalizing through indicators to rationalize "softly"

Far from being fixed and immutable professional bureaucracies, healthcare institutions today are in motion. On the one hand, the indicators are part of a professional dynamic: they are perceived as a *resource* mobilized by professionals in their activities and local relationships. On the other hand, they are part of a new external *constraint*, with a straitjacket of equivalence, transparency, surveillance, control and discipline. These two dynamics are indeed the two distinct but irremediably linked sides of the same process, which are intertwined to convey an increase in the formalization, codification, traceability, calculability and predictability of certain aspects of hospital activities. These two contrasting faces of rationalization thus benefit from being analyzed in their articulation, their complexity, their ambivalence and their paradoxes. The social power of indicators is therefore based on the interweaving of a "light side" and a "dark side" in the eyes of professionals, on their capacity to be mobilized as resources and constraints, to be perceived as professional and managerial devices, to arouse adhesion *and* anxiety, and to be grafted onto local *and* institutional uses.

This result leads to overcoming the opposition between the two theses discussed in this chapter. While each of them allows us to account for an essential dimension of the rationalization process at work, neither one alone captures the whole picture. The proponents of professional rationalization rightly insist on the ability of reflexive and strategic professionals to reapprove and locally adapt quality systems. However, the interpretive framework they propose leads to a reduction in the weight and effectiveness of the constraint that can be exerted on the stakeholders through metrological devices endowed with a certain rigidity, which the critical authors of *New Public Management* have examined with greater precision. This constraint, once it is relayed and internalized by the professionals through disciplinary processes, can lead to a powerful movement toward the standardization of practices, which an approach that is above all attentive to contingencies, strategic reappropriation and heterogeneity cannot fully grasp.

To overcome this schematic opposition, we can consider that the unexpected capacity of quality indicators to transform organized professional contexts comes to a large extent from their original modus operandi: they instill a *soft* rationalization. The deployment of these indicators on a local scale is far from being antithetical to the exercise of institutional constraints. The equivocal and unsuccessful external uses of indicators, their plasticity and their composite character allow a certain amount of play to exist at the local level around binding rules. Softness is a major condition of the capacity of institutional constraints to penetrate local contexts. Fueled by a multitude of factors, it gives multiple catches to the rationalization process, guaranteeing its deployment and effectiveness.

10.7. References

Belorgey, N. (2010). *L'hôpital sous pression : enquête sur le "nouveau management public"*. La Découverte, Paris.

Bertillot, H. (2014). La rationalisation en douceur : sociologie des indicateurs qualité à l'hôpital. PhD Thesis, Institut d'études politiques, Paris.

Bertillot, H. (2016). Des indicateurs pour gouverner la qualité hospitalière : socio-genèse d'une rationalisation en douceur. *Sociologie du travail*, 58(3), 227–252.

Bezes, P., Demazière, D., Le Bianic, T., Paradeise, C., Normand, R., Benamouzig, D., Pierru, F., Evetts, J. (2011). New Public Management et professions dans l'État : au-delà des oppositions, quelles recompositions ? *Sociologie du travail*, 53(3), 293–348.

Castel, P. and Merle, I. (2002). Quand les normes de pratiques deviennent une ressource pour les médecins. *Sociologie du travail*, 44(3), 337–355.

Castel, P. and Robelet, M. (2009). Comment rationaliser sans standardiser la médecine ? Production et usages des recommandations de pratiques cliniques. *Journal d'économie médicale*, 27(3), 98–115.

Desrosières, A. (2014). *Prouver et gouverner*. La Découverte, Paris.

Espeland, W.N. and Sauder, M. (2007). Rankings and reactivity: How public measures recreate social worlds. *American Journal of Sociology*, 113(1), 1–40.

Gadrey, J. (1994). La modernisation des services professionnels : rationalisation industrielle ou rationalisation professionnelle ? *Revue française de sociologie*, 35(2), 163–195.

Hassenteufel, P. (1997). *Les médecins face à l'État : une comparaison européenne*. Presses de Sciences Po, Paris.

Juven, P.-A. (2015). *Une santé qui compte ? Coûts et tarifs dans la politique hospitalière française*. PUF, Paris.

Mas, B., Pierru, F., Smolski, N., Torrielli, R. (2011). *L'hôpital en réanimation*. Éditions du Croquant, Paris.

Musselin, C. (2005). Sociologie de l'action organisée et analyse des politiques publiques : deux approches pour un même objet ? *Revue française de science politique*, 55(1), 51–71.

Pierru, F. (2007). *Hippocrate malade de ses réformes*. Éditions du Croquant, Paris.

Power, M. (2005). *La société de l'audit : l'obsession du contrôle*. La Découverte, Paris.

Segrestin, D. (1996). La normalisation de la qualité et l'évolution de la relation de production. *Revue d'économie industrielle*, 75(1), 291–307.

Timmermans, S. and Berg, M. (2003). *The Gold Standard: The Challenge of Evidence-based Medicine and Standardization in Health Care*. Temple University Press, Philadelphia.

List of Authors

Hugo BERTILLOT
HADEPAS
Université Catholique de Lille
France

Christian BOURRET
DICEN IDF
Université Gustave Eiffel – Paris-Est
Marne-la-Vallée
France

Sandrine CUEILLE
ECM-CREG
Université de Pau et des Pays de l'Adour
France

Jean-Louis DENIS
École de santé publique
Université de Montréal
Canada

Christine DUTRIEUX
IRTS Nouvelle-Aquitaine
Talence
France

Luigi FLORA
RETINES
Université Côte d'Azur
Nice
France

Jessica GHELLER
DICEN IDF
Marne-la-Vallée
France

Frédéric GILBERT
École des sciences de la gestion
Université du Québec à Montréal
Canada

Corinne GRENIER
KEDGE Business School
Marseille
France

Christelle HAVARD
CEREN
Burgundy School of Business
Dijon
France

Gérard MICK
P2S
Université Lyon I
France

Philippe MOSSÉ
LEST-CNRS-AMU
Aix-en-Provence
France

Norbert NABET
NEHS
Paris
France

Ewan OIRY
École des sciences de la gestion
Université du Québec à Montréal
Canada

Bertrand PAUGET
Karlstad University
Sweden

Tamara ROBERTS
Université de Bordeaux
France

Matthieu SIBÉ
EMOS
Université de Bordeaux
France

Delphine WANNENMACHER
CEREFIGE
Université de Lorraine
Nancy
France

Index

F, G, H

I

L, M

N, O

P

R, S

T

V, U

Other titles from

iSTE

in

Innovation, Entrepreneurship and Management

2021

ARCADE Jacques
Strategic Engineering (Innovation and Technology Set – Volume 11)

BOBILLIER CHAUMON Marc-Eric
Digital Transformations in the Challenge of Activity and Work: Understanding and Supporting Technological Changes (Technological Changes and Human Resources Set – Volume 3)

BUCLET Nicolas
Territorial Ecology and Socio-ecological Transition (Smart Innovation Set – Volume 34)

DIMOTIKALIS Yannis, KARAGRIGORIOU Alex, PARPOULA Christina, SKIADIS Christos H
Applied Modeling Techniques and Data Analysis 1: Computational Data Analysis Methods and Tools (Big Data, Artificial Intelligence and Data Analysis Set - Volume 7)
Applied Modeling Techniques and Data Analysis 2: Financial, Demographic, Stochastic and Statistical Models and Methods (Big Data, Artificial Intelligence and Data Analysis Set – Volume 8)

DISPAS Christophe, KAYANAKIS Georges, SERVEL Nicolas, STRIUKOVA Ludmila
Innovation and Financial Markets
(Innovation between Risk and Reward Set – Volume 7)

HELLER David
Performance of Valuation Methods in Financial Transactions (Modern Finance, Management Innovation and Economic Growth Set – Volume 4)

UZUNIDIS Dimitri, KASMI Fedoua, ADATTO Laurent
Innovation Economics, Engineering and Management Handbook 1: Main Themes
Innovation Economics, Engineering and Management Handbook 2: Special Themes

2020

ACH Yves-Alain, RMADI-SAÏD Sandra
Financial Information and Brand Value: Reflections, Challenges and Limitations

ANDREOSSO-O'CALLAGHAN Bernadette, DZEVER Sam, JAUSSAUD Jacques, TAYLOR Robert
Sustainable Development and Energy Transition in Europe and Asia
(Innovation and Technology Set – Volume 9)

BEN SLIMANE Sonia, M'HENNI Hatem
Entrepreneurship and Development: Realities and Future Prospects
(Smart Innovation Set – Volume 30)

CHOUTEAU Marianne, FOREST Joëlle, NGUYEN Céline
Innovation for Society: The P.S.I. Approach
(Smart Innovation Set – Volume 28)

CORON Clotilde
Quantifying Human Resources: Uses and Analysis
(Technological Changes and Human Resources Set – Volume 2)

CORON Clotilde, GILBERT Patrick
Technological Change
(Technological Changes and Human Resources Set – Volume 1)

CERDIN Jean-Luc, PERETTI Jean-Marie
The Success of Apprenticeships: Views of Stakeholders on Training and Learning (Human Resources Management Set – Volume 3)

DELCHET-COCHET Karen
Circular Economy: From Waste Reduction to Value Creation
(Economic Growth Set – Volume 2)

DIDAY Edwin, GUAN Rong, SAPORTA Gilbert, WANG Huiwen
Advances in Data Science
(Big Data, Artificial Intelligence and Data Analysis Set – Volume 4)

DOS SANTOS PAULINO Victor
Innovation Trends in the Space Industry
(Smart Innovation Set – Volume 25)

GASMI Nacer
Corporate Innovation Strategies: Corporate Social Responsibility and Shared Value Creation
(Smart Innovation Set – Volume 33)

GOGLIN Christian
Emotions and Values in Equity Crowdfunding Investment Choices 1: Transdisciplinary Theoretical Approach

GUILHON Bernard
Venture Capital and the Financing of Innovation
(Innovation Between Risk and Reward Set – Volume 6)

LATOUCHE Pascal
Open Innovation: Human Set-up
(Innovation and Technology Set – Volume 10)

LIMA Marcos
Entrepreneurship and Innovation Education: Frameworks and Tools
(Smart Innovation Set – Volume 32)

MACHADO Carolina, DAVIM J. Paulo
Sustainable Management for Managers and Engineers

MAKRIDES Andreas, KARAGRIGORIOU Alex, SKIADAS Christos H.
Data Analysis and Applications 3: Computational, Classification, Financial, Statistical and Stochastic Methods
(Big Data, Artificial Intelligence and Data Analysis Set – Volume 5)
Data Analysis and Applications 4: Financial Data Analysis and Methods
(Big Data, Artificial Intelligence and Data Analysis Set – Volume 6)

MASSOTTE Pierre, CORSI Patrick
Complex Decision-Making in Economy and Finance

MEUNIER François-Xavier
Dual Innovation Systems: Concepts, Tools and Methods
(Smart Innovation Set – Volume 31)

MICHAUD Thomas
Science Fiction and Innovation Design (Innovation in Engineering and Technology Set – Volume 6)

MONINO Jean-Louis
Data Control: Major Challenge for the Digital Society
(Smart Innovation Set – Volume 29)

MORLAT Clément
Sustainable Productive System: Eco-development versus Sustainable Development (Smart Innovation Set – Volume 26)

SAULAIS Pierre, ERMINE Jean-Louis
Knowledge Management in Innovative Companies 2: Understanding and Deploying a KM Plan within a Learning Organization
(Smart Innovation Set – Volume 27)

2019

AMENDOLA Mario, GAFFARD Jean-Luc
Disorder and Public Concern Around Globalization

BARBAROUX Pierre
Disruptive Technology and Defence Innovation Ecosystems
(Innovation in Engineering and Technology Set – Volume 5)

DOU Henri, JUILLET Alain, CLERC Philippe
Strategic Intelligence for the Future 1: A New Strategic and Operational Approach
Strategic Intelligence for the Future 2: A New Information Function Approach

FRIKHA Azza
Measurement in Marketing: Operationalization of Latent Constructs

FRIMOUSSE Soufyane
Innovation and Agility in the Digital Age
(Human Resources Management Set – Volume 2)

GAY Claudine, SZOSTAK Bérangère L.
Innovation and Creativity in SMEs: Challenges, Evolutions and Prospects
(Smart Innovation Set – Volume 21)

GORIA Stéphane, HUMBERT Pierre, ROUSSEL Benoît
Information, Knowledge and Agile Creativity
(Smart Innovation Set – Volume 22)

HELLER David
Investment Decision-making Using Optional Models
(Economic Growth Set – Volume 2)

HELLER David, DE CHADIRAC Sylvain, HALAOUI Lana, JOUVET Camille
The Emergence of Start-ups
(Economic Growth Set – Volume 1)

HÉRAUD Jean-Alain, KERR Fiona, BURGER-HELMCHEN Thierry
Creative Management of Complex Systems
(Smart Innovation Set – Volume 19)

LATOUCHE Pascal
Open Innovation: Corporate Incubator
(Innovation and Technology Set – Volume 7)

LEHMANN Paul-Jacques
The Future of the Euro Currency

LEIGNEL Jean-Louis, MÉNAGER Emmanuel, YABLONSKY Serge
Sustainable Enterprise Performance: A Comprehensive Evaluation Method

LIÈVRE Pascal, AUBRY Monique, GAREL Gilles
Management of Extreme Situations: From Polar Expeditions to Exploration-Oriented Organizations

MILLOT Michel
Embarrassment of Product Choices 2: Towards a Society of Well-being

N'GOALA Gilles, PEZ-PÉRARD Virginie, PRIM-ALLAZ Isabelle
Augmented Customer Strategy: CRM in the Digital Age

NIKOLOVA Blagovesta
The RRI Challenge: Responsibilization in a State of Tension with Market Regulation
(Innovation and Responsibility Set – Volume 3)

PELLEGRIN-BOUCHER Estelle, ROY Pierre
Innovation in the Cultural and Creative Industries
(Innovation and Technology Set – Volume 8)

PRIOLON Joël
Financial Markets for Commodities

QUINIOU Matthieu
Blockchain: The Advent of Disintermediation

RAVIX Joël-Thomas, DESCHAMPS Marc
Innovation and Industrial Policies
(Innovation between Risk and Reward Set – Volume 5)

ROGER Alain, VINOT Didier
Skills Management: New Applications, New Questions
(Human Resources Management Set – Volume 1)

SAULAIS Pierre, ERMINE Jean-Louis
Knowledge Management in Innovative Companies 1: Understanding and Deploying a KM Plan within a Learning Organization
(Smart Innovation Set – Volume 23)

SERVAJEAN-HILST Romaric
Co-innovation Dynamics: The Management of Client-Supplier Interactions for Open Innovation
(Smart Innovation Set – Volume 20)

SKIADAS Christos H., BOZEMAN James R.
Data Analysis and Applications 1: Clustering and Regression, Modeling-estimating, Forecasting and Data Mining
(Big Data, Artificial Intelligence and Data Analysis Set – Volume 2)
Data Analysis and Applications 2: Utilization of Results in Europe and Other Topics
(Big Data, Artificial Intelligence and Data Analysis Set – Volume 3)

UZUNIDIS Dimitri
Systemic Innovation: Entrepreneurial Strategies and Market Dynamics

VIGEZZI Michel
World Industrialization: Shared Inventions, Competitive Innovations and Social Dynamics
(Smart Innovation Set – Volume 24)

2018

BURKHARDT Kirsten
Private Equity Firms: Their Role in the Formation of Strategic Alliances

CALLENS Stéphane
Creative Globalization
(Smart Innovation Set – Volume 16)

CASADELLA Vanessa
Innovation Systems in Emerging Economies: MINT – Mexico, Indonesia, Nigeria, Turkey
(Smart Innovation Set – Volume 18)

CHOUTEAU Marianne, FOREST Joëlle, NGUYEN Céline
Science, Technology and Innovation Culture
(Innovation in Engineering and Technology Set – Volume 3)

CORLOSQUET-HABART Marine, JANSSEN Jacques
Big Data for Insurance Companies
(Big Data, Artificial Intelligence and Data Analysis Set – Volume 1)

CROS Françoise
Innovation and Society
(Smart Innovation Set – Volume 15)

DEBREF Romain
Environmental Innovation and Ecodesign: Certainties and Controversies
(Smart Innovation Set – Volume 17)

DOMINGUEZ Noémie
SME Internationalization Strategies: Innovation to Conquer New Markets

ERMINE Jean-Louis
Knowledge Management: The Creative Loop
(Innovation and Technology Set – Volume 5)

GILBERT Patrick, BOBADILLA Natalia, GASTALDI Lise,
LE BOULAIRE Martine, LELEBINA Olga
Innovation, Research and Development Management

IBRAHIMI Mohammed
Mergers & Acquisitions: Theory, Strategy, Finance

LEMAÎTRE Denis
Training Engineers for Innovation

LÉVY Aldo, BEN BOUHENI Faten, AMMI Chantal
Financial Management: USGAAP and IFRS Standards
(Innovation and Technology Set – Volume 6)

MILLOT Michel
Embarrassment of Product Choices 1: How to Consume Differently

PANSERA Mario, OWEN Richard
Innovation and Development: The Politics at the Bottom of the Pyramid (Innovation and Responsibility Set – Volume 2)

RICHEZ Yves
Corporate Talent Detection and Development

SACHETTI Philippe, ZUPPINGER Thibaud
New Technologies and Branding (Innovation and Technology Set – Volume 4)

SAMIER Henri
Intuition, Creativity, Innovation

TEMPLE Ludovic, COMPAORÉ SAWADOGO Eveline M.F.W.
Innovation Processes in Agro-Ecological Transitions in Developing Countries (Innovation in Engineering and Technology Set – Volume 2)

UZUNIDIS Dimitri
Collective Innovation Processes: Principles and Practices (Innovation in Engineering and Technology Set – Volume 4)

VAN HOOREBEKE Delphine
The Management of Living Beings or Emo-management

2017

AÏT-EL-HADJ Smaïl
The Ongoing Technological System (Smart Innovation Set – Volume 11)

BAUDRY Marc, DUMONT Béatrice
Patents: Prompting or Restricting Innovation? (Smart Innovation Set – Volume 12)

BÉRARD Céline, TEYSSIER Christine
Risk Management: Lever for SME Development and Stakeholder Value Creation

CHALENÇON Ludivine
Location Strategies and Value Creation of International Mergers and Acquisitions

CHAUVEL Danièle, BORZILLO Stefano
The Innovative Company: An Ill-defined Object
(Innovation between Risk and Reward Set – Volume 1)

CORSI Patrick
Going Past Limits To Growth

D'ANDRIA Aude, GABARRET Inés
Building 21st Century Entrepreneurship
(Innovation and Technology Set – Volume 2)

DAIDJ Nabyla
Cooperation, Coopetition and Innovation
(Innovation and Technology Set – Volume 3)

FERNEZ-WALCH Sandrine
The Multiple Facets of Innovation Project Management
(Innovation between Risk and Reward Set – Volume 4)

FOREST Joëlle
Creative Rationality and Innovation
(Smart Innovation Set – Volume 14)

GUILHON Bernard
Innovation and Production Ecosystems
(Innovation between Risk and Reward Set – Volume 2)

HAMMOUDI Abdelhakim, DAIDJ Nabyla
Game Theory Approach to Managerial Strategies and Value Creation
(Diverse and Global Perspectives on Value Creation Set – Volume 3)

LALLEMENT Rémi
Intellectual Property and Innovation Protection: New Practices and New Policy Issues
(Innovation between Risk and Reward Set – Volume 3)

LAPERCHE Blandine
Enterprise Knowledge Capital
(Smart Innovation Set – Volume 13)

LEBERT Didier, EL YOUNSI Hafida
International Specialization Dynamics
(Smart Innovation Set – Volume 9)

MAESSCHALCK Marc
Reflexive Governance for Research and Innovative Knowledge
(Responsible Research and Innovation Set – Volume 6)

MASSOTTE Pierre
Ethics in Social Networking and Business 1: Theory, Practice and Current Recommendations
Ethics in Social Networking and Business 2: The Future and Changing Paradigms

MASSOTTE Pierre, CORSI Patrick
Smart Decisions in Complex Systems

MEDINA Mercedes, HERRERO Mónica, URGELLÉS Alicia
Current and Emerging Issues in the Audiovisual Industry
(Diverse and Global Perspectives on Value Creation Set – Volume 1)

MICHAUD Thomas
Innovation, Between Science and Science Fiction
(Smart Innovation Set – Volume 10)

PELLÉ Sophie
Business, Innovation and Responsibility
(Responsible Research and Innovation Set – Volume 7)

SAVIGNAC Emmanuelle
The Gamification of Work: The Use of Games in the Workplace

SUGAHARA Satoshi, DAIDJ Nabyla, USHIO Sumitaka
Value Creation in Management Accounting and Strategic Management: An Integrated Approach
(Diverse and Global Perspectives on Value Creation Set –Volume 2)

UZUNIDIS Dimitri, SAULAIS Pierre
Innovation Engines: Entrepreneurs and Enterprises in a Turbulent World (Innovation in Engineering and Technology Set – Volume 1)

2016

BARBAROUX Pierre, ATTOUR Amel, SCHENK Eric
Knowledge Management and Innovation (Smart Innovation Set – Volume 6)

BEN BOUHENI Faten, AMMI Chantal, LEVY Aldo
Banking Governance, Performance And Risk-Taking: Conventional Banks Vs Islamic Banks

BOUTILLIER Sophie, CARRÉ Denis, LEVRATTO Nadine
Entrepreneurial Ecosystems (Smart Innovation Set – Volume 2)

BOUTILLIER Sophie, UZUNIDIS Dimitri
The Entrepreneur (Smart Innovation Set – Volume 8)

BOUVARD Patricia, SUZANNE Hervé
Collective Intelligence Development in Business

GALLAUD Delphine, LAPERCHE Blandine
Circular Economy, Industrial Ecology and Short Supply Chains (Smart Innovation Set – Volume 4)

GUERRIER Claudine
Security and Privacy in the Digital Era (Innovation and Technology Set – Volume 1)

MEGHOUAR Hicham
Corporate Takeover Targets

MONINO Jean-Louis, SEDKAOUI Soraya
Big Data, Open Data and Data Development (Smart Innovation Set – Volume 3)

MOREL Laure, LE ROUX Serge
Fab Labs: Innovative User (Smart Innovation Set – Volume 5)

PICARD Fabienne, TANGUY Corinne
Innovations and Techno-ecological Transition
(Smart Innovation Set – Volume 7)

2015

CASADELLA Vanessa, LIU Zeting, DIMITRI Uzunidis
Innovation Capabilities and Economic Development in Open Economies
(Smart Innovation Set – Volume 1)

CORSI Patrick, MORIN Dominique
Sequencing Apple's DNA

CORSI Patrick, NEAU Erwan
Innovation Capability Maturity Model

FAIVRE-TAVIGNOT Bénédicte
Social Business and Base of the Pyramid

GODÉ Cécile
Team Coordination in Extreme Environments

MAILLARD Pierre
Competitive Quality and Innovation

MASSOTTE Pierre, CORSI Patrick
Operationalizing Sustainability

MASSOTTE Pierre, CORSI Patrick
Sustainability Calling

2014

DUBÉ Jean, LEGROS Diègo
Spatial Econometrics Using Microdata

LESCA Humbert, LESCA Nicolas
Strategic Decisions and Weak Signals

2013

HABART-CORLOSQUET Marine, JANSSEN Jacques, MANCA Raimondo
VaR Methodology for Non-Gaussian Finance

2012

DAL PONT Jean-Pierre
Process Engineering and Industrial Management

MAILLARD Pierre
Competitive Quality Strategies

POMEROL Jean-Charles
Decision-Making and Action

SZYLAR Christian
UCITS Handbook

2011

LESCA Nicolas
Environmental Scanning and Sustainable Development

LESCA Nicolas, LESCA Humbert
Weak Signals for Strategic Intelligence: Anticipation Tool for Managers

MERCIER-LAURENT Eunika
Innovation Ecosystems

2010

SZYLAR Christian
Risk Management under UCITS III/IV

2009

COHEN Corine
Business Intelligence

ZANINETTI Jean-Marc
Sustainable Development in the USA

2008

CORSI Patrick, DULIEU Mike
The Marketing of Technology Intensive Products and Services

DZEVER Sam, JAUSSAUD Jacques, ANDREOSSO Bernadette
Evolving Corporate Structures and Cultures in Asia: Impact of Globalization

2007

AMMI Chantal
Global Consumer Behavior

2006

BOUGHZALA Imed, ERMINE Jean-Louis
Trends in Enterprise Knowledge Management

CORSI Patrick *et al.*
Innovation Engineering: the Power of Intangible Networks

Printed and bound by CPI Group (UK) Ltd, Croydon, CR0 4YY
15/09/2026
14962362-0003